THE ROLE OF THE AMERICAS IN HISTORY

Inquiries to   **John A. Loughney, Executive Director
Social Philosophy Research Institute
Westfield State College
Westfield, Massachusetts   01086, USA
(413) 568-3311**

THE ROLE OF
THE AMERICAS
IN HISTORY

by Leopoldo Zea

**Edited and with an Introduction
by Amy A. Oliver**

Translated by Sonja Karsen

Rowman & Littlefield Publishers, Inc.

ROWMAN & LITTLEFIELD PUBLISHERS, INC.

Published in the United States of America
by Rowman & Littlefield Publishers, Inc.
8705 Bollman Place, Savage, Maryland 20763

Copyright © 1992 by Rowman & Littlefield Publishers, Inc.

British Cataloging in Publication Information Available

Library of Congress Cataloging-in-Publication Data
Zea, Leopoldo, 1912-
[America en la historia.   English]
The role of the Americas in history / by Leopoldo Zea ;
translated by Sonja Karsen ; edited with an introduction
by Amy A. Oliver.
p.   cm. — (Social Philosophy Research Institute book
series. no. 8 Studies in Latin American social thought)
Translation of: America en la historia.
Includes index.
1. America—History—Philosophy.   2. America—
Civilization.   I. Oliver, Amy.   II. Title.   III. Series:
Social Philosophy Research Institute book series ; no. 8.
IV. Series: Social Philosophy Research Institute book
series.   Studies in Latin American social thought.
E18.Z4213   1991
970—dc20   90-23633 CIP

ISBN 0-8476-7720-6 (cloth : alk. paper)
ISBN 0-8476-7721-4 (pbk. : alk paper)

Printed in the United States of America

 The paper used in this publication meets the minimum requirements of
American National Standard for Information Sciences—Permanence of
Paper for Printed Library Materials, ANSI Z39.48–1984.

CONTENTS

EDITOR'S PREFACE

I would like to acknowledge with gratitude the contributions of a number of people who made this project possible. First, I wish to thank the many Mexican intellectuals and *universitarios* who have shared their ideas with me through their writings, *ponencias*, correspondence, and long, informal chats. I am especially grateful to Dr. Leopoldo Zea for his accessibility and *amistad*.

Among the colleagues in the United States to whom I am indebted are Robert Ginsberg of the Pennsylvania State University, who founded the Social Philosophy Research Institute Book Series, and whose internationalist vision includes an appreciation of Latin American thought. Professors Will H. Corral of Stanford University, Michael A. Weinstein of Purdue University, and Francisco Fernández-Turienzo offered valuable perspectives during the earliest stages of the project. I also wish to thank my colleague at American University, Jack Child, for his encouragement and support.

This project was partially supported by a faculty research grant from Mount Holyoke College. I also wish to thank Mary Heyer for early work on the manuscript, Michelle B. Butler, my research assistant at American University, for her careful proofreading, and Frank Connolly, Denise Brinker, and the staff of the Advanced Technology Lab at American University for their expertise.

Finally, I thank my spouse, Jack Loughney, for patiently serving as a sounding board for my ideas, and for his editorial suggestions.

TRANSLATOR'S PREFACE

The translator is indebted to Dr. Leopoldo Zea for a personal interview in Mexico City in 1971, when the author received the first chapters of this translation and for his letter of August 30, 1971, in which he indicated his approval of the English version.

I am especially grateful to the late Dr. Betty Morgan Popescu for reading the manuscript, making comments and offering suggestions for improving the English version.

Sonja Karsen

EDITOR'S INTRODUCTION

The publication of *The Role of the Americas in History* inaugurates a new book series on Latin American social thought intended to make contemporary Latin American ideas available to English-speaking readers. While numerous translations of Latin American fiction have been published in recent years, the world of ideas has a vitality of its own in Latin America that deserves wider recognition. Toward that end, this series should reveal a sampling of the innovative ideas burgeoning south of the United States so that northern readers can discover, appreciate, and perhaps profit from the thoughts of their neighbors in the Americas.

What follows offers a framework for appreciating this book in the contexts of the history of ideas and Leopoldo Zea's larger intellectual journey. After presenting some biographical information on the author, background details on the publication of this book, a brief history of Zea's major publications, and some discussion of the views of his critics and commentators, I will outline some of the central themes in *The Role of the Americas in History* and Zea's work as a whole. By situating Zea's thought in the context of the history of ideas, I hope to make the book more accessible for readers who are new to Latin American thought.

The author is professor emeritus at the National Autonomous University of Mexico where he directs the Center for Latin American Studies and serves as editor of the journal *Cuadernos americanos*. Author of more than fifty books on Latin American intellectual history, Leopoldo Zea explores the philosophical and ethical contributions that marginalized peoples can make to modern cultural life in general and to the institutions of the developed world in particular. Now seventy-nine, he has achieved international renown as a writer whose work enriches inter-American understanding and fosters dialogue between and within hemispheres. Zea has received honorary degrees in Madrid, Paris, Moscow, and throughout Latin America. He was awarded the Gabriela Mistral Prize by the Organization of American States in 1986, and currently coordinates

Mexico's National Commemorative Commission on the Quincentenary of the Encounter of Two Worlds, the International Federation of Latin American and Caribbean Studies, and the Latin American Society of Latin American and Caribbean Studies.

Leopoldo Zea's *América en la historia* was published in Mexico in 1957 and reissued in Spain in 1970. It was also published in French in 1990. Sonja Karsen's present translation, which is the first to appear in English, makes available to a broader audience a seminal essay in Latin American thought by one of Latin America's leading intellectuals. While the book was widely read in Spanish when it first appeared, *The Role of the Americas in History*, oddly enough, seems almost more timely today as notions of global interdependence are widely discussed. The book is especially relevant in light of the encounter of the Americas and Europe to be commemorated in 1992.

The Role of the Americas in History explores the meaning of the history of the Americas in relation to history in general, or "universal history." An unusual feature of Zea's analysis is that he does not consider Iberia to be part of the West since, as he will explain, Spain and Portugal do not form part of Western consciousness. The problems and conflicts of the Iberian and Western worlds, then, are analyzed as they pertain to the New World where they became the legacy inherited by North America and Latin America. The relationships between the Iberian and the Western world, as seen in their European and American manifestations, are examined as an expression of the relationship of the world in general to the West in particular; that is to say, the relationship of non-Western peoples, including the Iberians, to the so-called Western peoples. The book endeavors to reveal the relationships that exist between the particular history of Latin America and the history that has been and is being made by other peoples. Zea establishes a relationship with history in which Latin America's place is clearly recognized, and attempts to deal with the responsibilities imposed by the condition he calls "marginality." The experiences of Latin America are viewed as meaningful because of their possible validity for other peoples who find themselves in a similar historical situation.

An Overview of Leopoldo Zea's Work

One way to begin to understand Zea's essays is to highlight a particular historical moment in Latin American intellectual history. The Spanish philosopher José Gaos, a Catalonian disciple of José Ortega y Gasset, arrived in Mexico in 1938. Rather than view himself as an exile of Francoist totalitarianism, a *desterrado*, Gaos considered himself a *transterrado* and quickly focused his attention on his new "circumstance."[1] In his role as Leopoldo Zea's mentor, Gaos encouraged Zea also to devote himself to the study of their shared reality, Mexico.[2] Not for the first time, the arrival of a major thinker from Spain affected in still evolving ways the course of contemporary Hispanic thought in both the Americas and Iberia. While Joaquín Xirau and Eduardo Nicol, among others, come to mind as *transterrados* who have made similar contributions, Gaos was the key figure for Zea and his contemporaries.

Zea followed much of Gaos's advice and both his master's thesis, *El positivismo en México*, and his doctoral dissertation, *Apogeo y decadencia del positivismo en México*, published in 1943 and 1944, respectively, are considered classic works on nineteenth-century Mexican thought. Briefly stated, in these works Zea demonstrates that while positivism was confidently put forth as an "objective" and "scientific" doctrine which could most efficiently manage society, from the beginning certain members of the middle class reaped the benefits of the positivistic administration of Porfirio Díaz, *el porfiriato*, at the expense of the rest of the middle class and society. In addition to being a seminal contribution to the intellectual history of nineteenth-century Latin America, this emphasis on Mexican thought as it affected the nation socially and politically marks Zea's conviction that all philosophy arises from concrete individuals with particular historical circumstances and that "universal" truths are then suspect, points to which Zea returns repeatedly in his subsequent essays.

After the publication of *Apogeo y decadencia del positivismo en México*, Zea, then thirty-two, was able to continue his work on

---

[1]Leopoldo Zea, *La filosofía en México*, I (Mexico: Editorial Ibero-Mexicana, 1955), p. 82.
[2]Ibid., p. 84.

nineteenth-century thought during research trips to both North and South America. The North American travel arose somewhat coincidentally because of Alfonso Reyes's unfavorable reaction to a book which had just been published by William Rex Crawford, *A Century of Latin American Thought*, a consequence of which was that, at Reyes's recommendation, Zea received a grant from the Rockefeller Foundation to conduct research on Latin America in the United States.[3] These two trips substantiated Zea's belief that fundamental differences exist between the two Americas, ranging from world views to thought and culture, a premise which continues to characterize his critical stance.[4]   The research trip to North America was soon followed by a trip to South America during which Zea became acquainted with many leading Latin American intellectuals such as Francisco Romero, Arturo Ardao, João Cruz Costa, Guillermo Francovich, Francisco Miró Quesada, and Augusto Salazar Bondy, all philosophers in their own right who were preoccupied with similar problems.[5]

After these travels through the Americas, Zea published *Dos etapas del pensamiento en Hispanoamérica* in 1949. In addition to expanding his analysis from Mexican thought to the thought of Latin America as a whole, Zea included studies of romanticism and liberalism which he had undertaken in order to better understand the development of positivism. An English-language version of this work is available as *The Latin American Mind*, perhaps Zea's best-known work in the United States. *Dos etapas* was expanded further and published as *El pensamiento latinoamericano* (1965).[6]

---

[3]David R. Maciel, "An Interview with Leopoldo Zea," *Hispanic American Historical Review*, 65,1 (1985), pp. 4-5.

[4]Ibid., pp. 6-7. For an account of the differences which Zea perceives between North and South America in terms of interpersonal relations, notions of responsibility, and relationships to power, see his article "The Interpretation of the Ibero-American and North American Cultures," in *Philosophy and Phenomenological Research*, 9 (1948-1949), pp. 538-544. See also "Las dos Américas," in his *Filosofía de lo americano* (Mexico: Colección Cuadernos Americanos, No. 6, Editorial Nueva Imagen), 1984, pp. 64-77.

[5]See Risieri Frondizi, "Tendencies in Contemporary Latin American Philosophy," *Inter-American Intellectual Interchange* (Austin, Texas: Institute of Latin American Studies, 1943), pp. 35-48.

[6]*Dos etapas del pensamiento en Hispanoamérica* was translated as *The Latin American Mind* by James H. Abbott and Lowell Dunham (Norman: University of Oklahoma Press, 1963).

Zea found that the nineteenth century in Latin America is particularly worthy of study because it was a period in which, as Richard Morse has written, "colonial origins were never assimilated; the initial situation of external colonial dependence and internal colonial domination was never surpassed; the prolonged, inert past was impossible to digest as a present which could not be transformed into history."[7] Put succinctly, Zea concluded that *mental* political emancipation was only achieved when Latin Americans admitted both the impossibility of soon surpassing their colonial past and their inability to convert desirable futures into present reality.

In terms of intellectual development, much of Leopoldo Zea's work subsequent to this thesis has centered on the image and conditions of "marginality," a status in which he found himself, his culture, and society and of which he has been aware since the early stages of his career. The first phase of Zea's reaction to marginality began in the late 1940s and dealt with *mexicanidad*, a term which is at best awkwardly translated as "Mexican-ness," "Mexicanity," or "that which is Mexican."[8] In 1949, Zea formed the Hyperion Group, an intellectual circle which was crucial to the direction of Mexican philosophy in the following decades, to discuss systematically the question "What is a Mexican?"[9] As a result of the Hyperion Group's meetings and lectures, a book series called "México y lo mexicano" was begun in 1952. At the same time, Zea's more fully developed meditations on *mexicanidad* led to the publication of *Conciencia y posibilidad del mexicano* (1952) and *Dos ensayos sobre México y lo mexicano* (1952), books in which he clearly and polemically concluded that the Mexican does not possess a particular essence. In both essays, he made the more general philosophical points that there is no such entity as "human nature," and that the person is not something that already "is" but rather something that is in a process

---

[7]Richard M. Morse, *El espejo de Próspero*, trans. Stella Mastrangelo (Mexico: Siglo Veintiuno Editores, 1982), p. 22. The English translation is mine. Hereafter, all translations are mine except where noted.

[8]For a discussion of marginality in relation to *mexicanidad*, see Francisco H. Vázquez, "Philosophy in Mexico: The Opium of the Intellectuals or a Prophetic Insight?" in *Canadian Journal of Political and Social Theory*, IV, 3 (1981), pp. 27-41.

[9]In addition to Zea, the integral members of the Hyperion Group were Emilio Uranga, Luis Villoro, Jorge Portilla, Ricardo Guerra, Joaquín Sánchez MacGregor, Salvador Reyes Nevares, and Fausto Vega.

of "becoming."[10]   Thus Zea's interest in *mexicanidad* embodies
Ortega's dictum, "I am I and my circumstance," and stems from
Zea's concern with "autognosis," which, as Martin S. Stabb points
out, has led "more toward the consideration of *lo mexicano* as a
methodological problem than as a field for characteriological
analysis."[11] In short, through these two books, Zea's treatment of
mexicanidad, in contrast to the Adlerian analysis of Samuel Ramos in
Profile of Man and Culture in Mexico (1934) or the somewhat
disjointed psychoanalytical and sociolinguistic approach of Octavio
Paz in *The Labyrinth of Solitude* (1949), rejected the notion of a
Mexican national character. This stance can be viewed as the initial
phase of Zea's intellectual movement within twentieth-century
Mexican thought from the particular to the global.

In the only published book on Zea in English, at one point
Solomon Lipp argues that "character" or "personality" studies can
easily deteriorate into ugly stereotypes which contribute little or
nothing to the cultural empathy one might be trying to achieve, a
position which Zea implicitly has accepted.[12] Such overgeneralized
distortion occurs, for example, in *Distant Neighbors: A Portrait of
the Mexicans*, a generally well-reviewed (in North America) recent
analysis of Mexicans, in which Alan Riding makes copious
questionable generalizations assuming just such a value for national
stereotypes (such as "Mexicans need few friends because they have
many relatives").[13] In quite a different vein, as the Argentine
philosopher Arturo Andrés Roig has pointed out, Zea's concerns
with national cultural traditions are never privileged over the
concerns of the concrete person who cannot be generalized to
conform to supposed national characteristics.[14] Nevertheless, in his

[10]"El hombre no es algo hecho, sino algo que va haciéndose." Leopoldo
Zea, *Conciencia y posibilidad del mexicano* (Mexico: Editorial Porrúa, 1974),
p. 10.
[11]Martin S. Stabb, *In Quest of Identity: Patterns in the Spanish
American Essay of Ideas, 1890-1960* (Chapel Hill: University of North
Carolina Press, 1967), p. 195. Cf. Abelardo Villegas, *Reformismo y
revolución en el pensamiento latinoamericano* (Mexico: Siglo XXI, 1972), an
analysis of the same topics by one of Zea's disciples.
[12]Solomon Lipp, *Leopoldo Zea: From mexicanidad to a Philosophy of
History* (Waterloo, Ontario: Wilfrid Laurier University Press, 1980), p. x.
Lipp's study is useful if one wishes to analyze Zea's work primarily in relation
to nationalism and national stereotypes.
[13]Alan Riding, *Distant Neighbors* (New York: Alfred A. Knopf, 1985),
p. 239.
[14]Arturo Andrés Roig, *Teoría y crítica del pensamiento latinoamericano*
(Mexico: Fondo de Cultura Económica, 1981), p. 189.

books from 1952, Zea tended to use visions of *mexicanidad* present
in the works of the dramatist Rodolfo Usigli and the novelist Agustín
Yáñez as features of his polemic in favor of overcoming cultural self-
doubt within Mexican culture.[15] Zea can refer to Usigli and Yáñez
because they discuss such traits as hypocrisy and resentment more as
sociological or political phenomena than as absolute components of a
psychology inherent in all Mexicans.

Zea's interest in the *mexicanidad* described by Usigli and
Yáñez, then, is more indicative of his capacity for rigorous self-
criticism than of a possible contradiction in his analysis. Lipp's
larger point may be correct, and in these two books Zea appears to
partake of the tradition of national types, but his usage of Mexican
"characteristics" forms part of a larger argument about the need to
liberate Mexican thought from provincialisms. The goals of self-
knowledge and self-criticism are characteristics of Zea's analysis and
the study of *mexicanidad* in his hands, then, is a logical project in
the service of such values.

While marginality is the point of departure for *mexicanidad*, it
reappears in Zea's philosophy of history as he explores the place of
Latin America in world consciousness and world history in *El
Occidente y la conciencia de México* (1953), *América como
conciencia* (1953), *América en la conciencia de Europa* (1955), *Latin
America and the World* (originally published in 1965), and our
present work, *The Role of the Americas in History* (originally
published in 1957).[16] In these works, a Latin American vision of
history is contrasted with European and North American visions as
an exercise in emancipation or mental decolonization. Michael A.
Weinstein has commented that, for Zea, "the mental revolution is
more fundamental than any structural revolution, because without a
change of consciousness structural revisions will merely mask the
continuation of traditional social patterns."[17]

[15]See *Conciencia y posibilidad del mexicano*, pp. 35-39.
[16]See Raymond A. Rocco, "Marginality and the Recovery of History: On
Leopoldo Zea," in *Canadian Journal of Political and Social Theory*, Vol. 4,
No. 3 (1981), pp. 42-47.
[17]Michael A. Weinstein, *The Polarity of Mexican Thought* (University
Park: Pennsylvania State University Press, 1976), p. 52.

A third feature of Zea's preoccupation with marginality has been a critique of cultural imperialism and the development of a philosophy of liberation.[18]   Dependence and liberation, two important themes in Latin American thought today, are discussed in many of his works: *La filosofía americana como filosofía sin más* (1969), *Latinoamérica. Emancipación y neocolonialismo* (1971), *La esencia de lo americano* (1971), *Dependencia y liberación en la cultura latinoamericana* (1974), *La cultura y el hombre de nuestros días* (1975), *Dialéctica de la conciencia americana* (1976), *Filosofía y cultura latinoamericanas* (1976), and *Latinoamérica — Tercer Mundo* (1977).   A principal theme in these works is the struggle to authenticate Latin American thought and culture in the midst of pressing cultural and economic imperialism from the United States and, perhaps to a lesser extent, from Europe.   In these works, Zea has gone beyond the particular circumstances of Mexico and analyzes the more general phenomenon of Latin American culture.

Following his seemingly exhaustive analyses of marginality, Zea published *Filosofía de la historia americana* (1978), which both synthesizes and expands that concept as well as others that have been important to him throughout his career.   This study is divided into two parts, Western perspectives and Latin American perspectives, and essentially discusses history as a kind of text which has received a Eurocentric reading in "Western" consciousness.   The text of history, however, has been misread because the Eurocentric reading is not as comprehensive and "universal" as it purports to be.   Zea states, "The Eurocentric monologue needs to be replaced by dialogue between those who have been expansionist and those who have suffered the expansionism.   The philosophical and historical interpretation of the West [can be seen now] from the point of view of the philosophical and historical interpretation of the non-Western world."[19] For Zea, history in Latin America, in a certain sense, is still being reinterpreted and rewritten by a decolonized, autochthonous Latin American consciousness which is breaking out of its silence and marginality through this process of reinterpretation and its attendant project of liberation.   While Latin America is still the focus of Zea's analysis in *Filosofía de la historia americana*, he has also incorporated his view of the West's denial and

---

[18]For a discussion of Zea's contributions to philosophy of liberation, see Horacio Cerutti Guldberg, *Filosofía de la liberación latinoamericana* (Mexico: Fondo de Cultura Económica, 1983), pp. 161-168.

[19]Zea, *Filosofía de la historia americana*, p. 28.

misinterpretations of Latin America into a more inclusive vision of
history. His most recent meditation on this subject is *Discurso desde
la marginación y la barbarie* which can be viewed as a continuation of
The Role of the Americas in History.

The scope of Zea's concerns is still expanding as he continues
to write and publish. Yet, there continues to be a remarkable unity
to Zea's work, what Arturo Andrés Roig has called "a passion in
quest of synthesis," which can be described as an indefatiguable
effort to be comprehensive in his analyses.[20] As Zea's thought can
be said to possess a "recurrent character" insofar as he incessantly
strives for clarity about particular themes, his books have differing
emphases and are successively expanded according to what he rejects
or continues to maintain about the human condition. Thus, the
author may reiterate themes which are still fruitful, but always in
light of his current perspectives.[21] Roig uses the image of concentric
circles to depict Zea's intellectual development. As a thinker, Zea
has an intense urge to continually reexamine what he believes is true;
this evolving clarity is finally oriented toward the hope that historical
and social conditions will be transformed in favor of greater justice
and charity.

As an overview is necessarily sketchy and incomplete, the
preceding paragraphs simply serve to highlight some representative
essays and offer some themes and projects which have been critical
to the course of Zea's thought. What follows is a closer examination
of some of those themes and projects which are especially important
for understanding Zea's thought in *The Role of the Americas in
History* such as marginality, humanism, Catholicism and
Protestantism, philosophy of history, and liberation.

---

[20]Arturo Andrés Roig, *Filosofía, universidad y filósofos en América
Latina* (Mexico: Universidad Nacional Autónoma de México, 1981), p. 265.

[21]Carlos Real de Azua, in his "Filosofía de la historia e imperialismo,"
Latinoamérica, No. 9 (1976), notes the breadth of what Zea "reiterates" as
follows: "autonomy of peoples, peaceful coexistence, tolerance, control of
nature, respect for the dignity of the individual, conquest of material comfort;
industrialization and democracy ... as against inequality, poverty, ancestral
privilege, domination and intolerance" (p. 208).

Marginality

There is considerable consensus among critics that any discussion of Zea's intellectual contributions would underscore the importance of his analysis of "marginality," a key concept with an enormous range of social implications. Zea's treatment of marginality is a good example of how Latin American thinkers can discover and articulate critical perspectives that have great promise for enlightening discourse on social integration, stratification, personal suffering, and economic, political, and cultural inequality.

A marginal person "lives in two worlds but is not quite at home in either."[22] Traditionally, marginal peoples have been characterized sometimes by themselves and sometimes by others as those who "under the influence of European culture, are now in the process, sometimes slowly but more often rapidly, of being assimilated and incorporated into an emerging world-society -- the society which the expansion of Europe has brought into existence."[23] However, classic North American definitions of marginality, such those elaborated in Robert E. Park's *Race and Culture* and Everett V. Stonequist's *The Marginal Man: A Study in Personality and Culture Conflict*, overestimate the extent to which those who are already assimilated and incorporated into world-society are conscious of the lives of marginalized peoples.[24] For instance, the marginality of Mexican thinkers has been described as follows:

Mexican philosophers are aware that they are ignored by North Americans and also by most Europeans. The indifference toward them of those in the centers of Western intellectual life is an aspect of what they call the "marginalization" of their country and its culture. It became apparent in the second quarter of the twentieth century that, as the Mexican humanist Alfonso Reyes put it, Mexican intellectuals would not be

---

[22]Robert E. Park, *Race and Culture* (Glencoe, Illinois: The Free Press, 1950), p. 51.
[23]Ibid., p. 198.
[24]Everett V. Stonequist, *The Marginal Man: A Study in Personality and Culture Conflict* (New York: Charles Scribner's Sons, 1937).

invited to the banquet table of Western civilization, although they had many contributions to offer.[25]

The Peruvian philosopher Francisco Miró Quesada contends that Zea was the first Latin American thinker to tackle the problem of Latin American existence as a tension produced by the lesser existence which the European and the North American try to impose upon the Latin American.[26]

Philosophy produced by thinkers who feel themselves to be culturally or politically "marginal," then, is often different in significant ways from philosophy produced by people who perceive themselves as belonging to the "center." There are philosophers of the metropolis, whether or not they are aware of or refer to their position of privilege, and there are those who have been, as Octavio Paz puts it, "expelled from the center of the world and ... condemned to search for it through jungles and deserts or in the underground mazes of the labyrinth."[27] Zea consciously has articulated what it can mean to be among those who write from a position which is marginal relative to the metropolis, to the center.

Being marginal is not well grasped as finally a negative phenomenon, however. On the contrary, the fruits of marginality have been noted by Michael A. Weinstein and Deena Weinstein who have proposed that there is a bitterly ironic sense in which "the philosophy of marginality ... is a gift of the center to the periphery."[28] Since philosophy from the margin more easily lends itself to self-criticism, whereas philosophy from the center has no pressing need to criticize itself precisely because it is the center ("the universal"), marginal philosophy is frequently more thought-provoking and compelling. As Zea explains, "The great Greek, medieval, modern, and contemporary philosophers never had to worry about being original or about their cultures being strange since both their cultures and the people who created these cultures were

---

[25]Michael Weinstein and Deena Weinstein, "The Problematic of Marginality in Mexican Philosophy," *Canadian Journal of Political and Social Theory*, IV, 3 (1981), p. 22.

[26]Francisco Miró Quesada, "Realidad y posibilidad de la cultura latinoamericana," in *Revista de la Universidad de México*, XXVI, 6-7 (1972), p. 10.

[27]Octavio Paz, *The Labyrinth of Solitude*, trans. Lysander Kemp (New York: Grove Press, 1961), p. 209.

[28]Michael Weinstein and Deena Weinstein, p. 24.

considered universal."[29]   Zea finds evidence of an emerging awareness of marginality within "universal" culture, however, in a character in Jean-Paul Sartre's novel *Troubled Sleep* who says, "It was so natural to be French ... It was the others who had to explain why, either through circumstance or their own fault, they were not completely human. Now France is a giant broken-down machine. And we think: this was an accident of history. We're still French, but it's not so natural anymore. There has been an accident to make us understand that we were accidental."[30]

By embracing their circumstances in all of their marginality, Zea's mentors, José Gaos and Samuel Ramos, realized that the practice of self-criticism was essential to demonstrating that Mexican philosophy could not only elucidate Mexican culture but could also address questions of importance to non-Mexicans. In his treatment of marginality, Zea follows suit, ultimately maintaining that the problem of philosophy in Latin America "is the awareness that its existence is a marginal existence."[31]

As an example of the fruits of this awareness, Valeri Zemskov has analyzed how Zea's self-conscious meditations on marginality provide an ideological foundation for subsequent polemics over the Latin American interpretations of Shakespeare's *The Tempest*, a work whose thematics have sparked considerable interest in Latin America since the beginning of this century.[32] Using *The Tempest* as the basis for his classic essay *Ariel* (1900), the Uruguayan essayist José Enrique Rodó developed the images of Latin American *arielismo* in opposition to North American *calibanismo*. Rodó interpreted Caliban as the aggressive, practical, yet clumsy North American, and claimed Ariel as the embodiment of the more spiritual Latin American. For nearly seventy years, Rodó's vision generally provided the standard Latin American interpretation of *The Tempest*.

---

[29]Leopoldo Zea, *La esencia de lo americano* (Buenos Aires: Editorial Pleamar, 1971), p. 15.

[30]Ibid., pp. 15-16.

[31]Ibid., p. 19.

[32]See Valeri Zemskov's "Sobre las relaciones histórico-culturales de América Latina y el Occidente: el conflicto de Calibán y Próspero," in *Latinoamérica*, No. 13 (1980), pp. 115-178. This topic has become a literary battlefield, as can be evidenced in the polemic among Emir Rodríguez Monegal, Roberto Fernández Retamar, and others.

Unlike Rodó, the focus of Zea's work was not a Shakespearian play. Rather, Zemskov notes that beginning in the late 1940s, Zea studied the works of the "repentant" European intellectuals, Sartre, Camus, and Toynbee, and several intellectuals of Third World liberation, Frantz Fanon, Aimé Césaire, and Leopold Senghor. He then synthesized the ideas of the former group on universality and those of the latter trio regarding marginality, and convincingly articulated the philosophical abyss between Latin American and Western consciousness. During the 1950s and 1960s, Zea continued to develop the philosophical and historical implications of this existential gap. Among Zea's readers of this period were three writers who were becoming aware of his distinctions between those who have to "bargain for humanity" versus those who grant humanity, those who babble wanting to make the borrowed word their own versus those who own "the Word." These distinctions apparently reminded all three writers of the protagonists of *The Tempest*, Caliban and Ariel. Whereas Rodó viewed Ariel as the symbol of Latin America, these writers felt that Latin Americans could identify more easily with the savage Caliban, whose mother was a witch and whose father was a devil, than with Ariel.[33]

Thus, Zea's work, though indirectly, had more to do with *The Tempest* than he initially realized. In 1969, the three writers discarded Rodó's idea of *arielismo* and independently offered the image of Caliban as the symbol of Latin America: Aimé Césaire in "A Tempest. Adaptation of Shakespeare's *Tempest* for Black Theater," Edward Brathwaite in a poem entitled "Caliban" contained in his book *Islands*, and Roberto Fernández Retamar in his essay "Cuba hasta Fidel" which he later developed and published as *Calibán* (1971).[34] Zemskov's argument, then, is that Zea unintentionally anticipated this reformulation of Caliban's identity several decades before by describing the situation of the Latin American in a way that is almost identical to Caliban's situation.

[33]For further discussion of Caliban's transformation, see René Gotthelf, "Calibán como símbolo de la cultura latinoamericana," *Revista de filosofía latinoamericana*, II, 3/4 (January-December 1976), pp. 93-109, and Emir Rodríguez Monegal, "The Metamorphoses of Calibán," *Diacritics*, VII, 3 (Fall 1977), pp. 78-83.

[34]Zemskov, p. 117. Fernández-Retamar gives the same chronology in *Calibán: Apuntes sobre la cultura en nuestra América* (Mexico: Editorial Diógenes, 1972), p. 29. Fernández Retamar's *Calibán* appears in English in *The Massachusetts Review*, XV, 1-2 (1974), pp. 7-72. The essay also appears in *Caliban and Other Essays* (Minneapolis: University of Minnesota Press, 1989).

Zemskov believes that Zea was responsible for the new Caliban and that Zea's concern with expressing marginality led him, without specifically articulating it, to provide Césaire, Brathwaite, and Fernández Retamar with the ideological underpinnings for their reformulation of Caliban.

In his *Filosofía de la historia americana* (1978), Zea acknowledges the new Caliban in an epigraph in the second part of the book, "History in Latin American Consciousness." Keeping in mind that one function of an epigraph is to indicate a theme, it is important to note that Zea places the following epigraph in the second half of the book dealing with Latin America and not in the first half dealing with the West:

CALIBAN: I must eat my dinner. This island's mine . . .
Which thou takest from me. When thou camest first,
Thou strokedst me, and madest much of me . . .
And then I loved thee,
And showed thee all the qualities o' th' isle . . .
Cursed be I that did so!
For I am all the subjects that you have,
Which first was mine own king. And here you sty me
In this hard rock whiles you do keep from me
The rest o' th' island . . .
You taught me language, and my profit on't
Is I know how to curse. The red plague rid you
For learning me your language![35]

Humanism

Humanism is treated to some extent in nearly all of Zea's essays and signals a shift from *mexicanidad* to more general concerns. Moreover, Zea's thought, like that of fellow Mexicans Antonio Caso, José Vasconcelos, Samuel Ramos, and Alfonso

---

[35]William Shakespeare, *Shakespeare: The Complete Works*, ed. G. B. Harrison (New York: Harcourt, Brace & World, Inc., 1948), p. 1480.

Reyes, is pervaded by a rich humanistic discourse. Although it differs in some significant respects, Zea's particular brand of humanism is most inspired by that of the *erasmista* tradition of Spain's Golden Age, which, according to Angel Del Río, is characterized by a defense of personal religious beliefs, a return to a simpler Christianity devoid of complexities, the practice of charity as the basis for one's relations with others, and a return to the study of the ancient Greeks, all of which are characteristics in opposition to the scholastic traditions of dogmatic religious authority.[36] Zea does not directly refer to the writings of Desiderius Erasmus (1467-1536), but to the works of Spanish *erasmistas* such as Juan Luis Vives (1492-1540) and Francisco de Vitoria (1492-1546).

The *erasmista* influence in Zea's work has been modified by his encounter with important figures in the intervening centuries such as Simón Bolívar, Francisco Bilbao, Karl Mannheim, Karl Marx, Samuel Ramos, and Miguel de Unamuno, many of whose ideas Zea has incorporated into his own perspectives on Latin American circumstance. While the collection of essays *Latinoamérica, un nuevo humanismo* (1982) explicitly deals with humanism, Zea's humanism is perhaps most cogently revealed in *América como conciencia* (1953), *The Role of the Americas in History* (originally published in 1957), and *La esencia de lo americano* (1971).

Zea's humanism coincides closely with that of the *erasmistas* in terms of the practice of charity in interacting with others. He is seeking to place within the practice of global politics some principle of interaction which can be positively extended over all human conduct, a principle which is universal and whose implementation will benefit all people. Zea's critique of the West, especially the United States, is not a simplistic reactive stance which rejects Western ideals such as liberty, democracy, progress, and material comfort. On the contrary, he criticizes the West for its failure to exercise charity with respect to those ideals. In Zea's analysis, Western egoism has effectively prevented the universalization of Western ideals. He suggests that the West's perversity lies in inciting non-Western countries to aspire to its ideals while actively preventing such countries from achieving them: "The United States, so proud of its material progress and of the liberal banner which

---

[36]Angel Del Río, *Historia de la literatura española, I* (New York: Holt, Rinehart, and Winston, 1963), p. 242.

made such development possible, forgets this banner when Latin American countries have tried to attain the same successes under the same banner."[37]

Although Zea's humanism is also *erasmista* in its opposition to scholastic traditions of religious authority, he does not, as most *erasmistas* do, turn to the ancient Greeks for inspiration because he doubts the "universality" of the ancients as well as that of the Europeans and North Americans. If the Latin American is unable to recognize himself or herself in descriptions of the human being put forth by the ancients, Europeans, or North Americans, Zea argues, then such definitions of the human being are not universal.

Despite this emphasis on the conflicts between peoples and cultures, Zea's humanism has sometimes been called personalistic. While his humanism is not opposed to the *erasmista* defense of personal religious beliefs and a return to a simpler Christianity, these features are ends in themselves for the *erasmistas* whereas they are only possible means to an end for Zea. This Mexican philosopher's humanism evolves toward a notion of human freedom and dignity for each person as ends in themselves. Thus, his humanism arises more from a response to his social concerns as expressed in his discourse on marginality and from his identification with the dispossessed than from a metaphysical compromise. His Christianity is cultural rather than doctrinaire. He believes that a spirit of Christian charity can be beneficial to all without promoting Christianity as a religion that all should adopt. Similarly, though Zea is no Marxist, he does say that he finds that many features of Marxism are valuable tools for understanding reality.

Further arguing that Zea's humanism is substantially derived from the *erasmista* tradition, there are plausible and significant similarities between Spanish Golden Age culture and contemporary Latin American culture in terms of marginality, alienation, and quest for identity. José Antonio Maravall, in *Culture of the Baroque*, offers a perceptive analysis of these features of the Golden Age which fundamentally parallels Zea's interpretation of the human condition in contemporary Latin America. For instance, Maravall

---

[37]Zea, "¿Bondad norteamericana e ingratitud mundial?" in *Filosofía de lo americano* (Mexico: Colección Cuadernos Americanos, No. 6, Editorial Nueva Imagen), 1984, p. 186. This theory is developed further in *Dialéctica de la conciencia americana* (Mexico: Alianza, 1976).

maintains that Golden Age culture was a marginal culture of the dispossessed.[38] When Zea has explored concepts of marginality, he has often borrowed Emilio Uranga's image of the "occidentals" versus the "accidentals," in reference to Europeans or North Americans contrasted with the members of the Third World. The image of the dispossessed, the "wretched," especially as in the works of Frantz Fanon and Francisco Bilbao, is an important image in Zea's work and analogous to Ortega's image of the "shipwrecked" person, an image also present in Zea's more existentialist writings. Frantz Fanon's perspective can be quite similar as when he writes, "All the elements of a solution to the great problems of humanity have, at different times, existed in European thought. But the action of European men has not carried out the mission which fell to them, and which consisted of bringing their whole weight violently to bear upon these elements, of modifying their arrangement and their nature, of changing them and finally of bringing the problem of mankind to an infinitely higher plane."[39]

Suspension, the dehumanization of the dispossessed, and alienation provide, then, a common ground between Spain's Golden Age and Latin America's present. Maravall believes that baroque writers and artists felt somehow expelled from themselves, outside of themselves, and alienated. In discussing Latin American alienation and identity crises, Zea has pointed out the value of the alienation and disalienation concepts which he finds in the early Marx. Alienation, according to Maravall, resulted in baroque culture's providing a basis for people to be subjected to a culture which was not their own.[40] Similarly, Zea recognizes the impact of foreign culture on Latin America. For example, he writes, "The concern with adopting in America not only the European way of life, but also its products was a longstanding practice and had its roots in the Colonial period."[41] However, he stresses that Latin Americans have not adopted foreign culture, but rather they have adapted foreign influences according to their circumstance. Maravall believes the baroque is characterized by "extremes, suspension, and

---

[38]José Antonio Maravall, *La cultura del barroco* (Barcelona: Editorial Ariel, 1975), p. 429. This book is available in English as *Culture of the Baroque*, trans. Terry Cochran (Minneapolis: University of Minnesota Press, 1986).
[39]Frantz Fanon, *The Wretched of the Earth*, trans. Constance Farrington (New York: Grove Press, 1963), p. 314.
[40]José Antonio Maravall, op. cit., p. 429.
[41]Zea, *América en la historia*, p. 20.

difficulty"[42] while Zea similarly notes that history has placed Latin Americans between two worlds, neither of which is entirely their own.[43] It is perhaps in part because of the affinities between these two eras that Zea has focused on the humanism of the *erasmistas* rather than that of more contemporary figures. Put another way, his criticism emphasizes charity, anti-positivism, and living in history to such an extent that *erasmista* humanism is more consistent with his beliefs than, for instance, Comte's cult of humanity or Foucault's abstractions of human life from particular circumstances.

What Zea considers most important about the Golden Age remains "the spirit of the great Spanish *erasmistas* whose goal is to create a culture in which the best values of Christianity are joined to the best of modernity. A spirit which is contrary to the dogmatism and Hispanic absolutism which becomes apparent beginning with Philip II."[44] Evidently, one achievement of the *erasmistas* which Zea would like to see emulated in Latin America is the alteration of reality, in this case Latin American reality, by incorporating a new world view in which each individual forms an integral part of a community.

Furthermore, it has been argued that Zea tries to extract from the Iberian past as Latin America's patrimony the *erasmista* aspiration to universal equality free of all discrimination, viewing Latin American racial mixing as a key expression of their universalist spirit.[45] Zea himself recognizes that he is indebted to Golden Age humanism and its continuation during the Enlightenment when he writes that it is this humanism which gives the Latin American the ideological arms to fight for human dignity and each person's right to freedom.[46] Zea's admiration for the Spanish humanists is moderated, however, by his awareness that the Conquest took place in spite of their humanism and whatever effects it might have had in Spain. Paradoxically, Zea observes, the people who raised the cross which was to unite all people are the same people who created a new discrimination so brutal that it had never before been known to

---

[42]José Antonio Maravall, op. cit., p. 417.

[43]Zea, *La esencia de lo americano*, p. 45.

[44]Ibid., p. 42.

[45]Tzvi Medin, *Leopoldo Zea: Ideología, historia y filosofía de América Latina* (Mexico: Universidad Nacional Autónoma de México, 1983), p. 76. Zea's concern with racial mixing is also the topic of José Vasconcelos' well-known essay "La raza cósmica."

[46]Zea, op. cit., p. 101.

humanity.[47] Thus, a cultural crucifixion took place in terms of both personal and communal identity.

Obliged by historical constraints to modify his humanism so that it would jell with Latin American reality, Zea was inspired by a number of post-*erasmista* humanists, among whom Simón Bolívar was perhaps the most historically significant.   José Vasconcelos introduced Zea to some of the implications of Bolívar's ideas for Latin America in his *Bolivarismo y monroismo* (1937).   Zea eventually wrote his own book on Bolívar, *Simón Bolívar: Integración en la libertad* (1980).[48] Following Vasconcelos's lead, Zea believes that Bolívar's ideas are admirable because he manages to salvage some ideals of Spanish humanism which are still applicable to Latin America: "the old Hispanic-Christian ideal of the best Spain, with Vives and Vitoria, dreamed of an empire of equal people and equal nations, which is expressly stated in Bolívar's dreams.   An empire without the Spain of Pizarro and Cortés, but with the Spain of the *erasmistas* and Las Casas."[49]

Zea also derives from Bolívar his distinction between a society and a community. In a society, the individual tries to better society in such a way that his or her efforts also result in his or her own betterment. In a community, on the other hand, there is *convivencia* (an "experiencing together") and the members of the community feel united by an end that transcends them. Zea suggests that the society is the institution most characteristic of North America while the community is prevalent in Latin America.   Bolívar's dream is important because it is the expression of "different ideals from those of modern societies which exist to protect particular interests outside the community. The ideal of community could be extended to all nations of the world."[50] Besides Bolívar, Zea's distinction between community and society is also influenced by his reading of Ferdinand Tönnies's *Community and Society* (1887). In this book, Tönnies believes that the formation of families, friendships, and religious ties

---

[47]Zea, "Búsqueda de la identidad latinoamericana," in *Aztlán*, XII, 2 (Autumn 1981), p. 167.

[48]See also Víctor Andrés Belaúnde, *Bolívar y el pensamiento político de la revolución hispanoamericana* (Madrid: Ediciones Cultura Hispánica, 1959).

[49]Zea, *La esencia de lo americano*, p. 136.

[50]Ibid, p. 99.

(*Gemeinschaft*) reflect natural will whereas complex organizations and government (*Gesellschaft*) reflect rational will.[51]

The works of Samuel Ramos and Karl Mannheim are also influential in modifying Zea's humanism. In *Hacia un nuevo humanismo* (1940), Samuel Ramos advocates charity and rejects Cartesian dualism which he believes is positivistic and leads to the dehumanization and mechanization of society.[52] Zea, too, emphasizes existence as charity and antipositivism as a value, but he goes beyond Ramos and tries to formulate a humanism which better addresses his circumstance by taking into account exploitation, imperialism, and neocolonialism.[53]

Karl Mannheim's influence on Zea is apparent, for instance, in the latter's notion that exploitation and imperialism can affect perceptions of reality, an idea which was ironically presaged by Mannheim when he notes "the alarming fact that the same world can appear differently to different observers."[54] Such a statement might seem a truism were it not that Zea believes that imperialists choose to ignore or are not aware of differing perceptions of reality. With respect to Mannheim's observation, Weinstein has written that "the doubt that impels Mannheim's social inquiry is expressed in 'the challenge of developing a new pattern of orientation based upon a deeper and more genuine human truth'."[55] Like Mannheim, Zea seeks truth in values such as equality, tolerance, and respect for the individual as he continues to question that which is considered "universal" by undertaking a "cultural task which, with increasing comprehensiveness, coordinates diverse human expressions until reaching a profile of the person in which any person can recognize

---

[51]Ferdinand Tönnies, *Community and Society = Gemeinschaft and Gesellschaft*, trans. Charles P. Loomis (New York: Harper and Row, 1963).

[52]Samuel Ramos, *Hacia un nuevo humanismo* (Mexico: Fondo de Cultura Económica, 1962). See also the discussion of this work in Michael A. Weinstein's *The Polarity of Mexican Thought*, pp. 81-84.

[53]Zea's concerns with charity are influenced by Antonio Caso's essay "La existencia como economía, como desinterés y como caridad," in Caso's *Antología filosófica*, ed. Rosa Krauze de Kolteniuk (Mexico: Universidad Nacional Autónoma de México, 1957).

[54]Karl Mannheim (1929), *Ideology and Utopia: an Introduction to the Sociology of Knowledge*, trans. Louis Wirth and Edward Shils (New York: Harcourt, Brace and World, 1936), p. 6.

[55]Deena Weinstein and Michael A. Weinstein in "Intellectual Transcendence: Karl Mannheim's Defence of the Sociological Attitude," in *History of European Ideas*, II, 2 (1981), p. 97.

himself or herself and can recognize others."[56]   Zea's quest is described as follows by Tzvi Medin: "He seeks the recovery of concrete persons, the only human expression, by trying to transcend the prescribed notion of what is human which is supposedly embodied in only some people."[57] Recognition of all that is human can only come about, Zea believes, through solidarity and the negation of dependence.

Zea's concept of solidarity does not, however, involve banding together for purposes of more effectively resisting the evils of a particular ideology or a certain form of government.   Rather, solidarity for Zea is the hope that widespread awareness of the ideals expressed in his humanism will result in a dialogue based on the understanding that modernity has marginalized all humans to some extent. His ideal, which may be considered utopian, would be for citizens of North, South, and Central America, eastern and western Europe, Asia, Africa, and Oceania to recognize their common humanity and to work together for the good of all. Zea suggests that this ideal or some version of it, whether or not it seems realistic, should be regulative over our actions if we are to avoid devastation by war and other catastrophic or ugly scenarios of the future. Accordingly, he cites the horrors of the World Wars as crushing evidence that Europe no longer has a monopoly on humanity and is a threat to the rest of the world even as its colonialism recedes. These wars, according to Zea, have made everyone equal through solitude and suffering such that the need has arisen to resolve the urgent problems that plague each person simply by virtue of his or her being human.[58]

Thus, for Zea, neither dependence nor independence is acceptable. Dependence is disastrous for the victims of imperialism for obvious reasons, but it is not acceptable for the imperialists either because it questions their own humanity.   In this regard, within the North American context, the decadence caused by oppression's effects on the oppressor is perhaps most evident in the case of racism, a point which has been made eloquently by James

---

[56]Zea, *La esencia de lo americano*, p. 52.
[57]Tzvi Medin, *Leopoldo Zea: Ideología, historia y filosofía de América Latina*, p. 96.
[58]Zea, op. cit., pp. 104-105.

Baldwin in his essay *The Fire Next Time*.[59] Returning to the Latin American context, while dependence is flatly rejected by Zea, independence, on the other hand, whether it be personal or political, is also problematic because it negates fundamental relations among human beings and results in the individualist egoism and protection of certain interests which Zea has characterized in his description of society. As a result of these criticisms, Zea's vision has become one of an *interdependence* which he intends as the basis of charity and solidarity.

The concept of interdependence reveals that Zea's humanism is dualistic, with a profound tension between the individual and the community. Weinstein has observed that "Zea transcends the rationalism of modernity with a utopian vision of a planetary community united by existential awareness. For Zea, humanism is not necessarily demonic, because its meaning may be ministration to the finitude of each person, not the unrestrained will to control."[60] As a political philosopher, Weinstein generally disdains humanism because he believes that there is no way to reconcile individual freedom and social action. Thus, though he admires Zea's defense of human freedom, he goes on to imply that Zea's vision would be difficult if not impossible to put into practice. While his criticism of Zea is quite plausible, I think that there are some practical applications for Zea's vision as evidenced by the women's movement in the United States, for instance, which has sought to bring about change through the sort of consciousness-raising Zea advocates.

Zea's humanism may serve as a point of departure for living authentically because it offers a vision of liberation for all. His vision provides a compelling analysis of imperialism, marginality, and contemporary life, but he does not always make concrete proposals for resolving the problems he so keenly delineates. Analyses such as his are a necessary step toward change. Nevertheless, what remains unclear in Zea's thought is how to achieve his ideal of community, why the individual should work

---

[59]James Baldwin, *The Fire Next Time* (New York: Dell Publishing Co., 1962).

[60]Michael A. Weinstein, "Lament and Utopia: Responses to American Empire in George Grant and Leopoldo Zea," in *Canadian Journal of Political and Social Theory*, V, 3 (Fall 1981), p. 49. This article appears in Spanish as "Lamento y utopía: Respuestas al imperio norteamericano en George Grant y Leopoldo Zea" in *Nuestra América*, 8 (mayo-agosto 1983), pp. 145-164.

toward an end which transcends him or her for the good of the community, and what goal Zea is pursuing in pragmatic terms.

An understanding of Zea's humanism can result in moments of insight, liberation, and a sense of community, but such an understanding does not necessarily result in cultures of cooperation or societies of solace. Further examination of perspectives on the relationship between the individual and the community is needed to illuminate the limits of his humanism, establish a new problematic based on Zea's understanding of modernity, and evaluate the possibilities for social change.

Catholicism and Protestantism

The marginality of Latin America can be explained in part, Zea believes, by the marginality which, as a result of the Reformation, befell the countries that later colonized Latin America. Catholicism was in a sense isolated and then left behind in the Iberian peninsula as a marginalized religion while Protestant northern European countries such as England and parts of France eventually emerged as the primary representatives of the "modern age." In turn, the spread of a predominant Catholicism in Latin America and a predominant Protestantism in North America accounts in part for many of the differences between the two Americas. This notion of religious differences shaping distinctly divergent world views in the Americas figures extensively in *The Role of the Americas in History*, *Dialéctica de la conciencia americana, La esencia de lo americano,* and *América en la conciencia de Europa.*

Catholicism and Protestantism, as the dominant religions in Latin America and North America, respectively, are roots of opposing varieties of individualism. The individualism which characterizes many Latin Americans, according to Zea, is based on "personality," while North American individualism is more frequently based on "security." Reminiscent of his distinction between community and society discussed earlier in this chapter, Zea writes:

For the Latin American, it is important to be prominent in one's community, to serve others in serving oneself. The individual, far from respecting the proprieties of others, strives to reach out and grow with others. When people do not possess the desired personality, they latch on to those who do and incorporate the goals of the desired personality into their own. In this way individuals complement one another and live together in communities which foster interaction. This type of individualism gave rise to rule by *caudillo* in Latin American countries, the person with the magnanimous personality looking out for the interests common to all. The North American political leader is one who can bring about the greatest number of political, social, and economic advantages for other individuals. The Latin American *caudillo* is one who, through sheer force of personality, can rally support behind whatever cause. [61]

Within this analysis, the Latin American's social interaction is based on personality, while the North American fosters social relations in order to achieve that relative security of respect for process and property necessary to pursue the material success on which happiness appears to depend. In order to achieve such security, the individual yields a minimum of freedom to obtain maximum security. Thus, the North American is far more concerned with individual security than with the welfare of the community.

In Zea's view, Protestantism has contributed in significant ways to western imperialism and material comfort but at the expense of the misery of others. Catholicism is not without its flaws, but Zea believes that it is more likely to promote charity as the basis for interacting with others. The West has become Protestantized, which provides a convenient ideological justification of its imperialism and continued oppression of third-world countries. An apt and well-known historical example of such justification is the doctrine of "Manifest Destiny." According to Zea, Latin Americans view North Americans with both fear and admiration: "The America of 'Manifest Destiny' would be condemned as the personification of egotism and materialism, whereas the America that had given freedom and democracy to the world would be regarded as the model for the Latin

---

[61]Zea, *La esencia de lo americano*, p. 62.

American nations' loftiest ideals."[62] This ambivalent attitude toward North Americans is, of course, understandable because, due to historically verifiable interventions of one type or another, Latin Americans generally fear they can expect no charity from the North, only continued exploitation which will impede their efforts to realize the freedom and material and geopolitical comfort they so admire in the North.

Thus, Protestantism and its accompanying security-based individualism are seen as consistent with the pursuit of materialism. Zea presses the argument that the Puritan work ethic is particularly useful in justifying material comfort even at the expense of others. Thus Zea describes the Puritan world view to be ahistorical and departicularized:

> Beginning with his sense of self-sufficiency, the Puritan limited his sense of solidarity. All men were created equal and, if inequality existed, it was due to the weakness of the individual concerned. Some preferred to work and others to be idle. Circumstances had nothing to do with the individual's wealth or poverty, because man must be able to rise above them. The Puritan, therefore, did not see in the poverty of those around him a circumstance worthy of compassion and assistance, but rather as typical of a man's character, proof of his moral failure which, far from being pitied, ought to be condemned, because in that failure God has shown His condemnation of the unjust who have forsaken their mission. There was no reason, on the other hand, and regardless of the Catholic Church's condemnation, to make wealth the object of suspicion; it should rather be a cause of thankfulness because it bore witness to the Divine blessing on the just man who had fulfilled the mission assigned to him.[63]

This description of the Puritan world view is extended generally into that of the Protestant or western vision. In his analysis of this world view, Zea is very close to Max Scheler who in *Ressentiment* (1912) wrote that the world has "become accustomed to considering the social hierarchy, based on status, wealth, vital strength, and power, as an exact image of the ultimate values of

---

[62]Zea, *The Role of the Americas in History*, pp. 120-121.
[63]Ibid., pp. 119-120.

morality and personality."⁶⁴   Zea seems to detect Schelerian *ressentiment* in the collective materialism of the United States when he writes, "In the name of freedom and the ideals which encouraged the Revolution, they seek to maintain and justify their hegemony and material power."⁶⁵

It is clear from his criticisms of Protestantism that Zea believes that the culture of the United States embraces material growth within its own borders rather than the universalization of the ideals on which the country was founded.   Puritan morality rather than the ideals of 1776 guide the nation's actions.   Thus, Zea notes the increasing polarization of the world: "The chosen will live in democratic communities, governed by just laws in accord with their high aspirations.   The 'others,' poor, black, red, or yellow, if they are in some way destined to be saved, will have to do so by incorporating themselves into this community."⁶⁶   Of course, incorporating oneself into this community, even if it were a morally justifiable goal, is problematic because of all of the Sisyphusean elements mentioned above.

Philosophy of History

As a consequence of these meditations on imperialism and marginality discussed above, Zea's work culminates in a Latin American philosophy of history which is elaborated in his *Filosofía de la historia americana* (1978).   His philosophy of history searches for meaning in history: history ceases to be a chronicle of events or a mere collection of data and becomes a consciousness within the lives of people.   In other words, he admits the subjectivity involved in historical analysis, rejecting the naive but pervasive notion that historical objectivity is possible.⁶⁷   This realization is reminiscent of

---

⁶⁴Max Scheler, ed. Lewis A. Coser, trans. William W. Holdheim, *Ressentiment* (New York: The Free Press, 1961), p. 98.

⁶⁵Zea, *Dialéctica de la conciencia americana*, p. 92.

⁶⁶Zea, "¿Bondad norteamericana e ingratitud mundial?" in *Filosofía de lo americano*, (Mexico: Colección Cuadernos Americanos, No. 6, Editorial Nueva Imagen), 1984, p. 190.

⁶⁷As an unfortunate but useful example of cultural misunderstanding, William D. Raat insists that historians can be objective in his article

his earlier observation that although positivism was put forth as an objective doctrine that would scientifically manage Mexican society, it really was quite subjective in that it protected and privileged the interests of a few. Similarly, though they purported to be "universal," European versions of history told the story of some people in the world while ignoring that of others (which makes them perversions in terms of Zea's critique). Zea contends that his Latin American philosophy of history is a response and necessary complement to European philosophies of history which had been considered "universal history" and which, in their accounts of history, had excluded much of the non-European world. In Zea's work, this exclusionary bias is referred to as Eurocentrism.

Inherent in Zea's approach to history is the fundamental Hegelian point that to understand something entails a move beyond it. All interpretations of history entail interpretative strategies, what Zea would term "projects." Such projects involve formal notions that articulate what is important and which, through omission, relegate to unimportance the excluded elements. Thus, one way in which theories can fundamentally differ from one another is in terms of what they value and devalue. Every historian, and every theorist, is a conscious or unconscious servant of such projects, with each one's projects being determined by accidents such as personal psychology. Accordingly, Zea admits a concern with the meaning of history in relation to his *proyecto asuntivo* (project of transcendence) which is a desire for liberation. Thus, whereas Hegel posited consciousness of liberation as an end, for Zea such consciousness serves as a point of departure for altering reality.

Francisco Miró Quesada has noted that Zea's thought, "despite the fact that it is undoubtedly influenced by Hegel, is nevertheless

---

"Leopoldo Zea and Mexican Positivism: A Reappraisal," *Hispanic American Historical Review* 48, 1 (February 1968). (A Spanish translation of the article appears in *Latinoamérica*, 2, 1969.) In this article, Raat criticizes Zea for not being "objective" in his study of positivism primarily because Zea speculates about the meaning of positivism in relation to Mexico's present and future. Raat suggests that North Americans can be more "objective" than Latin Americans about Latin American history. Would it then follow that Latin Americans are more "objective" about North American history? Leaving aside the enormous metaphysical assertion Raat is making, he also failed to be epistemologically thorough in his critique of Zea. Tzvi Medin effectively refutes Raat's criticisms of Zea (see pp. 131-139).

far from being Hegelian."[68]   The Peruvian philosopher goes on to
say that although Zea makes use of Hegelian expressions to refer to
conceptual categories essential to his analyses, he uses these
expressions in a very special way, a non-Hegelian, if not anti-
Hegelian, way.   For instance, Zea employs the Hegelian term
Aufhebung (surmounting or overcoming); however, he does not
believe that Latin American history is characterized by particular
periods which are dialectically surpassed as Hegelian logic would
have it, but rather that Latin American history has dependence as the
dominant theme of its entire duration, an unfortunate dynamic which
has yet to be surpassed.   In commenting on Zea's senses of this
Hegelian category, Ofelia Schutte has categorized four meanings of
Aufhebung in *Filosofía de la historia americana*: the conscious
activity of humanity understood as the assimilation of what is
knowable in reality, the structure of historical processes, the
struggle for freedom, and the project of conflict resolution.[69]   These
denotations substantiate the essentially innovative, non-Hegelian
usage of the particular term *Aufhebung*; many Hegelian terms used in
similarly thoughtful but non-Hegelian ways appear throughout Zea's
work.

To return to the larger point of his critical examination of
history, *Filosofía de la historia americana* is largely devoted to the
analysis of six ideological "projects": Iberian colonization, Western
colonization, the liberating project, the conservative project, the
civilizing project, and the transcendence project ("el proyecto
asuntivo").   With respect to these projects, Zea analyzes the
Eurocentrism of philosophers of history such as Hegel and Marx and
Engels in ways which easily reveal his sensitivity to the implications
of this Eurocentrism.   Hegel dismissed Asia as "anachronistic" and
Latin America and Africa as "primitive."   The Eurocentrism of Marx
and Engels, according to Zea, was explicit in their approval of
conquests such as those of France over Algiers and the United States
over Mexico.   Within their Eurocentrism resides the idea of
industrialization which, with its implicit exploitation, creates the
conditions and the consciousness of true progress leading to the
inevitable historical annulment of the bourgeoisie, class equality, and

---

[68]Francisco Miró Quesada, *Proyecto y realización del filosofar
latinoamericano* (Mexico: Fondo de Cultura Económica, 1981), p. 142.
[69]Ofelia Schutte, "Hacia un nuevo mestizaje: Leopoldo Zea y la filosofía
de la historia americana," paper delivered at the Universidad Nacional
Autónoma de México in December of 1985.

the attainment of justice represented by "socialist man." Zea, of course, can never condone the incorporation or subjugation of non-European peoples into industrialized civilization through imperialist violence, cruelty, and domination even if judged by Marx or anyone else as but a necessary, evolutionary step on the road to eventual historical equality and justice. More fundamentally, Zea does not reduce life to the economic. Instead, Zea privileges charity over justice and, therefore, rejects Marxism. One way not to be a Marxist is to believe that charity, not justice, is the truth which should determine our human situations. For Zea, liberation is the triumph of charity (*caritas*) over circumstance.

Liberation

In an Unamunian sense, Zea's "hunger" for liberation has characterized the majority of his essays. He seems to think that human beings live in a world where meaningful issues are inextricably bound to social circumstances. Zea usually ties issues of human importance to the specific opportunities for expression and appreciation present in one's circumstances. As a result, traditional philosophical concerns with freedom lead, in Zea's world view, to questions of who within society determines the language, symbols, relational patterns, and myths of appropriate culture. He believes that imperialist domination and dependency need to be overcome before liberation will be possible:

> The freedom of the individual and the right of peoples to self-determination will not become a reality if they do not rest on equality which should exist among individuals and peoples. Freedom is not an abstraction, but is found in reality and this reality determines the relationship some individuals have with other individuals and some peoples have with other peoples. Inequality, within this relationship, simply impedes the possibility of freedom.[70]

---

[70]Leopoldo Zea, *Filosofía de la historia americana*, p. 39.

Zea's concerns with freedom make him a precursor of philosophy of liberation because he demonstrates that this preoccupation with liberation is not new in Latin America, but has been a central preoccupation throughout Latin American history. He believes that philosophy is always committed, and, with respect to freedom, philosophy is an instrument which can be used to understand and then end dependency. Miró Quesada has commented on Zea's pioneering role in the development of a theory of liberation:

> As early as 1956, Leopoldo Zea, as a logical consequence of the humanism which inspires his philosophy, clearly points out the existence of a culture of domination. From this period on, he begins to elaborate the basic concepts of a philosophy of liberation, an inevitable complement to the theory of the culture of dependency which was germinating in his writings of 1956 and which culminated in 1969 with the publication of *La filosofía americana como filosofía sin más*, in which he began a cordial polemic with Augusto Salazar Bondy. From this time on his contributions to philosophy of liberation are numerous and systematic.[71]

Horacio Cerutti Guldberg in his *Filosofía de la liberación latinoamericana* contends that Zea's "Dependencia y liberación en la filosofía latinoamericana," an article published in 1974, was the first written attempt, in a strict sense, to address philosophy of liberation in Latin America.[72]

Zea himself believes that Latin America is on the road to liberation from dependence and that, when such liberation is achieved, other parts of the world may benefit as well:

> The awareness of marginality in Latin America, which in the past was a negative reality, has taken on a positive sign. Rather than feeling inferior for not being completely western, Latin American thinkers are beginning to see that the small percentage of non-Westernness they possess is the foundation for Latin America's participation in the creation of a broader and more authentically universal culture.[73]

---

[71]Miró Quesada, *Proyecto y realización del filosofar latinoamericano*, p. 183.

[72]Cerutti Guldberg, *Filosofía de la liberación latinoamericana*, p. 25.

[73]Leopoldo Zea, *América como conciencia*, p. 124.

Exactly where this perceptiveness born of marginality will lead is not clear to Zea, but the moral bankruptcy of the developed world stands apart and is clearly different from the senses of community and human responsibility which he finds in Latin America as well as among marginalized peoples. Thus his point about liberation is both negative and positive: the industrialized countries possess the means to end human civilization, but, perhaps fortunately, from the disadvantaged peoples of the world there have arisen philosophies and attitudes of solidarity and interdependence which may bode well for all people in terms of arresting the process of dehumanization suffered by the contemporary person. In any case, Zea's concern with liberation seems to have led him to conclude that there are few other philosophical projects which are realistic and genuinely attractive. His sense of liberation, then, rests on a stance José Vasconcelos has termed "happy pessimism." Zea is happy because he has discovered and articulated a human sensibility in Latin American thought that can be extended to the rest of the world. His happiness is based on the realization that Latin America, far from being primitive and barbarous as it has usually been described in "universal history," may provide a vision capable of rescuing the West and the world from increasing mechanization and dehumanization. However, he is also skeptical because there can be no guarantee that such a humanistic vision will be appreciated; in that spirit, Zea also has sensed the possibility that liberation might never come to pass.

The issue of the importance of such liberation is found throughout *The Role of the Americas in History*. In at least its insistence on the possibility of genuine transformation through the advance of freedom, community, and respect for the plenitude of human types and cultures, such a work has much to suggest to the English-speaking reader.

Amy A. Oliver
American University
Washington, D.C.

PREFACE

Although the ideas which inspired my earlier studies of the Americas, *Dos etapas del pensamiento en Hispanoamérica* (1949) and *América como conciencia* (1953), have not changed, the present volume approaches the problem from a somewhat different and more ambitious point of view.[1] Here it is my endeavor to find the meaning of the history of Latin America and its relationship to history in general. I am speaking of the relationship that exists between our particular history and world history. Although it has come down to us in different ways, world history has become the history that is common to all peoples. In our own case, history begins by presenting itself in its European form: A history made by European peoples which in turn engendered our own. The history of the Iberian people on the one hand, and on the other of the countries constituting Western Europe. A history that is two-fold although it has the same beginnings: it is the history of Christianity, which inherited Greco-Roman culture. It is a history which branches off in modern times when Iberians and Western peoples confront each other as they follow different ideals: the former embracing Christian orthodoxy and the latter following a new Christianity centered on the individual. The problems and conflicts of the Iberian and Western

---

[1] *Dos etapas del pensamiento en Hispanoamérica* is available in English and will hereafter be referred to as *The Latin American Mind*. Trans. James H. Abbott and Lowell Dunham (Norman: University of Oklahoma Press, 1963). -Ed.

worlds were thus brought to the New World where they became the legacy inherited by Latin America and North America.

The relationships between the Iberian and the Western world, as seen in their European and American manifestations, are an expression of the relationship of the world in general to the West in particular, that is to say, the relationship of all non-Western peoples, including the Iberians, to the so-called Western peoples. This points up another facet of the relationship and meaning of our history with respect to what is generally referred to as history: Latin America, or our America, finds herself closely bound to peoples with whom until recently she was not concerned. Her position in present-day history is the same as that of other peoples in circumstances similar to her own and her problems tend to be the same. The West, in its expansion throughout the world, including Latin America, has set off reactions that have become common among all peoples affected by this expansion. Their individual histories are today merely part of a single and great history, the history of mankind. A history in which self-interest continues to be the dominant force that imposes its way of life on a person, a group of persons, or a people; but also a history where self-interest is in turn contained by the will of people who demand that they be given the same rights that other people claim for themselves. A history of affirmation and denial in which interests have been seemingly impossible to reconcile. A history, finally, whose conscience is the best indicator of the degree of humanity attained by its protagonists. A history that is common to Europeans, Americans, Africans, and Asians and, therefore, common to mankind.

This book endeavors to show the relationships that exist between our particular history, which we have tried to define in various studies dealing with the history of our ideas, and the history that has been and is being made by other peoples. A history of which ours is a part and in which, whether we like it or not, we are active participants. We shall try to establish a relationship with history in which our place is clearly recognized, and to deal with the responsibilities this imposes. That is to say, a history in which the experiences of our particular history are meaningful because they might have validity for other peoples who find themselves in a situation similar to our own.

L.Z.

CHAPTER I

HISTORY AND THE LATIN AMERICAN MIND

1. Concern with Originality

Originality is one of the major preoccupations of Latin American culture. Questions about the possibility of a Latin American literature, philosophy or culture are a clear indication of this concern with Latin American originality.[2] Originality as against what? Originality with respect to Europe, or Western culture. However, the expression "with respect to" (*frente*) should rather be interpreted to mean "in the presence of" (*ante*). Rather than to confront or oppose, what we want, what we seek, is recognition by the latter. Recognition by Western culture that other peoples exist, peoples on the Latin American continent, who also possess a culture. Recognition, not just by any culture, but Western culture, which means European culture.

---

2 See my book *The Latin American Mind.* Trans. James H. Abbott and Lowell Dunham (Norman: University of Oklahoma Press, 1963). See also José Luis Martínez, *La emancipación literaria de México* (México, 1955).

The preoccupation with the originality of Latin American culture is a concern which has its origin in a desire for recognition that only Western culture can bestow on Latin American achievement. Originality is not understood to mean the creation of something that is unique, special, different, or inimitable. We are not looking for something that is distinctive in order to hold it up to something else, but are rather trying to find points of contact. We are looking for diversity in relation to the whole of which it is a part. This whole is Western culture, and the Latin American knows that he is a part of it. When the Latin American asks himself whether there is an original Latin American literature, philosophy, or culture, he does so only in relation to what the word "original" means in its widest acceptance: place of origin. A culture that is original because of its origin, the person or people who express it, but not because of the way in which it is expressed, since the latter must be characteristic of the culture to which it belongs: namely Western culture.

For this very reason, the question about the possibility of a Latin American culture and what this means will be readily understood if it is expressed differently. Rather, the question is concerned with the possibility or ability of the Latin American to participate actively in the creation or re-creation of Western culture. The Latin American asks himself whether there is a possibility which would allow him to participate in Western culture in a way that is not merely imitative. He does not wish to continue to live, as Hegel would say, in the shadow of Western culture, but wants to become an integral part of it. His participation therefore, must be original. For this reason it must ensure the participation of the native-born American who, because of specific and happy circumstances, plays a part in the development of a culture that he considers to be his own and to which he contributes experiences based on the circumstances relating to existence. This is primarily the concern of the individual who wants to be more than a mere reflection or an echo of a given culture, but rather a person who wishes to participate in it.

This concern is noticeable, from the very beginning of the struggle for Latin America's political emancipation, in her attitude toward the mother country. The separation and rupture is nothing more than the result of the inability of the mother country to recognize the readiness of her colonies to participate in a task which should have been shared by the Empire. It was only when faced with Europe's lack of understanding of their cause that the Latin American liberators were forced to break the bonds that united them with their respective mother countries. The rebellion is not against the culture that is their heritage, but rather against the tutelage which the mother countries wished to impose on the colonies. Once the political ties were broken, Latin America's main concern revolved around the ability of Americans to again become an integral part of Western culture, but in a way that would not reduce them to a subservient role. Latin Americans, politically independent, want to play an active part in shaping Western culture. How can Latin Americans collaborate in shaping this culture so that it will not find itself in a subordinate position or merely be a reflection or echo? Their answer is: By being original.[3]

Latin America's cultural leaders point out that the characteristic trait of European culture is its originality. Originality is the only trait that Latin America ought to copy. Latin America must copy Europe precisely in its particular ability to be original. That is to say, in its ability to face reality, which enables it to analyze its problems and find ways to solve them. It is in this ability of the Europeans that European culture has its roots. Unfortunately, the Latin American has tried to repeat or faithfully copy the best European culture had to offer, instead of trying to emulate the spirit which inspired it. The imitation of this originality is not to be considered a break with the culture in which he hopes to play an active role.[4] "This does not mean that we renounce the progress of European science," states José Victorino Lastarria, "nor do we attempt to erase it in order to start anew on this long and arduous road which the intellect of the Old World has traveled in order to occupy the position it now holds."[5] No, but the question here is to try and adapt that same spirit which has made science possible in Europe and which in turn will develop it in Latin America: science, which like the European genius for originality, must be shared by Europe and Latin America alike, since both belong to the Western

---

[3] This is to be inferred from the answers by Spanish America's cultural leaders, such as Sarmiento, Lastarria, Bilbao etc. Refer to my book *The Latin American Mind.* Trans. James H. Abbott and Lowell Dunham (Norman: University of Oklahoma Press, 1963).

[4] Bolívar's teacher, Simón Rodríguez, said that Spanish America "must be original" in the sense that Europe was. Bolívar was neither more nor less important than Washington and Napoleon, each in his own environment and in accordance with his original goals.

[5] José Victorino Lastarria, *Discurso pronunciado en la Sociedad Literaria* (Santiago, Chile, 1842).

world. "Shall we be forced to repeat slavishly the lessons of European science," asks Andrés Bello, "not daring to discuss it, illustrate it with local applications or to stamp it as our own?" If we were to do this, he answers, we would betray the spirit of that very science, "which demands analysis, careful and close observation, open discussion and scrupulous certainty."[6] Still more important, what Europe expects of Latin America is not slavish imitation which contributes nothing, but a collaboration which can only be proffered if the Latin American applies to his reality the same spirit that the European has applied to Europe and from which originated the so-called Western culture. "Young Chileans," says Bello, "learn to judge for yourselves: strive for independence in your thinking. Drink at the source or at least in the streams closest to it . . . Question the achievements of every culture; ask every historian for conclusive evidence. That above all is the first lesson we must learn from Europe."[7]

The Latin American feels that only in this way can Latin America share in elaborating Western culture and participate as an equal among equals. Only by imitating its original and independent genius, but not the product of this spirit, can Latin America be something more than a shadow, an echo, a reflection of Europe, or a colony of the Old World. Until now, Latin Americans have not done anything but slavishly copy the results of this original and independent European spirit, instead of adapting it to create something of their own; achievements that would in turn contribute to their own culture, which is or should be the same for both Europeans and Latin Americans. It follows, therefore, that the recognition of the Latin American's ability to collaborate in shaping the culture to which he belongs can only succeed if he can demonstrate to Europe that he has her genius: an original and independent mind. Only then and not before, will Europe accept or ask for Latin America's collaboration. If Latin America does not adopt this outlook, she can only be a colony, the source of raw material which European science, by applying its genius, transforms into material goods designed to further the happiness of her people. "Our culture," says Bello, "will also be judged by its achievements, and if we see it copy slavishly from Europe, even in the things for which there is no application, what opinion will a Michelet or a

[6] Discurso en el aniversario de la humanidad (Santiago, Chile, 1848).
[7] *Autonomía cultural de América* (Santiago, Chile, 1848).

Guizot form of us? They will say that Latin America has not succeeded as yet in freeing herself from her chains; that she follows in our footsteps blindfolded; that there is neither an original thought nor something typical in her accomplishments: she copies our philosophy but fails to assimilate its spirit. Her culture is an exotic plant which as yet has not derived its sustenance from the soil which sustains it."[8]

What we say here about culture in general is valid for certain aspects of culture as well as for politics. Ideas like independence and national sovereignty will of necessity have their roots in the ideas which have been espoused by Western countries in their dealings with other nations. The great leaders of Latin America's political, intellectual, and cultural emancipation hold up to the West the spirit of independence which it has proclaimed before the world. It is precisely this point of view that we must assimilate, and not its end-product. If this way of thinking is adopted then we will reap benefits because of it. In North America, for reasons I will explain later, the assimilation of this outlook, and finally its immediate incorporation into the Western World, will be easy and almost natural; not so, however, for Latin America, which will have to overcome internal obstacles due to her cultural background and also obstacles placed in her way by the West, that same world which serves her as a model.

The main task of making the Latin American people a part of the Western World rests, therefore, on the assimilation of its spirit, which is characterized by originality, individual freedom, and national sovereignty. The result of this way of thinking in the cultural, social, and political sphere will come about by itself and emerge as a by-product of this philosophy. However, not all Latin Americans understand this, because there are many who make an effort to imitate or copy the achievements of the Western mind. It is an imitation that is beyond logic and will end in failure when faced with a reality for which it was not intended. It is an imitation that will reveal itself in the adoption of political systems, constitutions, enactment of laws, social order, art forms, philosophical systems, and so forth. Resistance to Latin American reality in order to conform to patterns not rooted in that spirit of originality and independence will be viewed in a negative way, or be taken for the

---

[8] Ibid.

inferiority which the West customarily sees in primitive peoples, that is to say as inferior races or immature human beings. Latin Americans whose efforts are bent on becoming a replica of Europe and the Western World will speak of themselves, their culture, and their country as primitive, inferior, and immature, because they are intent on imitating what that world has to give in the material sense, but do not wish to assimilate its philosophy. In these Latin Americans the idea that they live outside their own culture, history, and values will take hold. For them what is most important are material things but not the spirit that has created them. For this reason, aside from the material things produced by the European or Westerner, no culture, history, or human values exist. For those who take this point of view, Latin America can only be an expression of barbarism, on the fringe of culture; and its inhabitants, if native born, must be barbarians, savages, and primitives; and if they originally came from Europe, they are exiles, expelled from culture, history, and mankind.

2. Latin America on the Fringe of History

The idea of finding yourself on the fringe of history, and by this I mean the history of Europe or of the West, is felt by Americans both of Anglo-Saxon and of Latin descent. However, it is in the latter that this idea acquires greater impact and almost tragic proportions. The reasons for this attitude, its motives or origin, are what we are trying to show in this study. The former easily adopted the spirit which had made Western culture possible, and this in turn enabled them to create new forms of progress as well as to assimilate much of what Europe had to offer. For the Latins, the difficulty began with the assimilation of that spirit, which in turn made it hard for them to accept fully the achievements of European culture. North America not only assimilated the spirit of Western culture but became an extension of its natural development. Latin America, on the other hand, did not accept this spirit because she felt that to do so would lead to the renunciation of a way of life not in step with the so-called spirit of the West. The reason was that the Latin American related the problem of assimilating Western thought to its end product. For the Latin American, this outlook meant assimilating, absorbing the West's achievements exactly as they appeared in Europe or North

America: manifestations which in many ways represented the direct antithesis of the culture in which he grew up. He also belonged to European culture, but to an epoch when culture had passed through a crisis in order to develop a new cultural expression, the so-called modern or Western culture that arose out of an awareness of Western relations with the Orient at a time when the West was expanding and sought to conquer the whole world.[9]   The   Latin American was aware of the fact that the culture of Christian Europe which had shaped his education had undergone a crisis as a result of modern times. Spain and Portugal, even France, had resisted the challenge of this new world; they resisted and fought its ideas.   Spain, colonizer of most of Latin America, as well as her discoverer and conqueror, had been the champion of that world when Europe was in crisis. The triumph of modern times in Europe also signaled the defeat of Spain, which had opposed them.   Along with Spain, Portugal and the Latin World had been placed on the fringe of a new culture, the so-called Western culture. That is to say, on the fringe of history, on the margin of the new expression of man.

For the Latin American, therefore, again playing a role in history meant not only the adoption of the intellectual outlook which had made possible the modern and Western world but also the acceptance of its intellectual achievements. Thus in order to absorb this new spirit and its achievements it was necessary to renounce his own outlook and whatever else he had inherited from Spain and Portugal. As we will see later on, there were people who foresaw that the acceptance of this ideology was compatible with the inherited philosophy and its achievements; but what was incompatible was the introduction of new ideas and products of Western culture to the reality of Latin America, without their prior adaptation to the new environment.[10] However, the idea which was to predominate was that it was important to superimpose institutions and expressions of Western culture if in the end Latin America was to arrive at the same philosophy which had originated them, even if this meant that an inherited culture and a way of life were to be erased. This culture and its ideology were looked upon as the major obstacle, and prevented Latin America from becoming a full-fledged partner in the

---

[9] This culture, which is also referred to by its generic name, modern times, represents the opposite pole of Christianity which precedes it, and gives rise to the so-called liberal institutions and to the Machine Age through technology.

[10] See Chapter X.

history made by modern nations. Therefore, an investment was made by adopting certain ways which would make Latin America's participation in history possible, an investment which in the long run, however, was to prove fatal and produce results contrary to those that had been envisaged. The most enlightened Latin American intellectuals had always insisted that what was important was to adopt the independent and original outlook which had made the cultural, social, and political institutions of the modern world possible: this philosophy, if adapted to the realities of Latin America, would ultimately produce achievements, as it had done already in Europe and the United States. But other more impatient and less realistic minds found it easier to embark on the opposite course: they adopted the products modern culture had to offer first, in the belief that by their adoption they would ultimately acquire the outlook which had engendered them. [11]   They thought that merely by adopting the Constitution of the United States, any Latin American nation would end up being liberal and democratic. They also thought that by proclaiming free enterprise, free exchange, or free trade, which had contributed to the economic greatness of modern nations, the same conditions could be created for the nations of Latin America. The reality, however, was otherwise because the adoption of the United States Constitution in the Latin American nations did not lead to democracy, nor did free exchange contribute to their economic greatness.   The former only gave rise to so-called democratic dictatorships and the latter made these nations dependent on the economy of more powerful nations that were also more used to the struggles inherent in free enterprise.

The concern with adopting in America not only the European way of life but also its products was a longstanding practice and had its roots in the Colonial period. However, here too we should point out a difference between the spirit that animated the Anglo-Saxon colonizers of America and that which inspired the Iberians, particularly the Spaniards. The former hoped to find in America the fulfillment of a New World which could not be realized in Europe.

---

[11] This was indeed the outlook which inspired Latin American educators, such as those in Mexico, who found in Positivism a means to inculcate a practical turn of mind similar to that of the Anglo-Saxon, and the same sense of pride in personal work and in democratic institutions. See my books *El positivismo en México* (El Colegio de México, 1943), *Apogeo y decadencia del positivismo en México* (México, 1944) and *The Latin American Mind.* [The former two books were translated in one volume as *Positivism in Mexico.* (Austin: University of Texas Press, 1974) - Ed.]

We are dealing here with a new and different type of people, that is to say, those who did not have a definite place in the old European society of feudal origin. Many of these people saw in America the opportunity to create a new world of which they had only dreamed in Europe.[12] A new world in which their ideals would have a place. A world in which they would not have to fight vested interests. A new world which could be molded in accordance with the ideals of modern times. Those people, therefore, who were not in sympathy with the ideals of Christian Europe, and who were outside the established order, hurled themselves into an adventure from which they stood to gain a great deal and lose practically nothing. This advantage is symbolized by the colonization of America, a virgin land occupied inch by inch in accordance with the spirit of modern times. Here a world originally envisioned for Europe was created, a world which presented no obstacles except the natural ones, including the original inhabitants, the indigenous populations occupying those lands, who were merely another expression of nature that had to be tamed.

The situation was different, however, for the conquerors and colonizers of the lands that were to become a part of Latin America. The Iberians, far from severing their connections with the past, as had happened in the case of the Anglo-Saxons in America, embraced adventure in order to establish on the new continent a world similar to the one they had left behind in old Europe, Spain and Portugal. The only difference was, that in this world which they built for themselves in America, they occupied a social position they did not have in Europe. It was a world in which they could carve out for themselves a privileged existence, no longer possible in Europe where social position was firmly entrenched and had been for generations. It was a world in which the farmer could become a landowner, slaves could become masters, peons could become gentlemen, and the peasant could aspire to the nobility. It was a world similar to that of the Iberian Peninsula, but with other masters and other slaves, a world with new courts, castles, fiefs, land and subjects. It was a world in which a former servant could be a master. This is what the conquistadores and colonizers of Latin America were trying to establish.[13] They were not trying to create a

---

[12] Compare the Utopias of More, Bacon and Campanella.
[13] See José Durand, *La transformación social del conquistador* (Mexico, 1953).

New World but to reproduce the Old in order to find in it a place for themselves that did not exist in the original one.

In spite of all his efforts, however, the Latin American cannot avoid comparison of his achievements with those of the world which serves him as a model. It is this unavoidable comparison which produces disappointment. The new masters, the new Latin American aristocracy, were not satisfied; although they tried hard, they did not feel like the people upon whom they modeled themselves. In spite of imitating those men in their habits, customs, formalism, and protocol; in spite of their exaggerated endeavor to approach or even surpass the model, they knew they were different, very different from the men who belonged to the old established aristocracy of the Peninsula. All was in vain, because there was something in America which prevented the establishment of the same kind of society that existed in Europe. New Spain could never be Spain. All efforts were spent in a useless repetition which sooner or later became a caricature. And this because the Latin American, unlike the Anglo-Saxon, had no intention of creating a New World, rather he wished to repeat the one he left behind.

The idea that they were exiles from history was already being developed by these people. Latin America began to be looked upon as a place of exile. This idea was even more accentuated in the sons of conquistadores and colonizers, the *criollo* or native born. For the latter, exile was not a desired banishment, as it was for their fathers. In Latin America they paid the penalty for a guilt that was not theirs. They were men who found themselves in a world they did not choose and all this because of an ambition they did not share.[14] Native born and *mozambos*[15] tried without success to recreate a world abandoned by their parents. Whatever they did, they were always confronted by bad copies, bad imitations of a world to which they belonged and which had cast them out through no fault of their own. The ambition, the frenzied rebelliousness of conquistadores and colonizers who refused to accept their rightful place in the Old World in order to create another like it, gave rise to a guilt for which their children and grandchildren paid, an original sin which all Latin

---

[14] See Fernando Benítez, *La vida criolla en el siglo XVI* (Mexico, 1953).
[15] The term refers to African blacks in the New World. See Manuel Alvarez Nazario, *El elemento afronegroide en el español de Puerto Rico: Contribución al estudio del negro en América*, 2nd edition, (San Juan: Instituto de Cultura Puertorriqueña, 1974), p. 356. - Ed.

Americans inherited and had to atone for.[16] That they were exiled from history, thrown out of the Paradise of European culture, is precisely what was felt by the various cultural generations that have risen in Latin America from Colonial times to the present.[17]

These feelings of guilt today are apparent in the new generations of *criollos* born in nations like Argentina, where European immigration to Latin America is still relatively recent. People who, like earlier generations of native-born Latin Americans, still resist belonging to a world they do not accept as their own. "Latin America," according to Murena, "is an exile from a place in history." The Latin American is merely an exile from the limits of the intellect, "because Latin America is the expelled European soul from the oldest place in history, exiled she contemplates her remote asylum, restrained by a secret, incessant question about the reasons for the present guilt, which were responsible for her banishment." And this guilt similar to that of the former conquistadores and colonizers, was the ambition, the arrogance of people who, in the adventure of seeking gold and wealth, saw a way to attain the privileges which Europe denied them within the established order of things. People who sold their birthright, the fact of belonging to culture and history, for a plate of gold and wealth which did not compensate for the loss. This is the heritage that Latin Americans have received, this is the sin of Latin America and the Americas. The heir of this guilt, states Murena, tries in vain to escape reality by looking for subterfuges that will make him forget it. Some try to place themselves in the future, others in the past, but in either case in order to avoid accepting a present which they do not acknowledge as their own. According to Murena, "Latin America is a grown son without experience, a senile young man who lives in the shadow of his parents, barren, in whose brutal and silent life banquets alternate with erudite but unending empty speeches all of which symbolize lifelessness and a lack of courage."

Today's native-born Latin American, like those born of earlier generations, complains not so much because of what he does not have, but because of what he could have and lacks. Belonging as he did to European culture, shaping as he did part of history par excellence, world history which has produced and produces the

---

[16] See H.A. Murena, *El pecado original de América* (Buenos Aires, 1954).
[17] See Alfonso Reyes, *Ultima Tule* (Mexico, 1942).

European or Western man, he has left it because of his forebears in order to create a different kind of history: a history that is different from the history par excellence, to which the native-born has not been able to contribute but which he now feels compelled to achieve. The native-born does not wish to rewrite history, but simply to participate in history being made which, as Hegel pointed out, means analyzing oneself, reading oneself into a book written since the dawn of time. Therefore, whatever is outside of this way of thinking can only be an imitation of history. "We Latin Americans," continues Murena, "are the outcasts of the world, the scum of the earth, the most wretched among the poor, we are the dispossessed. We are dispossessed because we left it all behind when we came from Europe and Asia, and we abandon it all because we are leaving history behind." We Latin Americans "have neither history nor a father." Our secret is to go "from everything to nothing." Absolute banishment, a fall from grace because of a guilt for which everyone now has to pay. "At one time we lived on a continent called Europe fertilized by the mind, " continues Murena, "but suddenly we were exiles, and came upon another uncivilized continent, a vacuum of the intellect which we came to call America . . . At that particular moment we were on the threshold of history and the sap and wind of history nourished and excited us, because they gave a meaning to each object we touched, each word we spoke, each inch of land we walked on, and everything was a challenge; now we live in nations situated outside the magnificent circle of historic events, nations touched by history only because of their material resources, so that history acquires a material significance for us and it follows, therefore, that our relationship to it ends by being without importance and ultimately degrading. "From all that man can attain, we have gone almost to not being able even to be men. From a seed sown in good earth we have developed into a seed that has fallen among thorns."[18]

3. An Awareness of History

The awareness of banishment, of separation from history is, as will be shown more fully later, a knowledge of history which is

---

[18] H.A. Murena, op. cit.

unlike what modern man in Europe or America thinks of as history. The American will try from the very beginning to sever his relationship with a history for which he is not responsible. This, however, does not apply to the Latin American: he wants no part of a history, whether Christian or modern, that does not encompass that part of the world from which he originally came. Modern man, and with modern man the creator of Anglo-Saxon America, who is his ultimate expression, does not want to know anything about a history in which he did not participate. History, if it is to exist, has to begin with him. He does not accept the blame for others, he does not feel guilty about anything, because he has not accomplished anything yet. For this very reason he places himself within the ahistoric sphere. He is innocent, and the mere fact of being blameless is an ahistoric state of being. Innocence is not conscious of the past, has nothing to do with it, and is not to be blamed for its actions. Cognizant of this fact, modern man is determined to appear before the world as free from blame, as a man who is not to be held responsible for what his forebears have done. Actually, he has no forebears, since history begins with him: he is the inventor of history. He embraces the future unencumbered, not weighted down by anything that is not the direct result of his own actions.

This, however, does not apply to the Latin American, who not only wishes to assume the mistakes of history, but would consider it a shortcoming not to be affected by them. The Latin American conquistador and colonizer came to America with very different intentions from those of his Anglo-Saxon neighbor: his mission was not to create a new world, but to recreate and enlarge the old one from which he originated. History must continue its onward march in America, since it represents its future, but a future that is closely tied to Europe's past, and to modern times or present-day Europe. The Latin American, the Iberian of the Peninsula, and to a large extent the Latin as well, oppose cutting off any part of history, although, in the long run, for reasons that will be explained later, they realize or at least try to understand that most absurd of amputations. Modern man, on the other hand, starts out from the present and sees it in relation to his past, and as a part of a past that is already serving him and not vice versa. This, however, does not apply to the Latin American, who, forced by circumstances and not finding the harmony between the Christian past he has inherited and the modern times he would like to inherit, tries to cut off his past, in order to be deserving of the future he covets. This struggle between

his past and his future, between what he is because of the
achievements of his forebears and what he wants to be in the future,
exhausts the possibilities modern man has developed without
worrying over a break that he knows is impossible to avoid.

The Latin American, determined to make Latin America a new
Christian Europe, finds that Europe has ceased to be Christian in
order to pursue a new course. The same zeal he evinced in making
America an extension of Christian Europe he will now deploy to
make her into a modern Europe, by turning her people into countries
similar to the great modern nations that are coming to the fore in
Europe and Anglo-Saxon America. Europe has seen and achieved its
transformation by renouncing its Christian past; the Latin American,
too, will have to renounce this past if he wants to reach the level of
the emerging nations, leaders of civilization and culture. But there is
something that the Latin American does not learn, and that is the way
in which this renunciation is used by modern man in order to create
his new world. Modern man, and this is shown by the greatest
philosophers of history such as Hegel, equates denial with
assimilation, which means preserving the attained level of the
experience so that it will not have to be repeated. But to preserve an
experience does not insure its validity, except that it avoids repeating
that experience.[19]   Europe has ceased to be medieval, feudal, and
Christian in order to be modern, but in so doing, she has not
forgotten what she was. Thus, the past continues to be a part of the
present and is a function of the future; but not in such a way that it
creates a disturbance, a hindrance, or an obstacle; on the contrary, it
is experience that has made the present possible and will allow the
future; Europe is what she has been, and for this very reason she
does not have to continue in a way different from the one she
followed in the past. The Latin American will not understand the
renunciation of this kind of assimilation, which can be preserved
only by the manner in which we discard. The Latin American is still
trying to effect the assimilation of the Christian world he brought to
America with the indigenous world he has found there, but feels he
must renounce this assimilation in order to establish another kind of
world which seems a negation both of the one he has inherited and
the one he has found.[20]   The Latin American compares his situation

---

[19] These Hegelian ideas and their relationship to America were developed
in my book *The Latin American Mind* from which I quoted before.
[20] According to Antonio Caso, "Mexico, instead of following a uniform
and graduated dialectical process, has proceeded cumulatively . . . So far we

with the goals attained by modern nations and sees that he is far removed from them. He feels that this distance can only be bridged if he cuts the tie that binds him both to an inherited cultural world which is no longer valid and to the primitive world he found in America. He thinks that it is sufficient to cut himself off from this past which has become the present in order to join the modern world without much ado. The individual who formerly felt guilty because he was unable to develop fully the forms of the inherited Christian culture now feels guilty that he has been unable to develop those of the modern world. He holds the primitive world against which he has struggled responsible for his earlier inability; for his new inability and the fact that he inherited a culture which was even then outside of history, he blames the modern world.

The Latin American thinks that it is sufficient to renounce American barbarism and the Iberian heritage, for the double guilt he feels disappears and thus makes him an integral part of world culture and history. In order to achieve this end he renounces first one and then the other as if he had nothing in common with them, not even in their old form, an impossible renunciation because one or the other will become noticeable in a way that as yet has not been understood. The experience that is being lived does not as yet belong to the past, but rather to the present, because the experience has not concluded as yet. The Latin American, like modern man, wants to enter the threshold of history in a state of innocence, without assuming any guilt for the past, by refusing to accept the guilt of his forebears. But unlike modern man, he feels that past as guilt, an inherited and special guilt, but guilt just the same: guilt which modern man does not feel because he has made of it something unique and personal. For modern man the past is a necessary experience, something that he has to undergo in order to arrive at the stage where he is at present, but not something that determines or indicates, as original sin marked Adam's children by limiting their possibilities. No, the past for modern man is not a limitation, but rather the point of departure for a future whose development depends on man's ability to achieve his ends. Modern man does not carry around the guilt of his forebears, only their experience and this he uses, making it serve

still have not solved the problem which the conquest has bequeathed us, nor the question of democracy, and yet we have already addressed socialism, as a part of the historical discussion, in its most acute and pressing form." These ideas can also be applied to all Latin Americans. See A. Caso, *México, apuntamientos de cultura patria* (Mexico, 1943).

his ends, because it tells him what he must not do so that he will not repeat the mistakes. But nothing more, because the future is his creation, his personal and unique creation, the creation of a society of which he is a part. Modern man, as I said before, refuses to accept as his own a past for which he is not responsible; but he accepts it in the sense that it has allowed him to become what he is and as a point of departure, has enabled him to change. The Latin American, on the other hand, in spite of all his efforts, feels that he cannot escape the past; his forebears, his dead, continue to live and impose certain conditions on him, restricting his possibilities and burdening him with their guilt. He cannot be innocent like modern man; he cannot begin his own history; he has to take on the one he has inherited, yet he suffers because he cannot accept modern history for which he is not responsible either.

While for modern man the past is something useful, for the Latin American it constitutes an obstacle. Modern man emphasizes the present which applies the experience gained in the past, and from which a better future will be forged. This, however, does not apply to the Latin American, who emphasizes what he might like to be, yet at the same time makes of the present a permanent battlefield against a past which for him represents an impediment to the desired future. Modern man blends the various periods of history harmoniously and thus continues to build a more perfect world all the time. This, however, is not true of the Latin American who cannot bridge the gap between what he is and what he has been and what he wants to be. Modern man, in an ever active present, states what he is as a consequence of what he has been, and a basis for what he may become. This does not apply to the Latin American, who denies the present because it is the result of something that has been and that he does not accept as his own, or that exists in relation to a future which cannot be. The one looks upon the past and the present as the basis for his development, whereas the other considers these same periods as an obstacle preventing it. For modern man the present is, therefore, the daily fulfillment of the future, a natural and logical consequence which finds its basis in the achievements of the past. For the Latin American such a thing is not feasible, because he forges out of his present the impossibility of his future and therefore, makes of the future a mere utopia, that is to say, something that does not exist, without place, without topos; something that can only be produced by a miracle. It can be said that the Latin American is a millenarian; a man who waits for the

Messiah-like arrival of a future he does not think he deserves, because of what he is and has been: a guilty Adam, in permanent recrimination, who waits for the dispensation of grace which will place him among the chosen of history, a history of which he is a shameful part, the history of the Western world.

4. America Seen as a Utopia

The Latin American's awareness of his history has, as we may suppose, its roots in a reality which is his very own and original if we compare it with that of nations where modernity has come to the fore.   This reality has been approached in a negative way when comparing it with those nations.   Certain symbols came into being with the advent of modern times for judging people whose background was different from the background of those describing them.   When it spread to the rest of the world, the West created its own interpretation of history, which is merely an interpretation of its own history in relation to that of other peoples, even when these, like the Latins or the Iberians, were a part of that history.   However, as we shall see in greater detail later, the history of the Latin and Iberian people is merely a part of the history that the West has denied, assimilated, and considers of little importance.   It is history, genuine history, which in accordance with this criterion has shaped the West.   Others, the rest of mankind, other nations, have made history but no longer make it; or they may eventually be able to make it, but as yet do not make it.   The great nations of Asia (India, China, etc.), are nations that have made history but are no longer making it; the primitive tribes who live in Africa and Oceania are people who perhaps in the future will make history, but as yet do not participate in it.   The only people who make history, based on their achievements and in relation to what can be done, are the so-called Western people, the people who have spread over the confines of the earth creating the only true history, a history in which other people have participated in the past and in which others may perhaps collaborate in the future.[21]   But what is important is the actual

---

[21] In *The Philosophy of History*, Hegel defines the role of all peoples in history, eliminating the non-Western peoples such as Latin Americans because

situation, the present; and right now the only history being made is made by the West. The past is a memory, the future a prophecy; what is important is the present.

Within this interpretation of history by Western philosophers, Latin America occupies a special place; and one that North America does not occupy.   Latin America in general, because of its topography, fauna, flora, and original inhabitants, is a world that can be compared with Africa.   A virgin land, full of potential, a world of the future; but, a future which can soon turn into the present because of the work accomplished by Western man, who is determined to make history in America.   It is a continent still immature, but one that can develop with the help of Western man. Western man sees it as his mission to make these lands a part of the history of the West.[22] It is in his hands to make of this world of the future a world of the present.   Such is the meaning of American colonization. This ideal, obvious to Europeans, is in the process of being realized by the men who are colonizing North America.   That part of America is entering history in a big way and soon the West will have to take notice.   This is not what is happening in Latin America, that part of America which was colonized by the Spanish and Portuguese, who, although Europeans like the Anglo-Saxons, are merely the last and stubborn defenders of a past that has no longer any reason to continue indefinitely.

That is precisely why the past and the present meet in Latin America. What may be is here joined to what has been. But what is lacking is the amalgam of a present which fuses one with the other, as has happened in Europe and is taking place in North America. Latin America, like the rest of America, holds the key to the future, but a future that does not take into account the stimulus of the present, as is happening in North America and in Europe, where the modern world is in the process of being created.   Latin America's present is nothing more than a permanent holding-on to a world that once existed, an experience that is no longer necessary to repeat

---

they have been insignificant since the decline of their indigenous civilizations, and only in the future will they come into their own again.

[22] See Antonello Gerbi, *Viejas polémicas sobre el Nuevo Mundo* (Lima, 1946).   In this book various European theses about America are analyzed; among them there are some that see the need for America's Europeanization through the direct influence of Europeans working there. [*The Dispute of the New World: The History of a Polemic, 1750-1900*,   trans. Jeremy Moyle (Pittsburgh: University of Pittsburgh Press, 1973) - Ed.]

everlastingly; a world situated between extremes which cannot be linked; a potentially rich world that is without the necessary resources at present to exploit its possibilities; a world endowed with enormous natural wealth that brought greatness to the people of Europe and America, but which could not assure the economic well-being of the stern Latin American colonizers, who insisted on keeping a conception of the world and of life which denied the importance of such wealth. These men resigned themselves to repeating the pageantry, pomp, and courtesy of their decadent cities instead of creating new dynasties, new forms of pageantry and courtesy. They left untouched the marvelous world of wealth and well-being which was within their reach and were bent on repeating a past which no longer existed, except in their memory. Such is the unfused past and future of the Latin American world, which is simultaneously all that it can become and all that it no longer has any reason to continue being. It is a world of the future, a Utopia, since Latin America has no place in a reality that might make this vision come true. It is a form without content, a desire without the necessary strength to fulfill itself. That is to say, a mere nothing, although theoretically Latin America could be anything she chooses to be. That is the idea Western man has of Latin America which, he believes, remains on the fringe of history like the rest of the world. There is the hope, however, that it may become a part of history through exploitation and power, as already are, or are in the process of being, those civilizations which made history in the past, such as India, China and the Orient; or developing nations which can become that history but have not done so as yet; Africa and Oceania. This applies to all of these people, Orientals, undeveloped nations and Latin Americans who for one reason or another find themselves on the fringe of history, outside of what Hegel called "what is and must be."[23]

Latin America thus remains full of possibilities waiting to be realized by more talented hands. It is a resource to be developed, as has happened or is happening to other countries equally unfortunate because of their marginal position in history. It is a world of the future, but a future that cannot be realized unless it becomes a part of that history whose future it is: a history in which Latin America participated but can no longer engage in, for lack of ability to make her collaboration an effective experience. Like the world which

---

[23] See Georg Wilhelm Friedrich Hegel, *The Philosophy of History*.

shaped Latin America, the modern world has been feudal and Catholic in a period of history when it was necessary to be just that; but this is no longer true, except that we know that phase existed. This, however, does not apply to Latin America, which has insisted on participating in history in the same role she played in the past. She has not stopped being what she was in order to become something different. But her new attitude of renouncing what she has been, in order to become something else, is worthless too, because this renunciation, far from making the past an experience that will help her in her development would transform her into something that has never existed. And along with this past turned into nothingness there exists a present that tries to be nihilistic. There remains but one future, a future without possibilities, because these have vanished with the past and the nihilistic present; an empty future without substance, unsuited to the Latin American reality, which rejects the realities that could give it substance, because she considers them inappropriate to that future. Latin America lacks the assimilation of her own true history, the awareness of a history to which she aspires but has not made. She lacks that awareness and that assimilation of history typical of her model, the West, of her own history, as personal and true as the history of any other country, a history which has placed others on the fringe of history, a specific and definite history. The Latin American, therefore, like other peoples in the world who happen to be in his situation, has fallen into the trap set by the West in order to justify its expansion and control, thus making the Western peoples the expanders and controllers par excellence of history, culture, civilization and mankind.

There is a lack of awareness of her own history, of the history that Latin Americans are making day and night in their struggle against the world or against themselves. A history which the Latin American, like all people, makes in order to achieve certain ends and values, without attaching importance to the order in which, according to evaluation statistics, these come. A history, which in a sense is also the history of the West, because of what the West represents in her past, present and future; but even more than the history of the West, it is simply the history of man; the history of man in certain specific and definite circumstances which make him different from others, but neither inferior nor superior, except on the balance sheet which records his work. It is this lack of historical awareness with respect to his own role which has permitted the Latin American to accept a marginal situation; but marginal in relation to a history that is not his own, except for what it was or might be; but not in relation to the history that is shaping up as something definite and personal, and not as a desire for action pure and simple. It is this lack of historical awareness that prevents him from making history the way Western man does, which in essence is nothing more than an awareness of history and of his own actions. The history of Western man depends only on the past or the future, but never on the present. The original and unique history of Western man at all times is par excellence the center of history; it is never marginal, except when it alone can be marginal.

In his strong desire to become a part of European or Western history, the Latin American forgot that the best way to join, not European or Western history, but history as such, is to imitate that history by being original as some of the leaders of Latin America's intellectual emancipation have pointed out. This means, in other words, the ability to make out of something personal, something universal, valid for other men in a situation similar to one's own. Western man was aware of this from the very beginning, only he was not satisfied merely to share his experience with men in situations similar to his own, but in addition wanted to benefit men whose circumstances might be entirely different. It is an awareness of the history of the West which made, out of a particular situation, a situation valid for all men who accepted it. This eventually led to the subjection of countries which as yet had not developed an awareness of themselves and their history.

5. America's Inclusion in History

However, as we pointed out earlier, Latin America has also taken another attitude: that of people who are well aware of Latin America's position in history; people who understood the true essence of the attitude which permitted the West to become the pattern of the modern world; people who spoke to their contemporaries of the need to understand the mood behind this attitude, but not its results. These people, like all Latin Americans, hoped to become a part of the history of the Western world, because of the lofty humanitarian ideals it embodied. They hoped that our America would also be a world which would be based on honor and decency; that they would create a world which like the West, would be concerned with harnessing nature to serve man. A world in which respect for the individual and achievements would be uppermost. A world in which coexistence, based on mutual respect, would prevail in America. The Americas, like Europe free and sovereign, without further restrictions except those which the freedom and sovereignty of other nations would impose. A world in which the cultural and historical past of the Iberian countries would be assimilated for their future use and development. A world which, without renouncing the universality implied by participating in a task common to all nations, would strive to preserve individuality and originality of expression. This originality would be a contribution to the tasks which mankind is jointly undertaking, regardless of whether there is an awareness of it or not.

Those people of yesterday, like many today, were concerned with establishing in America the highest ideals which the West had contributed to the history of mankind. They tried to introduce these values without forcing their acceptance. On the contrary, they attempted above all to enter into the reality they found. Modern yes, but without renouncing their heritage, a heritage that was no more than an accumulation of experiences, so that it would not be necessary to relive them. They were Catholic or Christian, but without renouncing the future which permits man to expand his ability to learn, to advance in order to be ever more human. That it what Western or modern man had achieved, for although he had placed the emphasis of his actions on the future, he had known how to assimilate the past. That was the spirit which prevailed in the Iberian Peninsula and in the America created by the Iberians, the so-called "Erasmians" and the "New Christians," the followers of the Philosophia Christi. The same was true for the "eclectic" Iberians and Latin Americans during the eighteenth century, the followers of Bolívar, San Martín, and Hidalgo who set out to win the independence of Latin America; as well as for those who in Spain and America faced a past which resisted being classified simply as experience. In Spain, this same spirit encouraged the "Krausistas," followers of Krause, and their disciples, who were bent on including Spain in history, but without surrendering its identity.[24] A Spain of

---

[24] Karl Christian Friedrich Krause, 1781-1832. - Ed.

"flesh and bone," as Unamuno used to say. The same spirit encouraged and encourages in Latin America those who look for a reconciliation between the inherited world and the one they wish to build. All these thinkers desire for their world the same kind of material well-being and the same freedom that Western man aspires to and tries to achieve for his people.

Such is also what we would like to express in another sense, when we speak of incorporating Latin America into history, that is to say, a history which follows along the paths of individual dignity and material comfort for there is no reason why these should not be enjoyed by all nations. There is no reason why individual dignity and material comfort, which the modern nations, the nations of the West claim for themselves should not also belong to other nations. There is no reason why there should be nations outside or on the fringe of history, to whom the right of attaining this or that goal is denied. The fact that it was the West which probably became aware of these aspirations for the first time does not imply that it is the only part of the world with the capacity to enjoy them. The West, in claiming respect for these rights, fostered awareness of them by other nations. Such an awareness the Latin American had from his earliest beginnings in history; an awareness which was also based on those values, apparently overthrown by the modern world which enabled him in turn to be more aware of honor, individuality, and human freedom; an awareness which in modern man became an egotistical individualism, which ended by making of his ego a dehumanized ego, the focal point of history its principle and end; and every occupation its goal. That objective point of view of which Romantic idealism spoke, and to which we owe the moral justification of all the aggression, plunder, and suffering to which it subjected other men, and other nations which for this reason could not develop because that ego, transformed into spirit, culture, and progress, were nothing more than instruments for its own development, pastures for its own insatiable appetite.

The individualism in which the modern world culminated also generates the most violent opposition to making that part of the world a partner of the one in which we used to speak of human dignity, and the material happiness of the individual. People and nations who used to speak of this dignity and happiness for themselves are the first to oppose its realization by other people and other nations. They will be the first to oppose it, because its realization would mean a reduction of their material advantages and likewise, the renunciation of a theory they invented: namely progress, understood as meaning an infinite accumulation of material goods for the benefit of a single privileged individual or group of people, for whom a moral justification will be found, thus making them acceptable to everyone, even to those individuals or nations who used to belong to the underprivileged group, or to those who contributed through their efforts and good toward the well-being of the underprivileged.[25]

This individualism is certain to object to other nations becoming an integral part of the history which they created, or to admit them except in a subordinate role.   Asia, Africa, and Latin America are excluded from the sphere of modernity under various pretexts.   In Latin America, this exclusion has its pathetic side, since the nations excluded from the new history know that they rightfully belong to the modern world because of their European origin. Nevertheless, they are not the only people of European descent who are excluded; even in Europe other nations, such as Spain, were excluded, although Spain represented one of the most brilliant periods of European and world history.   Spain no longer played that role; her achievements belonged to the past, to a past which did not need to be repeated.   To that same past belonged the Spanish and Portuguese colonies in America.   The nations to which they gave birth carried the stigma of sin because they belonged to a period in history which had passed.

Confronted by this rejection, the Latin Americans turned against themselves, trying to find within themselves, in their system, their heritage, the reason for their rejection. I have already mentioned the efforts that will be made in those countries in order to break with a past which they considered a hindrance.   These countries, in order to escape their past, a past to which they were not resigned, would have to resort to violence against each other, but at the same time they would have to struggle against the resistance surrounding their active inclusion in history, which is endorsed by the very nations which serve as examples, the nations in the vanguard of history.   For this reason, the history of Latin American culture is one in which men constantly burn ships, constantly

---

[25] See Chapter IX, "Puritanism as a Component of the North American Mind."

renounce what they are, in order not only to achieve what they are not, but to avoid becoming what they might be. In this history, admiration for the great nations which serve as a model alternates with bitter resentment of the attitude of these nations towards their admirers: people who, in order to bring to their countries the democratic and liberal institutions which modern nations uphold as a sign of superiority, have to fight not only against the difficulties imposed by their own reality and their still living past, but also against countries that refuse to recognize their ability to maintain those institutions; people who, because they established in their own countries the forms of freedom of which nations like England, France, or the United States are the guarantors, must not only fight against the most conservative groups in their own countries, but also against the very countries which they admire and which serve as their model, because these have become a force that not only encourages the forces opposing their endeavors, but even defends such forces, sending for their support all the material assistance necessary for their preservation and triumph. In order to become modern, they will have to fight the forces of the modern world which will side with the old and apparently dead feudal forces to stop them succeeding. Why? The modern world itself is the reason for this attitude. It is the same reason that underlies the origin of a Western culture capable of spreading all over the world, as no culture before has done. The why and wherefore of this situation and its impact on Latin America, the efforts that Latin America has made to join the modern world, which was making its power felt, will be discussed in the following chapters.

CHAPTER II

HISTORY VIEWED AS AN INVENTION OF THE WEST

6. Innocence as an Ahistoric State of Being

Latin America outside history. Outside what history? Outside history par excellence is the usual answer. And by history we mean the history of the Western world.[26] History begins in a small area located in the Western part of Europe and comprises a small group of nations among which the prominent ones are England, France, Holland and in later years Germany. It is a history that begins about the middle of the sixteenth century, reaches its peak in the nineteenth century, and becomes universal because of the ability of these countries to expand all over the world. A world that is incorporated in and subjected to the aims of the history pertaining to these countries.

In spite of this, it has been said (and this is stated, of course, in contemporary Western philosophy), that if the person has a particular nature, it is historical. The person is a historical entity par

---

[26] See Arnold J. Toynbee, *A Study of History* (London, 1934-61).

excellence. If something characterizes and defines the person, it is precisely his lack of definition, in the sense that he is permanently "self-made" until his death. Only death can define him, handing him over to the idea which "others" have formed of him, an idea he can no longer refute, transform or change. Seen from this angle, any person is a historical entity. The person is history and his achievements will become history as well. History is something that belongs to the person, to all people who, like all societies and cultures, are historical and have a history.

However, this idea, this definition of what is human and valid for any person, has not been held by all mankind. Although mankind, societies and cultures are historical, not all people, societies and cultures have been aware of that historical nature. The person is a historical entity who has not always been conscious of this fact. Furthermore, if we analyze the history of ideas which describe the thoughts the person has had about himself, we find that the idea of historicity is a recent one, only too recent: it belongs to the present. Within the same culture from which Western culture developed, this idea of historicity is somewhat contemporary if taken in the radical sense in which it is understood today. Classical antiquity and Christianity shun the idea that the person is a historical entity, fluctuating without permanent form: the person is reason, idea, substance, something that does not change, nor can it be otherwise; or else an "image of God," a creature made "in the image and likeness of God," which cannot be different either unless it ceases to be a human being. The change here is essentially negative since it can contribute to divesting the person of human attributes. That the person is precisely the opposite of what antiquity thought him to be is a relatively recent idea, but one that is prevalent today.

Since the person is a historical being, the discovery or rather the invention of his historicity, is the work of modern man, of the individual who has created what we call Western culture, that culture which began during the sixteenth century with the modern period. An awareness of history, as we shall see later, begins as a negation of the past which is not accepted as our own, of a history which is considered to be another's, in order to begin a history that is new and for which modern man, the man who sees himself as "new," alone wants to be responsible. Only today does man realize that it is impossible to renounce history in any form if he wants to be responsible for the history he accepts as his own. This awareness of his historicity becomes more apparent every day and has been called philosophy of history, a term invented by Voltaire, a Frenchman formed in the Western tradition during the eighteenth century, a century in which the expansion of the West took a firm hold on the world. Thus history is viewed simply as the passage of time which does not alter what is intrinsically human; as something accidental, for it can be found in all people, all societies and all cultures. In this sense, the chronicle is history, and we find it in all cultures and societies. Philosophy of history, as a form of awareness of that history, as an awareness that is typical of man and his way of expressing himself, is an invention of the West, if by "invention" we mean discovering something that has always been a part of our daily lives, but of which we had not become conscious until the advent of modern times. Looking at history from this point of view we can say that it is an invention or a discovery of the West, discovery or invention which now appears very natural, characteristic of man, and essential to human life.

Dilthey, going back to the past in order to seek the origin of this conception of history, finds that it begins only with Christianity. This is an idea of history that our ancestors did not have in the form in which modern man acquires it. Ancient man was preoccupied with the present, with life, but not with what he had been, nor with what he might become. He was life in the way Parmenides understood it: someone without beginning or end; someone who, in himself, was all, beginning and end, and could not be anything else. In Herodotus, the past, or the fable, is a part of the present in the Hellenic world which historically is just beginning; in Thucydides, the future is imprisoned, bound up with a world in crisis. A history of man and his culture does not exist; it is merely a collection of anecdotes describing the troubles man has endured. It has been said that the Greek world is a "miracle." It rises like a brilliant present and fades away in the same way. There is nothing that precedes it, except a nothingness of which one cannot even speak and is therefore nonexistent, as stated by Parmenides and as demonstrated by the great masters of the Greek world, Plato and Aristotle. It is a nation, a culture, without a sense of guilt.[27] What they considered typically human begins and ends with them. The idea of guilt, of original sin, of an inherited historical guilt, appears only with Christianity.

[27] Refer to my study "Superbus Philosophus" in *Ensayos sobre filosofía en la historia* (Mexico, 1948).

For this very reason the "state of innocence" is viewed as an "ahistoric" state of being. The Greek, who finds within himself the beginning and end of his being, does not feel subjected to any past because he has no relationship with something that is other than himself. The past, viewed as movement and history, is what is accidental, indefinite, indeterminate; whatever is nebulous and marvelous, of which we cannot even speak because it is not a part of reason that defines, affirms, and gives "being." The Christian is the first to show an awareness of history as his past, as an inevitable heritage even though it may be ominous. The Christian feels the past as something that concerns him, as his guilt, his sin. St. Augustine, whom we may call the first great philosopher of history, sees in history the guilt of man, original sin inherited from the first man and passed on to all men without exception. But, here again, the "miracle" appears, the "grace" which redeems and makes of a historical event something merely accidental. Once again, whatever is human acquires definite characteristics, outside of which man degrades himself and ceases to be human. Through "grace," guilt disappears and one enters into a new "state of innocence," an innocence that has nothing, absolutely nothing to do with the past, which is viewed as an expression of sin now erased. In Christianity, therefore, the consciousness of history becomes diluted and does not attain the sharp outline it takes on in modern times. In Christianity, once "grace" has erased the "guilty past," everything reaches out for the kingdom of universal salvation, toward God, where everything becomes one, something definite, secure, permanent or eternal. In this eternity, history, the concrete reality of man's existence is merely an insignificant incident.

It is modern man who, once his relationship with that eternal life in God is placed in jeopardy, sees in history a guilt which he refuses to accept as his own; but ultimately accepts as a means to affirm himself in the present and as a justification for the future. In his ahistoricism as well as his historicism, however, modern man is aware of history as something that can no longer be evaded. The fable, miracle, or grace which made that escape from history possible, evident in ancient man and Christian alike, have been eliminated from human life. Now, man alone is responsible for his existence and the form it takes; outside forces on which he had discharged his guilt have been eliminated by reason, a reason centered on the ego, the man who thinks and loves. For this man, "innocence" is no longer possible, although he covets it or pretends he can attain it. He has an awareness of history that prevents him from feeling he is innocent. Man is born guilty because he is born to form a part of history. From Descartes to Rousseau, this sense of guilt associated with history is evident. This guilt which no "grace" can erase, except for the impossible return to the origin of human existence; to that period when man must have been an innocent being, unstained, without a past, the so-called "natural man" or "naive savage," the imaginary man whom utopians and romantics situate in America. Jean Jacques Rousseau, the seeker of innocence in modern man, said, "man is born good." It is history, the past, that has made him guilty. The philosopher from Geneva therefore, proposed a return to the natural state of innocence by means of legal subterfuges. Man is history, but he ought to begin history anew and not accept the history that has been made. For this purpose, a "contract" which would erase the entire past would be sufficient, and would indicate how the future should develop; this then is how history would be made.

7. History Viewed as a Continuous Upward Line

The man who has discovered history and has a clear awareness of it is the same man who is looking for a justification of his in the new world he is creating. The first thing that he comes up against is history which traditionally justifies the feudal aristocracy. The new man, the creator of Western culture, finds himself outside of the tradition in whose name he justifies the feudal aristocracy. The new man, the creator of Western culture, finds himself outside the tradition in whose name he justifies his superiority over a particular group of people; outside a past for which he is not responsible, and his aspirations and predominance vis-à-vis the aristocracy and the medieval church are therefore without justification. Naturally both the aristocracy and the Church claim their justification in the past, in a tradition they have inherited.

Thus history becomes conscious of modern man as someone who justifies the present and, therefore, can also justify the future. That is why modern man insists on a history that justifies his future, a history that must begin in the present once we accept that history as it exists, or the past, has nothing to justify it. This is why he insists

on not accepting history as a dimension of the past, because it is a
history he did not make, but rather it has been made by others. He
only wishes to answer for what he does and is capable of doing.
Starting from this premise, history ceases to be a tradition, a
retelling of the past, in order to become a tool for justifying the
future, a future whose history the new man is ready to embark on, a
planned, oriented and directed history, and one in which the past will
be merely a stepping stone, a stage in the interminable march of man
toward the future whose goal is always infinite.

In this way, the past which did not justify the new man's
aspirations toward predominance becomes in the present a justifiable
stage on the way to his future. The past is not and never has been
anything but a necessary stage for giving birth to the new man, the
appearance of a new world with its new values. The past is
something that was, but has no further reason for existing;
something that has passed or is passing in order for the new culture
to develop so that the new man can appear and realize his potential.
This new culture is Western culture. It is a culture responsible for
the great philosophies of history, and through them will try to prove
its preeminence, a preeminence that is viewed as an improvement
over the past and as a permanent goal for the future. These
philosophies of history see in the past a simple guarantee for the
development of Western culture. They view the present merely as an
expression of the ever-growing development of that culture to the
exclusion of any other: endless development of Western culture in a
continuous, upward line.

History, once it is renounced as a past that is only an obstacle,
becomes an upward line with Western man as the sole protagonist.
Western man and his culture. This linear and upward interpretation
of history begins, significantly, during the eighteenth century,
known as the Enlightenment. It is the same century in which new
social groups, who displaced the old aristocracy of feudal origin and
the Church, began their forward march. In that century, too, began
the consolidating of Western expansion initiated during the
seventeenth century. In this period the West was to consolidate its
economic and political superiority over the people of the millenary
culture. It was the period also which saw the appearance of the first
philosophers of Western history, Voltaire, Turgot, Condorcet, and
Gibbon, who searched for a justification of the already brilliant
future of the Western world in its history and its past. This

justification is based on a philosophy of history which sees it as a line of endless progress.

In this way modern man avoids the obstacle that history represented for him. History thus ceases to be a negative element in his eagerness for reform. The obstacle that history represented disappears. The old privileged classes can no longer defend their situation in a history which only justifies the future. History viewed as the past thus no longer determines either the present or the future. The feudal nobility and the Church can no longer support one another in a history viewed as the past. History which prevented social, political, economic, and religious change, was transformed into an ally of the new man when emphasis was placed upon the future relative to events still in the making. History no longer shapes the future, rather it is the future that determines the past. The past is what it is in order to make the future possible, and that future is to be found in modern man and his culture.

How has man been able to achieve such an inversion of history? How has he been able to shift the emphasis from the past to the future in order to justify a new present? To achieve this process, he begins by feeling "innocent" or unrelated to a history for which he is not responsible. This enables him not to accept the social reality which confronts him at the beginning of history. That reality is not his reality; he is not to be blamed for what it is or could be. This is the reason for his ahistoricism of which we spoke earlier. This is also the reason for his rejection of history, as it was so frequently rejected during the seventeenth century by René Descartes, the father of modern philosophy, for whom history is the cause of all inequalities and the source of all human misunderstandings and responsible for all wars and fanaticism which fomented them.[28] Therefore, in opposition to history conceived as the past, a return to its origins, the Golden Age, the lost Eden, or the world in its natural state, one must begin as if nothing had existed before. History must begin anew and another history must evolve.

In this way, the new man negates history as it exists but not in order to remain in the ahistoric or "innocent" state. He knows that man is guilty by nature, but he wants him to assume guilt for

---

[28] We are aware of this preoccupation in the creators of the great Renaissance utopias. See *Utopías del Renacimiento* (Mexico, 1941).

something that he considers his own. Therefore, he talks about returning to nature, the natural state, not to remain in it but rather to start on a new road which will take him to a world where he can occupy a position of preeminence, or the best of positions. He knows what history is and is fully conscious of it, and so looks for a way of making it a tool rather than an obstacle. That is why he does not accept history as it already exists, because the only acceptable history is the one he makes himself. Going back to the beginnings is only a return to the starting-point, from which he can take the best of all available routes. Not wishing to be burdened with the responsibilities of a world he has not made, he wants to begin as if nothing had existed before, criticizing everything that does not originate in his desire to create anew.[29] Modern man thus abandons the past as a justification for the present and the future by placing the emphasis on the future as a justification for a new present. To insure the greatest success of this inversion he has recourse to a new idea, to something of his own and exclusive creation. Something that will be the expression of potential history, a history not yet made but to be made, a history that is no longer the exclusive right of an established order but within the reach of all people and therefore also available to the new man. Something that will eliminate all discrimination, that will be valid for all men without distinction. This something, this new idea, is the idea of progress.

With the idea of progress the new man will be able on the one hand to justify his ideal of equality in place of a world that haggled over his privileges, and on the other hand to establish a new kind of justification for the inequality within the world he is creating and in which he will occupy a privileged position. Progress is something that is within reach of all people without exception, but it also depends on them and on their ability. From this point of view, all people are equal, alike, and with the same opportunities, but only opportunities that are within the reach of their individual abilities. Nothing that is not the personal and unique effort of each separate person can justify the idea of progress. But here we come to the other aspect of this idea, which invalidates the equality with which we begin. Progress is something coveted by all people without distinction, but it is also something which only a group of them, namely the most able, the best or most competent will achieve. Understood this way, to progress is already a distinctive

---

[29] See René Descartes, *A Discourse on Method* (New York, 1949).

characteristic. It is a way to differentiate between those who are fit for progress and those who are not. What is done will depend on each individual or group. It is man himself, man as an individual, who is responsible for his own well-being and progress. The well-being and the happiness of man on earth cannot be anything but the product of the effort he himself expends. It is something personal, concrete, unique, and therefore unquestionable. All people, merely because they exist, are potentially able to successfully achieve progress, and on this potential their equality rests. The actual achievement of progress is something else again and depends on the ability of the individual. In Western culture this ability is transformed into the source of a new type of social and cultural discrimination.

Discrimination, or the differences between people apparently alike, will be based on another kind of justification. The differences between people which the new society will establish will spring from the assumed nature of man. It has been said that only two kinds of people exist in society: those who have ability and those who do not. Equal in their natural origins but different because of the ability with which nature has endowed them. In modern as in ancient and medieval society, privileges continue to exist; only now, privileges are of natural and not historical origin. They are not inherited: they are acquired, and they represent a genuine effort by people who exist and whose ability is obvious. Privileges not based on man's natural ability have no place in the new society. However, there is another aspect of the idea of progress which comes to mind here and which will justify a new type of heritage. Modern man talks about going back to the start, to nature, to begin the race toward endless progress, but once that race has begun it does not begin again as if nothing had existed. That is a privilege of the pioneers because the rest will have to begin again with what was achieved by their forebears, until they attain a new goal which in turn will serve as a point of departure for other people, the best among them in this endless march of progress.

To progress, therefore, means to accumulate; an endless accumulation of material goods which are tied in with social, political and economic privileges. Progress thus acquires a wider dimension than a purely personal one for the individuals who make it possible, and becomes the task of a group or social class. Within this group or social class, what it has achieved or how it has progressed is merely a point of departure for what still remains to be done. Whatever has been amassed is received not as a simple inheritance but rather as an aggregate of wealth which will help individuals to accumulate more. The individual's ability to increase what he has received will depend on his belonging to a privileged class or social group. However, it is not sufficient to receive or inherit wealth because it is also necessary to increase it endlessly, in an upward line which transcends personal needs.

History again finds its position in society as a justifiable tool, as an instrument of an always open future. Whatever has been amassed, the history that has been made will only serve to increase that accumulation. In the new history the passive privileges that were simply received no longer have any justification; it will be necessary to uphold them in a continuous struggle in which the best will invariably win. In this new history, in the end, those who are competent are nothing more than mere instruments of an entity that transcends them. An entity which takes shape in the interpretations of history by modern philosophers. An entity that derives its origin from individuals who act within a historic reality that transcends them. An entity which begins to take shape within that idea of progress as something objective, impersonal, foreign to the very individuals who initiated it. Something similar to the God that modern man has placed in parentheses, but because of his origin is somewhat dependent on man. It is like the deification of man prior to his dehumanization. A God in whom all men become deified without actually being any one of them. It is with the idea of progress that the creative activity of man becomes deified.[30]

In this way, modern man, while justifying his new social situation, gives his activities a transcendental meaning, which in turn also justifies a number of privileges that he has attained or may attain. Thus his personal privileges as well as those he receives as a member of a social group, class, or nation, are also justified, giving them a new kind of transcendence. A new God, a new Deity, justifies modern man, as in former times another idea of God justified early man. The old Determinism is replaced by another: a Determinism no less absolute than the first, based on the least defined or created being, man. Man and his efforts; man and his

---

[30] See Chapter III which deals with Liberalism as a philosophy of expansion in which there is a more detailed analysis of this point of view.

ability to triumph. Abstract man, given various names by philosophers of history: progress, an objective spirit, mankind, civilization, culture, the complete man, etc.

8. A New Determinism

The new man, remote from the Determinism which may be called heteronymous, that is, external and contrary to his freedom, creates a new type of Determinism which originates in his own will. It is a Determinism that can be called autonomous. From a certain point of view man is presented as the tool of an entity that transcends him; whether it is called God, progress, or the objective spirit. Only here this transcendent entity cannot completely dissociate itself from man who invented it. This entity, whether we like it or not, is dependent on man. Contrary to the Christian God who creates man, this entity is a god created by man. It is an entity whose existence depends on man himself. Man makes it possible, is responsible for its existence, and defines it by his action. God, the Divinity, irrespective of the name he is given, exists because man creates him through his work. God is the sum of man's work. Without man's actions, the Divinity would not exist, divine goodness would not be felt, progress would stop, or the spirit would cease being aware of itself. Without men, nature, even if it existed by itself, would not exist. Nothing and nobody would be a witness to Divine goodness, glory, or justice, nor would there be an instrument to realize these attributes. This spirit, God, nature, or whatever its name, would merely be an undetermined blind force, without definite expression, without goals or even the most useless values.[31] God here is dependent on man. Man is in the last instance the creator of God. The latter is merely an expression of the power of man. He is all that man has been, is, and can become. God is thus absolute human possibility, its future, its permanent power to be; that endless goal which modern man has invented to justify his existence.

---

[31] With reference to this aspect Max Scheler and the Philosophy of Values stress the importance of values in relation to the reality in which they occur. See Max Scheler, *Der Formalismus in der Ethik und die materiale Wertethik* (Halle, 1913-16) and Nicolai Hartmann, *Ethics*, trans. Stanton Coit (London, 1932).

God's relationship with man, that is to say, the relationship of the universal with the concrete being that is man, is clearly shown in Romanticism. "The true essence of Romanticism," stated Novalis, "is to make absolute, universal, and to classify the moment or the individual situation." Romanticism elevates what is particular, concrete and unique to the absolute and universal. The individual, expressing himself as such, expressed universality although this seems paradoxical. The individual is like a mirror which makes it possible for the universal entity par excellence, or God, to know himself. Without this awareness both Romantics and philosophers of history who make Romanticism their point of departure believe the Divinity would not exist. God ceases to be a purely natural and blind entity when he is reflected in man's consciousness. According to the great German Romantic poets, the gods would be unhappy if there were not an awareness that would make their existence and happiness known. Furthermore, they would not exist without the awareness that makes them known and gives an account of them. Therefore, these poets say, the gods had to create mankind. They need the recognition accorded them by mankind. "Certainly," said Hölderlin, "the sacred element needs for its complete glory a human heart that feels and recognizes it, in the same way that heroes feel the need to be singled out and crowned with laurel."

Schiller also expressed this relationship between the absolute and the individual when he said: "The great Master of the world was unhappy, something was lacking in his Divinity, therefore, he created the spirits that are the happy reflections of divine beatitude." Hölderlin, for his part, shows the Divinity's tragic need when he says: "Alone and solitary, deaf and sad, the Divine Father would be in darkness in spite of his omnipotence, in spite of being the sum of all thought and all fire if he could not see himself reflected in man, if mankind had no heart to praise Him." The supreme song of mankind is action revealed in history. The Romantics say that God, the Divinity, manifests Himself in history, culture, and the humanization of nature. They further state that the Divinity needs the heroic deeds of man, who confronting the natural world to transform and convert it to culture, gives the Divinity an awareness of His existence. Without the only possible history, the history of man, the gods would tire of an immortality similar to that of the stone, an immortality without feeling, mute and sad. "The gods," says Hölderlin, "weary of immortality, need one thing: the heroism of mankind. Yes, they need mortal man, because the celestial beings have no awareness of their own existence. We may say that they need someone to reveal their existence to them."[32]

It is in Hegel, the philosopher of the Prussian state, that this Romantic interpretation of history, this idea of history whereby God becomes a part of man or man becomes deified, finds its highest expression. For the German philosopher of history, history is merely a becoming through which the mind is gradually made aware of itself, thus breaking away from its natural state. It is in the history made by man that the Divinity becomes conscious of its existence. History is not the mere accumulation of historical facts, but rather an awareness of their existence and a search for their meaning. This is the role of the philosopher of history. This is the role of a man whose name is Hegel, but he may also be called Comte, Spengler or Toynbee, men who reveal an idea that possesses them. It is through the rationalization of the historical element that the Divinity acquires an awareness of its existence. God is eternal, but it is only after reading an account of what happened by the philosopher of history that he is aware of his eternity. According to Hegel, "it may be said of universal history that it is the exhibition of spirit in the process of working out the knowledge of that which it is potentially . . . there is nothing superior to the spirit, bringing it to consciousness and realizing it. And this aim is none other than finding itself coming to itself and contemplating itself in concrete actuality."

It follows, therefore, that "the goal of world history" or man's task, according to Hegel, is that the spirit "realize its potentiality, make itself its own deed, its own work, and thus it contemplates itself as an objective existence." For this reason, when people of flesh and bone try to attain their own ends, they achieve the goals of the spirit. As Hegel has said: "Individuals undoubtedly partly want universal goals: they want a benefit." Only here we are dealing with goals of a limited nature, but it is through them that the spirit realizes itself. "In world history an additional result is commonly produced by human actions beyond that which they aim at and obtain or that which they immediately recognize and desire. They satisfy their own interest; but something further is thereby accomplished,

---

32 See Alexander Gode-Von Aesch, *El romanticismo alemán y las ciencias naturales* (Buenos Aires, 1948). Arturo Farinelli, *El romanticismo alemán* (Buenos Aires, 1948).

latent in the actions in question, though not present to their consciousness, and not included in their design." This something is what permits the spirit to realize itself. "In world history," Hegel adds, "satisfaction undoubtedly also exists; but the latter is not what is called happiness, because it is based on the satisfaction of those goals which rest on individual interests. The goals that are important in world history have to be fixed energetically, by means of an abstract will. Certain individuals of importance to world history, who have pursued such goals, have undoubtedly been satisfied, but they have not wanted to be happy."[33] In this way, the man of flesh and bone can become an agent of Divinity, an instrument of the spirit, civilization, democracy, of freedom in the abstract. He ceases to be a man, his will and his goals cease to be individual ones, in order to become an agent for a will whose ends are abstract and universal.

Modern man thus becomes an agent for what is universal and, in part, an instrument of God. His action will be, to a greater or lesser degree the action of God, progress, or the spirit. God speaks through him or expresses Himself in his works, regardless of how tangible or personal they might be. Therefore, whatever this man achieves acquires a transcendental aspect. He is what he is, what he must be, and he cannot be any other way. Man himself produces elements of his transcendence. His concrete action transcends his human limitations. Man becomes deified by injecting into his work transcendental qualities. This man, as a man, dies, disappears and physically turns to nothingness; but by what he does he remains and becomes eternal. He becomes immortal through his work, through which speaks that God whose expression man is. Man has become an instrument of God, a springboard of progress, or consciousness of the spirit. Man with a capital "M" stands above all men real or imaginary, beyond his limited passions, desires and aspirations, that must be sacrificed in order to realize the high goals pursued by man who is the expression of the new Deity. The goals of this man cannot but be those of God, progress, or the spirit. For this reason, only when the passions, desires and aspirations of man coincide with those ends, can any of his actions be successful. On the other hand, any action which deviates from these ends will fail. And this is so

---

[33] Georg Wilhelm Friedrich Hegel, *The Philosophy of History* (New York, 1956), pp. 17-18, 25, 27, 73-74.

because nothing can stop or change God's forward march, nor that of progress or the spirit.

Thus, out of modern man's frail being there evolves a new Determinism, a Determinism which considers his concrete and definite action the work of the Deity, whatever its name. An action which becomes an orientation, direction, or guide for all work done by man. An action with a meaning that transcends the interests of man's actual work, in order to act in accordance with the real meaning of the Divinity which is operating within him. However, behind this so-called transcendence, behind this deification of what is human, there lies hidden an aggregate of interests no less concrete than those one speaks of transcending. The goals, the interests, that fight each other are those of certain people, groups, or social classes. This new Determinism serves to justify the interests of the new man and the new social class which has reached the threshold of history. Man, who has taken the initiative in that new world, the modern world, makes of the actions and goals he pursues action par excellence, the only valid action and the sole objective to be attained. Any actions or interests which deviate from that goal will have no meaning and, therefore, no support in the new order. In the event that they lack justification because they are not in agreement with those of the new social groups, they will have to withdraw or be separated. Social groups, societies, nations, or individuals whose interests are in opposition, or perhaps different, will have to submit or be liable to expulsion. Their destiny, if they wish to survive, will be to serve as tools aiding in the growth of individuals or groups who see themselves as the incarnation of the highest divine ends, progress, or the spirit. Those ends must be their own. Only within the new theological order of the Puritans, or within the order established by nations which appear as the standard-bearers of progress, or within the order established by nations in which the spirit of Western culture is defining itself, is survival possible. Outside this order there is death, exile, the loss of the soul, barbarism, the marginal and nonhuman. People, countries, or nations that withdraw from this order will finds themselves outside the established one, because the existence of an order different from the one established by modern man is not acceptable since man would be on the outside of whatever is meaningful in his existence. These men will merely be an expression of what is negative, of evil in its various forms, such as barbarism or animality.

Therefore, any action against these people, countries, or nations is not only justified but is also seen as an action that is necessary, as an expression of something that God, progress, or the spirit has recommended to man or to the society with which he identifies. This man or social group has as one of its missions to destroy evil wherever it is found, to control barbarism and to conquer nature in all its forms. Regardless of opposition, his mission is to establish the kingdom of God on earth, the dominance of culture, progress, or civilization; the rule of freedom and democracy over everything that opposes it; and whatever is not in conformity with these interests will be in opposition to the ideals of the man or social group representing them. Thus, to eliminate evil in its various forms and to include other men and nations in the kingdom of God, progress, or the spirit, will become the lofty mission of man or of privileged nations, of people and nations that see themselves as the incarnation of the highest values of the transcendental. As representatives of these values, their action will be crowned by success since they are predestined to triumph always. Good will always prevail over evil; civilization over barbarism; the rights of those who are superior over those who are inferior. Any success that is achieved will be merely an expression of the good. On the other hand, any obstacle, any resistance placed in the way of success, will be seen an an expression of evil; therefore, any obstacle presented by the latter will be overcome always; the people and nations whose symbols they are will distinguish themselves precisely by their success. This is the way it is, and it cannot be otherwise. It is so stated in the book of eternity. Nothing and nobody can alter what is written in that book. The new man, Western man, and his culture see and introduce themselves to each other as entities predestined to triumph, to achieve success over people and nations that do not fall into line voluntarily.

9. History and the Displacement of the Non-Western World

Starting with the premise that modern man has gone beyond history, all people, social groups, nations, and civilizations can be displaced if they do not serve his particular interests. The old enemies of the Western bourgeoisie, the aristocracy and the Church, will be the first to remain outside of history. Both belong to the past, to a past that is not to be repeated. The Western world, as we have seen already, does not accept this past, but rather seeks to justify it in terms of the future it is creating. It and it alone is the creator of this future. The past is merely a stepping stone for the future in that interpretation of history in which modern man sees himself as the personification of all values. In fact, history begins with this man and the world he creates. Greece, Rome, and Christianity are related to the Western world, but only in relation to the extent to which this world has been able to develop. It is like a ladder whose steps it has been necessary to climb without implying that this proves their soundness. Now, we have to press forward, without looking back at a past that has already existed. Modern man has emerged largely because he confronted the past, and the people who insisted on keeping that world intact.

Speaking of the West, therefore, does not imply that we are referring to a world whose cultural history includes Christian and classical civilization. No, this world actually begins during the sixteenth century and extends into the present. It is a world that, although rooted in Christianity and Greco-Roman culture, pretends to be different, so different, in fact, that it begins by renouncing this very past, as if it were a new world and its people about to begin their history, the true history of mankind. And only by starting with this idea do they accept the past. Modernity as a cultural expression of the Western world appeared symbolically in the period of history known as the Renaissance and is introduced as opposing Christianity. It opposes its order, its estates, its morals, and almost all its forms of cultural expression. Modernity only accepts the past provisionally as did Descartes, intending to change it to something new, to transform it into something that would best accord with the new conception of the world and the life of the new man.[34]

But the philosophy of history, an invention of Western culture, not only relegates the world from which it arose to the past, but also thus relegates other cultures and other worlds encountered by Western man in his uncontainable expansion. Outside of history, a creation of the West, there will remain all those cultures, peoples, and societies which do not belong to Western culture, the self-styled protagonist of history. The nineteenth century, a century in which

---

[34] Toynbee also believes that the West, although tied to a Christian and Greco-Roman past, presented a new idea of life and the world during the sixteenth century, as shown by its great contributions, democratic institutions and industrialism, during the eighteenth and nineteenth centuries.

the conquests of the West over the rest of the world became firmly
established, is also the period in which the great philosophies of
history which serve as a justification for that expansion develop. It
is the century in which a Hegel and a Comte, among others,
guarantee Western culture historically for the present, while
prolonging that present into the future. Once the preeminence of the
West over the rest of the world has been attained, the great
preoccupation of her philosophers and historians is to justify her
superiority in the future, an endless future which has espoused the
idea of progress. The idea of progress in a continuous ascending
line, which we have analyzed, is good, but it is not sufficient
because it is necessary to insure that progress become a permanent
component of a given group, a given class, a given person, people,
or nation so that, in the future, the person, social group, or country
in question will not be displaced as were those who preceded them.
Greece and Rome disappeared, and so did Christianity. It is up to us
to prevent the same thing from happening to Western culture and to
the world of which it is an expression.[35] Already in the eighteenth
century Gibbon had written his *Decline and Fall of the Roman
Empire* in order to show the British how they ought to organize their
empire, an empire that would avoid the mistakes made by the Romans
in Antiquity and thus ensure its permanence. Progress, yes, but with
a permanent and stable component: Western man.   History's
protagonist, once its old components, such as the feudal aristocracy
and the Church had been in the past, were eliminated, would always
have to be the class which had given rise to the new social, cultural,
and economic order: the bourgeoisie. The only aspect that would
change with history would be the ability of that class to progress, an
ability constantly renewed. The spirit most prevalent in this constant
and forever renewed eagerness to accumulate wealth in an endless
sequence is therefore described by Hegel as an "insatiable devourer."
It is upon the same dissatisfied, purposeless spirit that the Faust
myth centers. It is the spirit of the Western world, the "Faustian"
spirit, which Spengler said characterized the West in the twentieth
century.

All progress, all that man might become or achieve, will be
determined by the priority of interests assigned by that insatiable

---

[35] This is precisely the basic concern of Toynbee's great contemporary
work, which sets out to show the Western world how it can avoid the death of
its civilization by not making the mistakes committed by other civilizations in
the past.

devourer, the Western world. The history of Western culture, therefore, will be the only one possible, the only one that we may properly call history. Persons, peoples, and cultures not included in this history which represents itself as world history will belong to the past, to something that, because it has already been, need not be repeated, or they belong to a remote future which cannot even be discussed because it has not been nor can it exist as yet. Therefore, the non-Western peoples, not only those who existed, but those who exist and with whom the West has clashed in its world-wide expansion, will become a part of that past which now is merely a legend, a story, or nonexistence, or a part of what they might become: prophecy, imagination, utopia, or simply nothingness.

Like few philosophers of history, Hegel has shown this displacement of non-Western peoples and cultures in relation to Western culture, a displacement which he justifies even from the naturalist point of view, following the ideas of naturalists like Buffon and De Pauw, who greatly criticized America because of its supposedly innate immaturity.[36] The true theater of history, says Hegel, is therefore the temperate zone, or rather its northern half. By analyzing all the possible places in the world which would correspond to that temperate zone, Hegel presents many other natural obstacles which will hinder its development, as in Europe, or will make of that history simply a past. In the great division he establishes between the New World and the Old, he begins by eliminating the New World or America as one to be discussed in the future. "As to the political condition of North America, the general object of the existence of this state is not yet fixed and determined, and the necessity for a firm combination does not yet exist . . . North America is no proof in favor of a Republican regime. Therefore, neither that nation, nor the other American states that are still struggling for their independence interest us.   Only their external relation with Europe is of importance; in this respect, America is an annex that collects the surplus population of Europe. When America established contact with us, she had already partly ceased to be. Now we can say that she is not yet fully developed." What then does America represent in that history whose main protagonist is Europe, that is, the West? "America," answers Hegel,

---

36 See Antonello Gerbi, *Viejas polémicas sobre el Nuevo Mundo* (Mexico, 1960). [The Dispute of the New World: *The History of a Polemic*, 1750-1900. Trans. Jeremy Moyle (Pittsburgh: University of Pittsburgh Press, 1973) - Ed.]

"is therefore the land of the future where, in the ages that lie before us, the burden of the world's history shall reveal itself, perhaps in a contest between North and South America. It is a land of desire for all those who are weary of the historical lumber-room of old Europe . . . It is for America to abandon the ground on which hitherto the history of the world has developed itself. What has taken place in the New World up to the present time is only an echo of the Old World, the expression of a foreign life, and as a land for the future, it has no interest for us here for, as regards history, our concern must be with that which has been and that which is. In regard to philosophy, on the other hand, we have to do with that which, strictly speaking, is neither past nor future, but with that which is, which has an eternal existence, with reason, and this is quite sufficient."[37]

Africa remains outside history because nothing has been done for her as yet, a continent which does not as yet have the future envisaged for America. It belongs to a part of the world which, according to Hegel, "has no historical reality. For this reason we leave Africa, not to mention it again. It is not a historical part of the world; it has no movement or development to exhibit. Historical movements in it, that is, in its northern part, belong to the Asiatic or European world. Carthage displayed here an important transitional phase, but it does not belong to the African spirit. What we properly understand by Africa is the unhistorical, undeveloped spirit, still involved in the conditions of mere nature and which had to be presented here only as on the threshold of the world's history."[38] Africa is thus on the margin of history, of that history whose only protagonist is Western man. Africa is the land of children, and for that reason, beyond self-conscious history. In Africa, says Hegel, "consciousness has not yet attained to the realization of any substantial objective existence . . . This distinction between himself as an individual and the universality of his essential being, the African in the uniform, undeveloped oneness of his existence has not yet attained . . . he exhibits the natural man in his completely wild and untamed state . . . there is nothing harmonious with humanity to be found in this type of character." According to Hegel, this is also the reason for the contempt which the African has for man. "The undervaluing of humanity among them reaches an incredible degree

---

[37] Georg Friedrich Wilhelm Hegel, op. cit., pp. 80, 85, 86-87.
[38] Ibid., p. 99.

of intensity. Tyranny is regarded as no wrong." From this order
stems the naturalness with which slavery is accepted. "For it is the
essential principle of slavery that man has not yet attained a
consciousness of his freedom and consequently sinks down to a mere
thing, an object of no value." Other than slavery Africa has no
relation with Europe. She is merely the purveyor of slaves for the
Western world. "The only essential connection that has existed and
continued between Negroes and the Europeans is that of slavery." Is
this relationship unjust? It is, answers the German philosopher, but
it cannot be otherwise. "Slavery is in and of itself injustice, for the
essence of humanity is freedom, but for this man must be matured.
The gradual abolition of slavery is therefore wiser and more
equitable than its sudden removal."[39]

With Africa eliminated, what happens to the rest of the Old
World? There is Asia, "the real theater of world history." In Asia
there exists an awareness of themselves for themselves. But Asia is
only the past. She is the source, the antecedent of Europe, of the
West, but nothing more. She is related to Europe as the past is
related to the present. Nothing that was produced here "this land has
kept for itself, but sent over to Europe." The most important part of
Asia for Europe, in Hegel's opinion, is the Anterior Asia we now
refer to as the Middle East, which has served as a link between the
rest of Asia and Europe. But this part of Asia is also the past which
has been given power in the European present. "In this part of Asia
we find the rise of principles which have not been perfected in the
land of their birth, but have been clearly developed in Europe. This
part of Asia is the origin of all religious and political principles, but
Europe has been the scene of their development."[40]

In this way the non-European world, the non-Western world,
is eliminated from history, which leaves only Europe as the sole
protagonist of history hovering between a past that, because it has
been, can no longer be, and a future that as yet does not exist. "The
European is the most universal." No natural principle is imposed on
the European and he is, therefore, the freest and most universal,
according to Hegel. An expression of freedom is that transcendence
beyond what one is, that going beyond oneself which characterizes
the European and shows itself in his relationship with the sea. The

---

[39] Ibid., pp. 93, 95, 96, 98, 99.
[40] Ibid., pp. 99, 101.

sea as an element has been taken into account by the European only
in order to extend himself, to expand and go beyond himself. "This
stretching out of the sea beyond the limitations of the land is wanting
to the splendid political edifices of Asiatic States . . . For them the
sea is only the limit, the ceasing of the land; they have no positive
relation to it." On the other hand, in Europe, the relationship with
the sea is important, and here we have a lasting difference. "Without
the sea, a European state could not be conceived . . . The extensive
tract of eastern Asia is severed from the process of general historical
development, and has no share in it."[41] Therefore, the principle of
individual freedom has become the guiding principle of life in
European nations.

Once the preeminence of the West in relation to other ancient
and modern nations had been established, there only remained
justifying the expansion of that world over nations that had arrived
too early or too late to witness a history that had as its sole
protagonist the European. The philosophy which justified this
expansion is Liberalism and it has been called that as well as other
names. It was a Liberalism that differed, as we shall see later, from
the one that appeared in Spain, and the Iberian countries. It was a
Liberalism which, in the name of that freedom of which Hegel
speaks, set out to justify the hold over countries that as yet had not
reached that stage of development. They were countries which for
one reason or another had not been able to overcome their natural
state. They were countries that were immature or anachronistic.

---

[41] Ibid., pp. 81, 87, 87-88.

CHAPTER III

LIBERALISM AND THE EXPANSION OF THE WEST

10. The Western Model

What kind of world was it from which the non-Western peoples were displaced? The world of freedom and the conquest of nature. The world of the liberal-democratic institutions and material comfort achieved through industrialism. These were the two principal contributions of the Western world, and they characterized it. According to Toynbee, the two great trends that give the Western world its character are these two institutions: "the Industrial System of economy and a hardly less complicated system of politics which we call 'Democracy' as a short title for responsible, parliamentary, representative government in a sovereign, independent, national state. These two institutions, the one economic and the other political, attained a general supremacy in the Western world at the close of the age preceding our own because they offered provisional solutions for the chief problems with which that age had been confronted."[42] Both institutions are an expression of what Hegel

---

[42] Arnold J. Toynbee, *A Study of History* (London, 1934), Vol. I, p. 1.

called the freedom of the spirit, so characteristic of the Western world. Freedom with respect to nature in its social, political, and economic aspects. These were the two institutions that showed the non-Western world why the West was the leader of a history whose permanent goal was progress. All countries should strive for that world of freedom in its political and economic aspects if they wished to become a part of this history. It was a history to which they did not belong because of immaturity or anachronism. The West showed the rest of the world what could be done in a free society, except for those obligations that accompanied freedom, to create a world in which nature had been placed at the service of man for his greater happiness on earth, a world in which happiness was a personal matter, something that could be acquired through personal effort. Democracy and industrialism, as an expression of the conscious domination of man over nature, were the means of a personal happiness never achieved in other periods. The goal was a world of free and rich people. Freedom and material wealth were the gifts that the Western world offered to the rest of the world. All people, said the world's foremost philosophers, could be free and therefore equal to any people in the world. Freedom and wealth were within the reach of all individuals and all countries. All that was required was to follow the example of modern nations as a pattern of freedom and wealth.

These were the same nations that had fought and defeated countries which continued to maintain attitudes contrary to freedom. These were the same nations that had criticized Spain for the spoliation of her colonies; the same nations that had condemned and continue to condemn "black Spain," which had brought political despotism and religious superstition to her colonies. These were the same nations which, in Africa and Asia, had subjected peoples who, by their subordination to nature and the despotic institutions which governed them, clearly lacked personal identity. These were the nations which brought civilization to those peoples who, for one reason or another, had remained outside of history. These were the same nations which had decreed the freedom of the seas by eliminating Spain; these were the very nations which now advocated freedom of trade in all parts of the globe bombarding the harbors of countries that refused to do business with them. These were the nations which had stimulated the political emancipation of the Spanish colonies in America in order to create a vacuum later filled with obligations and concessions, so as to be able to exploit economically a world which the mother country did not know how to exploit. The Latin American countries which had achieved political freedom like those of Asia and Africa had felt the impact of Western civilization and soon realized that it invariably exacted a price for the slightest help given. This price took the form of concessions made on the basis of the wealth of these independent or civilized nations. Entrance into history was not free, and the freedom which they seemed to have attained had a price: a new kind of subjection, namely the subjection of immature or anachronistic countries because one could not go impulsively from the past to the present, nor advance towards the future. According to Hegel, "in order to exercise freedom, a certain level of maturity is required." With respect to slavery, its "gradual abolition is more equitable than its sudden removal."

These countries could not do anything to make the spirit of freedom a reality for themselves, except to be incorporated in a state where freedom was to be found, so that within this new dimension they might reach the standard set by that new world in a natural and progressive way. But this was something that concerned those countries alone. It was up to them, and only them, to develop an awareness of freedom as had been done in Western countries, without assistance and through their own efforts. In the meantime, by maintaining their position of immaturity, as countries closer to the spirit of their original state than to that of freedom, they would become an instrument of the free spirit symbolized by the West. This whole philosophy would develop with liberalism, in the liberal philosophy of Western origin which expressed itself in the institutions we have already mentioned: democracy and industrialization.

11. Liberalism as a Philosophy of Expansion

What is liberalism? According to Harold J. Laski, "it is not easy to describe, much less to define, for it is hardly less a habit of mind than a body of doctrine."[43]   More than a definable rational doctrine, it is a way to experience and live the life of the so-called Western man. In the preceding chapters we have already had some glimpses of that conception of life and the world which we will try to explain here by viewing it from another angle, by looking at man's idea of freedom in relation to the apparent freedom of other people and other countries. It is an idea of freedom that coincides with his idea of history, which he sees as progress, as a new kind of justification felt in his eagerness to dominate, first, within the realm of the society to which he belongs and, later, in his relations with other societies, peoples, and nations.

An individual, a nation, a people cannot do anything for the progress of other individuals, nations, or peoples. In the modern world individuals, like nations, are the sum total of their own effort. People and nations are self-made: they are the most tangible product of freedom, their freedom. As we have already stated, all people, like all nations, are equal. There is nothing in the past that would justify an inequality in the present, except the inability to achieve that progress. It is a march in which individuals and nations show their ability and lack of ability. There are nations like individuals, ready for progress with all that this implies in terms of freedom and material well-being; but, on the other hand, there are also nations and individuals who show their inability to win those benefits. Inequality is merely an expression of the ability or inability of individuals or countries to gain possessions that can contribute to their spiritual and material well-being.

Modern man, therefore, has little or no sympathy for individuals or countries that, in accordance with that point of view, have not acquired the ability to conquer nature in its political and technical aspects.   He does not understand, nor does he try to understand the real reasons for this apparent lack of ability.   For him, there are only competent or incompetent individuals and countries. Difficulties in overcoming obstacles are seen as a sign of inability, an inability which is also taken as a sign of sub-humanity. There must be something wrong with men and countries that can neither achieve democracy nor overcome nature; this certain something places them on a lower rung of the human ladder with

---

[43] Harold J. Laski, *The Rise of European Liberalism* (London, 1958), 3rd ed., p. 15.

respect to individuals or countries that have achieved democratic institutions or have succeeded in conquering nature. The difference between those who are able and those who are not in turn justifies the attitude the former adopt towards the latter. Beyond any consideration that would enable us to understand the position of the latter, is the fact of their inability and their unimportance in terms of the relentless march of progress.

The wealth of nations and the well-being of individuals thus depends on their ability to attain these ends. "Every man," says Adam Smith, "is by nature first and principally recommended to his own care."[44] The freedom and prosperity of countries and individuals depends on their own ability to attain these goals and to safeguard them. Social welfare and national wealth have their origin in the care individuals exercise in handling their own interests, and from this care derive in turn social well-being and national wealth. What the individual achieves for his own benefit is transformed into social benefit. The individual cannot want for society something he would not want for himself, inasmuch as he is a member of that society. Kantian ethics and the liberalism he represents take on a practical character in Adam Smith. The individual who depends freely on his obligation to exist, originates that new world of wealth and social welfare. The position of the individual is reflected in the social world of which he is the center. It is the world of the great businessmen, merchants, and industrialists, who are the real benefactors of society, because they contribute to its greatness and are responsible for its prosperity and national wealth. These are men who do not have, and ought not to have, any bond or limitation other than that of their own conscience, based on the assumption that they would not want for society anything they would not want for themselves. A nation will be prosperous when important business deals can be transacted. Since the only thing it wants or covets is a steadily increasing wealth and material well-being, the entire nation will benefit as a result of these deals.

Confronting these people and nations in love with progress are, of course, people and nations that have not made a large enough effort, or any effort at all, to achieve well-being and wealth. The internal or external reasons for their apparent inability are not

---

[44] Adam Smith, *Theory of Moral Sentiments* (London, 1759), as quoted by Harold J. Laski in ibid., p. 178.

accepted and only the concrete fact of their poverty is valid. Therefore, people who regard themselves as creators of their own wealth and well-being, as originators of the greatness of their country, will not feel any sympathy for people and nations who have not made wealth and material well-being the goal of their existence, or as happens in the non-Western world, because of their social position and cultural background they encounter difficulties in the way of achieving that wealth and material well-being. In their continuous upward march, the nations established by these people who consider themselves to be competent will encounter countries that lack these attributes. They will not think highly of these countries, nor of individuals in their own society, who have lacked the ability to succeed. Ideologically this attitude manifests itself in liberalism of which the great Western nations are the standard-bearers. In analyzing this doctrine, Laski has stated: "Liberalism has always been affected by its tendency to regard the poor as men who have failed through their own fault."[45] And what one thinks of individuals is also applicable to countries.

Of course, unsuccessful individuals, like nations, and particularly the poor ones, occupy a special place in modern Western society, namely that of subordinates, a position which is merely an expression of their inability to rise to the top as individuals or nations. The great English philosopher Locke, known as the father of modern liberalism, used to divide society into two large segments: the rich and the poor, and assigned to each a specific function. This philosopher, who speaks of science as a tool for making nature the servant of man, tells us also that "Knowledge and science in general are the business only of those who are at ease and leisure."[46] That is, of those who already have the means or necessary wealth, and along with it that minimum of leisure which is essential in order to acquire knowledge and to study the sciences in general are those destined for government service, or positions of leadership in society, that is to say, a society which will profit from the ability of such individuals. As for those other people, the poor, who are unable to avoid poverty because of a lack of means and time to become acquainted with science as a liberating force, there remains one role only, that of "pious and useful obedience."

---

[45] Harold J. Laski, ibid., p. 259.
[46] As quoted by Harold J. Laski in ibid., p. 91.

Therefore, what is said about individuals can also be said about countries that have conquered poverty and countries that continue to be poor. For this reason the whole world, except for the countries that make up the so-called Western nations, is composed of countries that, for different reasons, try to maintain values which are different from those that have contributed to the greatness of modern nations. These countries have not understood the importance of science as a liberating force; for one reason or another they have fallen behind in the race which leads to the harnessing of nature by man. There are countries where the work of the individual has not contributed to the greatness of the nation. There are countries, finally, on the fringe of progress whose forward march is guided by the West; countries that must of necessity be in the position of subordinates.

It is precisely over those countries that Western man maintains his right to expansion. It is a strange right which cannot expect the approval of countries affected by such expansion, an expansion which, far from being rejected or resisted, must be accepted and praised as a kind of inclusion in progress shared by all countries, regardless of the position they hold. Western countries, far from looking upon this expansion as something negative, see it as a gift granted to countries that have done nothing to join the modern world. Westerners say that ultimately those countries will also be able to conquer their poverty and achieve the well-being and wealth characteristic of the modern world. Of course, everything will depend on their ability to achieve these ends within the limits imposed by free enterprise to which they have to adhere as members of the new order. An order in which the best, the most able, win, starting from the hypothesis of an apparent equality which here is due to the fact that they belong to the Western world as a result of its expansion. Free competition in everything characterizes this world, and all countries join in, irrespective of how they feel about it. It is an order in which it is useless to speak of obstacles of any kind. The fact that we are dealing with countries whose cultural background is vastly different from a way of life which permits success or at least adaptation to an order previously alien to them, does not count.

There was no time to wait for the adaptation of these countries to the new order. Whether they liked it or not, they were part of a new order in which freedom in its various forms reigned. One of these was free enterprise, a kind of freedom which had led to the greatness of modern nations. Why would it not have the same result in the new countries if they were able to compete successfully? It was free enterprise that had made possible the appearance of powerful nations like England, France, and the United States. What did the countries directly affected by the expansion of those nations expect in order to participate in that new world? What hopes did the young Latin American nations have of participating in that free enterprise once they had broken with their respective mother countries which had prevented this development? Their position in the new order now depended on their ability to face competition. They would have to gain that position by fighting for their interests, just as the English, French, and North Americans had done before them. Their place in the new order depended on their ability to defend their interests and, if necessary, impose them upon alien interests. It was this kind of resourcefulness that had contributed to the greatness of the new nations. Now if because of their education or background, as happened in the case of Asian and African nations, they showed an inability to participate in that struggle and lost, so much the worse for them! Nothing and nobody could do anything to improve their lot. It was their own business and in their own interest, just as it was the business and in the interest of those with whom they had to compete.

The outlook of the Western nations in international affairs was the same as in domestic matters which, as we have already seen, amounted to acceptance of a society divided into rich and poor. Rich people and poor people, equal by nature, by unequal in their ability to accumulate wealth and acquire well-being. An ideal equality which justified inequality. A fictitious equality which justified the inevitable results of uneven competition. The poor person, who did not belong and had never belonged to the middle class that had given rise to the bourgeoisie, which now imposed its outlook on society and the world, could not do anything with a declaration that spoke of his equality, since he lacked the material means to assert his equality against individuals who had more than they needed. A fictitious equality, since in this competition into which he was forced he could only avail himself of his physical strength whereas his opponent had already accumulated the material tools, techniques, and means of production; they were the same means which had made it possible for him to triumph over his old enemies the aristocracy of feudal origin and the order represented by the Church.

Consequently, a class that could have destroyed the old medieval order by supplanting it did not exist in a relationship of equality between classes, or between social groups whose only wealth was their ability to work. Work might or might not be accepted, on an individual basis, by the class in whose hands production was concentrated. This was exactly what happened to the countries the West encountered in its expansion. These countries found themselves with a high degree of material inequality when they merged with the modern world. Some of them, like the Latin American countries, were seduced by the illusion of free enterprise in a world to which they were latecomers, a world in which material leadership was already in the hands of the Western countries. In this so-called competition into which they were drawn by the West, they were already at a complete disadvantage. Countries that had no other resources than their eagerness to acquire wealth were compelled to compete with countries that had already accumulated sufficient wealth to impose their outlook and their interests. Countries that began by reëducating themselves in order to adapt to the modern world had to compete with countries responsible for creating that world. It was a competition between rich and poor countries, between countries at the height of their economic and political expansion and those that had nothing more going for them than their ambition to be like their great Western models which, far from providing them with any stimulus, represented an obstacle that had to be overcome. The desire of the poor countries to emulate them strengthened the rich countries' spirit of expansion. It represented a challenge to their uncontrollable ambition for enrichment, which might be diminished in case the new nations were successful in imitating them. There was no longer any room in the world for the enrichment of other countries, nor any possibility of arriving at an agreement regarding a new distribution of the world's wealth once a group of nations had attained absolute control. All that remained was the competition between the powerful and the weak, a competition that was merely a means of justifying the plunder by the former of the latter, since the powerful were in possession of the means necessary to insure success. A sure triumph, in which the word "competition" was merely a way of justifying the morally unjustifiable.[47]

---

[47] The Puritan origin of this desire for moral justification will be analyzed in a later chapter.

How then was it possible that this injustice and inequality derived from liberalism, a philosophy that seemed to be its exact opposite? Referring to this point, Laski tells us as a doctrine, "no doubt, it is directly related to freedom for it came as the foe of privilege conferred upon any class in the community by virtue of birth or creed." In other words, it is directed against the old aristocracy of medieval origin and against the Church. "But the freedom it sought had no title to universality, since its practice was limited to people who had property to defend." Freedom is understood as freedom for one's own enrichment, as liberating with respect to any obstacle which might limit this enrichment. Freedom with respect to the government or any other institution of a social character which might try to limit the right to free enterprise. "It has sought, almost from the outset of its history," Laski continues, "to limit the ambit of political authority, to confine the business of government within the framework of constitutional principle, and it has tried, therefore, fairly consistently, to discover a system of fundamental rights which the state is not entitled to invade." Rights, however, that will be exploited by other groups or classes which can hinder the growth of the class which has espoused liberalism as its doctrine. "But, once more, in its operation of those rights, it has been more urgent and more ingenious in exerting them to defend the interests of property than to protect as claimant to their benefit the man who had nothing but his labor-power to sell. It has attempted, where it could, to respect the claims of conscience, and to urge upon governments the duty to proceed by rule rather than by discretion in their operations; but the scope of the conscience it has respected has been narrowed by its regard for property, and its zeal for the rule of law has been tampered by a discretion in the breadth of its application. "Liberalism," Laski continues, "has always taken a negative attitude towards social action." Thus, "though it has expressed itself always as a universal, it has, in its institutional result, inevitably been more narrow in its benefit than the society it sought to guide. For though it has refused to recognize any limit in theory, whether of class or creed, or even race, to its application, the historic conditions within which it has operated effected a limitation despite itself." That is the way it had to be. It could not be otherwise. Liberalism was merely a doctrine whose ultimate end was to justify the emergence of a new class which appeared when the medieval order disappeared. "What produced liberalism," Laski continues, "was the emergence of a new economic society at the end of the middle ages. As a doctrine, it was shaped by the needs of that new society and, like all social philosophies, it could not transcend the medium in which it was born. Like all social philosophies, therefore, it contained in its birth the conditions of its own destruction . . . by which the new middle class rose to a position of political dominance." It invented, as a kind of social relationship between unequal groups, the ideal of contractual freedom which existed whenever there was a so-called equality between contractors. "It never understood, or was never able to fully admit, that freedom of contract is never genuinely free until the parties thereto have equal bargaining power. This, of necessity, is a function of equal material conditions. The individual whom liberalism has sought to protect is, within his social context, always free to purchase his freedom, but the number of those with the means of purchase at their disposal has always been a minority of mankind. The idea of liberalism, in short, is historically connected, in an inescapable way, with the ownership of property."48

The idea which the middle class as the originator of the liberal doctrine had of its relationship with other social groups will also be seen in the relationship the nations it created have with countries of a different origin and background. These countries, as has been seen, were compelled to participate in an enterprise based on a so-called equality between competitors, a competition that was neither free nor among equals, but rather forced upon those who were not equals. The inability of these countries to engage in such competition, far from limiting expansion, came to justify it. Their inability showed that they were too immature to come to terms with the modern world, and this gave the West the right to accomplish in those countries what they were unable to do alone; however, it was solely to benefit the West. These countries, weak as they were to engage in a competition supposedly among equals, thus demonstrated their inequality, or rather their inferiority. Such countries were not even accorded the status of nations. No, they were simply not nations nor were their inhabitants people, at least not people like those who had made freedom and progress possible. Rights like sovereignty, which Western nations always invoked in their relations with non-Western peoples, would therefore be denied them. These countries lacked rights because of their weakness and all that it meant in relation to

---

48 Harold J. Laski, op. cit., pp. 15, 15-16, 17, 17-18. Juan José Arévalo has analyzed this same relationship with respect to the role played by the weak versus the powerful nations in his book symbolically entitled *The Shark and the Sardines* (New York, 1961).

the concept of progress. Only the influence of Western nations on these countries could finally achieve their inclusion in progress and all that progress implies in terms of rights and freedom. These Western nations were the world's standard-bearers of freedom and progress. Therefore, in the name of progress, civilization and freedom, their expansion into other countries would be justified. It was an expansion that was merely a means of integrating the non-Western world and making it a part of the world of freedom and progress. This was the justification for the expansion of nations and individuals who had achieved those values in their own countries. They were going to be the standard-bearers of those values for the rest of the world, and at the same time were its only beneficiaries.

12. World Expansion

The development of the middle class which created the modern world shows that it began by subordinating the interests of other classes and groups to its interests. The basis for its development was enrichment, the accumulation of wealth, from which modern capitalism originated. It was wealth that began by being wrested from the weakest classes in the nations that embarked upon that road. Soon the effect of this attitude was felt. An economic disaster threatened England, the nation that had led the way. The enrichment of a small group was bringing poverty to the majority of the population. The poverty of the weakest threatened to stop the growth of wealth of those who thought of themselves as the best or the most able in vying for power. Furthermore, not only did this threaten to put a stop to the accumulation of wealth, but also to plunge the whole nation into poverty which without exception would touch all groups. But it was little, progressively less, that could be extracted from a majority that had been thoroughly exploited. The attitude of laissez-faire proved deceptive. The idea that the search for wealth in itself went hand in hand with the welfare of the people began to be doubted in countries like England, where it had been put into practice.

Agricultural and urban workers began to distrust the doctrines of a social group which, in the name of so-called social progress and through free enterprise, was creating the poverty of groups that were not a part of the new elite of businessmen and shopkeepers. One could not look with sympathy upon a class whose doctrine only justified the sacrifice of the worker and the consumer in order to obtain ever-increasing profits for itself. The social groups that had only their labor to offer had supported the liberal revolution because at least in theory it stood for freedom and human dignity. But they could no longer accept the consequences of its interpretation of freedom, a freedom which permitted the free exploitation of the weaker by the stronger social groups, on the hypothesis of an apparent equality that was purely theoretical in character. The so-called free enterprise did not operate among equals but between groups, classes, and individuals that were unequal economically, politically, and socially. Some had nothing more to offer than their work, whereas others had the tools needed for work, the wealth produced through work, and the protection of the state, which regarded them as social benefactors. Referring to a liberalism which in fact justified inequality on the hypothesis of an apparent ideal equality, Laski says that "it has always suffered from its inability to realize that great possessions mean power over men and women as well as over things. It has always refused to see how little meaning there is in freedom of contract when it is divorced from equality of bargaining power."[49] Awareness of this fact among the largest weaker social groups was shown, therefore, in an ever-increasing resistance against the class which, in the name of freedom and equality, was progressively reducing their dwindling profits.

The industrial revolution began in England during the eighteenth century and marked the beginning of the rise of the Western bourgeoisie. This revolution was the signal for greater production and resulted in greater profits. However, the English experience was to herald a failure in the first half of the nineteenth century. The results of this experience were negative. The industrial revolution, far from obviously leading to social well-being and national wealth, led the country to unemployment and poverty. And this happened because the bourgeoisie in its growth, which was to lead to capitalism, had relied on the exploitation of its fellow-citizens, on those who belonged to the poorest classes of the nation. The poorest groups in England saw themselves forced to pay the price which industrialization and capitalism demanded. The Western

---

[49] Ibid., p. 259.

bourgeoisie which originated in England grew and expanded, but at the expense of the poorest among them and the weakest social groups in the country. According to Fritz Sternberg, "this expansion was primarily at the expense of pre-capitalist forms of production at home."[50]

The result was a crisis that threatened to slow down the march of capitalism which had produced it. A great impoverished mass with a majority of unemployed was bound to be a bad market for the products which had made the industrialization of the country possible. What could be the solution? How could this problem be solved? The only solution was expansion to other lands, the non-Western countries, where they would not encounter the competition already felt in other Western nations. England chose this way out since she had this possibility in her colonies, which she would now try to develop. Purveyors of raw materials, the colonies were also to serve as a market where they could be sold as manufactured goods. The colonial people in the non-Western countries were now to bear the burden and pay the price of enabling the British nation to acquire wealth and achieve greatness.

Now the social and economic well-being which the English bourgeoisie had offered the nation would become possible, since other groups, weaker and more unfortunate than her own citizens, were going to pay for that long-hoped-for prosperity. The countries of Asia, Africa, Oceania, and Latin America were going to pay for this prosperity. Soon France, Holland, and the United States would follow this useful method. It was a way that avoided the experience of the British failure in its first period of industrialization and capitalization. It resulted in a period of great prosperity for the West, particularly England, during the second half of the nineteenth century. In a letter written to Marx on October 7, 1858, Engels declared: "The English proletariat is in fact becoming more and more bourgeois, so that it looks as though this most bourgeois of all nations will end up having a bourgeois aristocracy and a bourgeois proletariat as well as a bourgeoisie."[51] The West's expansion permitted the establishment of a nation that was one hundred percent bourgeois but kept its internal differences; it was a much better

---

[50] Fritz Sternberg, *Capitalism and Socialism on Trial* (New York, 1951), p. 57.
[51] As quoted by Sternberg in ibid., pp. 100-101.

situation than the West had established in its colonies. The people in these colonies represented the proletariat that had made possible the bourgeois standard of living in their respective mother countries.

Sternberg says that "the 'bourgeois' workers of Europe, on the other hand, grew up in a period of tremendous capitalist expansion and imperialist exploitation . . . At the same time hundreds of millions of people in the colonial and semi-colonial countries had a standard of living far below that of the European workers. It was not only the workers of these colonial and semi-colonial countries, who were often 'free' only in name, who lived in conditions far inferior to those prevailing in Europe, but ninety percent of the whole population of the colonial and semi-colonial countries; in other words, the majority of the population of the world. It was, in fact, the relationship between the metropolitan capitalist centers and the colonial and semi-colonial countries which represented one of the most important factors which made the working classes of the European countries so 'bourgeois'."[52]

Western capitalism included not only people like the Asians and Africans, to whom the conception of the world and life on which this expansion was based was alien; it also included nations which were trying to follow the example of the West, and countries which kept their political independence, like Russia and Japan, but lacked the tools to participate in that expansion; it also spread to countries recently emancipated politically, like the Latin American countries, which were trying to emulate the example of the great Western nations. Industrialization which had made possible the greatness of nations like England, was to encounter difficulties in other countries intent on following England's example. "England was the country in which capitalism was most highly developed, and it then became the country in which the destruction of pre-capitalist forms of production was most thorough," according to Sternberg. "In this period capitalism in England was not merely dominant, it was practically the only system," while in countries where its development was late in coming as, for instance, in the nations of Western and Central Europe, it developed rapidly. This is true particularly with respect to Germany. Around the middle of the nineteenth century "this

---

[52] Fritz Sternberg, ibid., p. 101. In our own time we have seen how a Socialist party like the one in France adopted a policy of aggression against colonial countries like Egypt and at the same time was averse to extending the same rights French workers have to those born in Algiers.

capitalist expansion into sovereign states which retained their
sovereignty, such as Russia and Japan, in which pre-capitalist
production forms dominated ... went parallel with a further extension
of the capitalist mode of production at home . . . Imperialism is
characterized by capitalist expansion into areas which it dominates
politically and turns into colonies of the capitalist metropolitan
centers. This colonial drive, which was largely European, reached a
certain culminating point in the nineteenth century with an extension
of colonialism in Asia and a particularly strong drive from Europe
into Africa in the last quarter of the century." In those regions,
therefore, the interests of the capitalist "motherlands" decided the
desirability and the degree of development. At that time capitalism
had "expanded into areas which had previously hardly been settled at
all," particularly in the United States but also in Canada and other
'white' colonies; but it "did not break into a system of feudalism to
undermine it and destroy it in part, as European capitalism did."[53]

To these we would have to add the recently emancipated
countries that were a part of the Spanish and Portuguese empires in
America, where the economic capitalist penetration of the West began
once they had broken their ties with the Spanish and Portuguese
mother countries. This penetration imposed on them a new type of
colonial subordination, the economic imperialism of the West as
represented by England, France, and later the United States.

13. Reaction as an Instrument of Progress

In the expansion of the West over the rest of the universe, it
became clear how little she was interested in the negation of her
ideals in another world, if this helped to strengthen her interests. It
became clear that one kind of conscience was operative for internal
and another for external use. The bourgeois standard of "do unto
others as you would have them do unto you" had no validity for the
West's relations with countries outside her sphere of interests. It
was one thing to have a relationship with her own citizens, and quite
another with those of other countries. "The double ethic," says Max

---

[53] Ibid., pp. 34, 36-37, 79.

Weber, "has permitted here what was forbidden in dealings among brothers."[54] Peoples who, in their own countries had fought against feudalism, the Church, and other institutions as symbols of reaction supported them in subjected countries so that these might not attain a degree of progress prejudicial to the advancement of the West. In this way, reaction became a tool in the service of Western progress. This was considered necessary from the Western nation's point of view since they were interested in their own development, even if this meant poverty for other countries. The way this would turn out had been shown by the experience of industrialization in England.

The expansion of Western capitalism all over the world had slowed the danger revealed during the early phase of its growth in England. This growth was to continue, but no longer at the expense of poverty for her own citizens, since other countries would pay for it. The prosperity promised to the Western nations by the bourgeoisie had become a fact, but this prosperity would not touch the countries that were merely to be the tools of a wealth that eluded them. In this way, capitalism came to represent progress in the countries where it originated, but not in the countries that felt its impact and paid with their poverty for the prosperity which the world gradually achieved under the capitalist system. According to Sternberg: "This undeniable economic progress of capitalism is only one side of the picture . . . since progress did not take place all over the world equally. On the contrary, as against the tremendous progress in the capitalist centers, in what are known as the 'mother countries,' though their real role was anything but 'motherly,' there was little or even no progress, and sometimes even a decline, in those countries which they had turned into their colonies or which were otherwise more or less politically, economically, and financially dependent on their decisions . . . Capitalist progress brought about a considerable growth in the national incomes of the capitalist centers, but no approximate increase in the national incomes of the colonial and semi-colonial countries, not even an improvement beginning at a very much lower level. On the contrary, the gap between the capitalist metropolitan centers and their colonial and semi-colonial dependencies increased quite considerably."[55]

---

[54] Max Weber, *The Protestant Ethic and the Spirit of Capitalism* (London, 1930), p. 57.
[55] Fritz Sternberg, op. cit., pp. 30-31.

Various theories were advanced to justify this inequality, such as the inferiority of the races inhabiting the colonial countries. The fact is that capitalism, or the Western world, based its prosperity on the poverty of other countries. This poverty did not undermine the West's prosperity, as had happened when the Western countries tried to nurture it on the poverty of their own weakest classes. "The speed of capitalist imperialist progress," adds Sternberg, "was based to some extent on the exploitation of the colonial and semi-colonial peoples, and in consequence the gap in the standards of living between the two groups was made still wider." But something else occurred in addition. This accentuation of differences between the mother countries and their colonies developed into a carefully planned program which the former carried out on a permanent basis. It became a necessity to maintain this inequality, to maintain poverty in the colonies so as not to endanger the prosperity of the mother countries. The wealth of the latter was to depend in the future on the inability of the colonies to overcome their poverty. This is the reason for the Western nations' opposition to an integration of their colonies or semi-colonies into a world which they hold up as an example and a moral justification for their expansion. Within this prosperous world the non-Western peoples merely occupied the position of inferiors, of people who were exploited. This would permit the maximum development of capitalist countries but would prevent the same process from taking place in the colonial and semi-colonial countries. "Further, capitalist development in the metropolitan centers was accelerated," says Sternberg, "to some extent by the fact that industrial development in the colonial and semi-colonial countries was prevented, or deliberately slowed when it could not be prevented altogether."[56] Non-Western countries were deliberately prevented from developing the strengths which would allow them to succeed in the competition which, in the words of Westerners, was responsible for the greatness of nations. The champions of equality deliberately maintained an inequality which befitted their expansion and ever-increasing superiority.

In order to prevent the non-Western countries from attaining a level higher than that of subordinates, the representatives of Western capitalism and progress in those countries neither had nor felt any moral misgivings about establishing alliances with representatives of the reactionary forces in those nations which were the equivalent of

---

[56] Ibid., p. 32.

feudalism in the West. The most backward-looking groups and forces which, for one reason or another, opposed Western progress in their countries received the support of Western representatives. The forces which insisted on maintaining the old status quo found support in groups which symbolized their negation. The modern West entered into an alliance with feudalism in the non-Western countries in order to prevent them from becoming modern nations. "At the same time it also became necessary for the imperialists," says Sternberg, "to look around for reliable allies among the colonial population. Now, the only social strata where such allies could be found was amongst the old feudal ruling classes, and therefore imperialism began to support these elements, and where they had begun to decline it even encouraged their resuscitation." In this way forces similar to those against which the Western countries had fought in Europe were turned into allies; an alliance which prevented the distribution of prosperity and wealth which the West wished to monopolize. According to Sternberg, "This alliance . . . had certain important economic results: it greatly slowed industrial and economic development in general in the colonial empires."

Thus, the countries which represented modernity and progress, far from supporting the countries trying to emulate them, formed alliances with citizens opposing such cooperation. The old forces against progress, which had been defeated in the West, were encouraged by the West in countries where they still existed, or were strengthened where their existence seemed in danger. Chieftains, small dictators, and oligarchies of all types were supported in Asia, Africa, and Latin America. In this way the West tried to ensure that its citizens would not suffer in the so-called march toward progress by making other countries pay for it. Nehru said, "The cost in human suffering was paid . . . and paid in full by others, particularly by the people of India, both by famine and death and vast unemployment. It may be said that a great part of the costs of transition to industrialism in Western Europe were paid for by India, China, and the other colonial countries whose economy was dominated by the European powers."[57]

---

[57] Ibid., pp. 42, 43, 67.

14. Justification for the Inequality of Other Countries vis-à-vis Those of the West

How could the inequality imposed on the non-Western countries be justified? Was there a philosophy which, while it spoke of freedom and equality, could also justify the inequality in other countries and for that very reason their subordination? Yes, it existed and we have mentioned it in other parts of this book. A philosophy which started from the assumption that all men are created equal was later firmly to maintain the most difficult of all inequalities to overcome, namely, the natural or biological one. Men who were equal essentially by virtue of their reason, mind, or "talent" as Descartes called it, were denied equality by what seemed to be accidental: man's biological make-up. The father of modernity had stated that all men are equal by virtue of their reason or talent but that they are different because of a series of circumstances, simple accidents outside of man's true essence. The accidental, which seemed a circumstantial element, is what determines man's essence in the modern world, the inequality within the so-called equality. All men are equal and similar, but it happens that some of them for reasons beyond their control were born in a certain country and not in another; in a certain cultural setting and not in another; and were educated by certain teachers and not by others.

But there was something much more serious than all that, something that not even education could overcome: this reason or "talent" existed only in a particular body. That this reason or "talent," by an accident over which man had no control, could also be found in a black, brown, copper, or yellow body and not only in a white body; that instead of blond hair and blue eyes, the reasoning head would have black hair, dark and slanting eyes: that of course, was an accident which did not change the equality of that reason or "talent" in an ideal sense, but it altered its actual expression in the world. It was a simple but fatal accident, because that "talent" or reason could not exist in a body which did not fulfill the conditions which had permitted other talents or reasons to develop. This body, therefore, became a kind of prison which prevented one kind of reason from developing like others. Western inequality was therefore an essential inequality because it could not be divided. In spite of the equality of all people, there was in fact an inequality which must have originated somewhere. In spite of all the ideas of equality, there existed superior and inferior people in the world.

Superiority depended largely on the race to which people belonged: it showed up when white people met people of color.   In free enterprise, the struggle for life in which the best and most able always win, white people had shown their superiority.   The non-Western countries were unable to resist the impact of the Western nations that were superior because of their race.

The people of color also revealed a lack of competence in the limited ability they had shown in adopting the spirit which had made the triumph of countries inhabited by the white race possible.   Many of the people of color had opposed the march of progress.   On the North American plains, for example, the Indians had often refused to let wagon trains pass and railroads be built because they preferred a life that followed their old Nomadic customs; these were tribes that lived by hunting on the plains that did not belong to anybody in particular, that belonged to no one and had no boundaries.   There were also many tribes in Africa that, in one way or another, opposed the march of progress in which their place was that of slaves.   And the same happened to India, China, and the Arab countries, because they did not understand that their heritage of ancient and outstanding cultures was outdated, and tried to maintain habits and customs which far from helping the march of progress hindered it.

Beginning with this assumption, liberal philosophy, which discussed free enterprise among equals, changed little to that other philosophy of which one of the highest expressions was Positivism, particularly in the form of Darwinism.   Free enterprise became the struggle for survival, a struggle in which the strongest, the best, or the most able invariably triumphs.   A struggle as highly developed in the animal world as it is in that of man.   After all, man is merely an animal who has evolved and progressed.   Therefore, by means of various stages of evolution that separate the animal from man, the differences that exist among humans can be explained.   People are equal but different, and what matters here are distinctions, in the sense of what it is that makes people different or unequal, an inequality that originates in the biological, physical, or natural world.   A distinction, an inequality, which finally denies the humanity of some people while upholding that of others.   If man is an animal that has evolved, the inability of some people to progress indicates that these are not people as yet, that they are still not ready to advance in order to qualify as human beings.   These tribes must still be far from being truly human.   A strangeness which manifests itself even in the pigmentation of the skin. This is the way in which the moral problem that might have been discussed by the people who discussed freedom and equality is solved. They could continue to speak of it without loss: Freedom and equality among people, as proper values of the person, but there was no reason why they should be granted to those who could not be considered human as yet.

Racial inequality based on biology leads therefore, to denying the humanity of some people while favoring that of others. Human beings who are different because of their skin, habits, and customs must be something other than people, since their skin, habits, and customs resemble so little, or not at all, those of people who regard themselves as human prototypes. Those beings can only be things, objects to be dominated like those other objects in the world that constitute nature, that nature which Western man has tamed and made to serve him. Those beings should be exploited like the rest of nature with which man comes in contact. Says Arnold Toynbee:

> When we Westerners call people "Natives" we implicitly take the cultural color out of our perception of them. We see them as trees walking, or as wild animals infesting the country in which we happen to come across them. In fact, we see them as part of the local flora and fauna, and not as men of like passions with ourselves; and, seeing them thus, as something infra-human we feel entitled to treat them as though they did not possess ordinary human rights. They are merely natives of the lands which they occupy, and no term of occupancy can be long enough to confer any prescriptive right. Their tenure is as provisional and precarious as that of the forest trees which the Western pioneer fells or that of the big game which he shoots down. And how shall the "civilized" Lords of Creation treat the human game when in their own good time they come to take possession of the land which, by right of eminent domain, is indefeasibly their own? Shall they treat those "Natives" as vermin to be exterminated, or as domesticatable animals to be turned into hewers of wood and drawers of water? All this is implicit in the word "Natives" . . . evidently the word is not a scientific term but an instrument of action; an a priori justification for a plan of campaign . . . In short, the word "Natives" is like a piece of smoked glass which modern Western observers hold in front of their eyes when they look

abroad upon the World, in order that the gratifying spectacle of a "Westernized" surface may not be disturbed by any perception of the native fires which are still blazing underneath.[58]

In this way everything will be morally justified. The philosophy which speaks of the equality of all people has not been changed. People continue to be free and equal, masters of all their rights. Inequality does not exist among people; only the natural inequality exists between people and things. And man has been created to take advantage of things of his world, to conquer nature and place the physical world at his service. The inhabitants of those lands where Western man has arrived in his expansionist march are merely things, objects to be dominated. Something that must be tamed like the rest of nature to achieve greater happiness for man. The native who inhabits those lands, because of his difference, which is an indication of his subhumanity, must serve the man who has discovered and conquered him. Nothing and nobody can change this situation, which is a consequence of nature's evolution, a design of the Divine. The Western world can belong only to Western man. But, what are the people in the non-Western countries going to do, faced with a situation to which a new Determinism condemns them?

---

[58] Arnold J. Toynbee, *A Study of History*, Vol. I, pp. 152-153.

CHAPTER IV

THE UNIVERSALIZING INFLUENCE OF WESTERN CULTURE

15. The West as a Universalizing Agent

Countries, like people, cannot expect anything from others that they do not expect of themselves; this is the West's message to the world. The non-Western countries have learned something they did not know before: the position they occupy in the world. When the West expanded it created a universal sphere of influence hitherto unknown to the rest of the world. Within this sphere each country can see how it compares with other nations, a standard which merely assists in gauging the ability or inability of a given country and reveals the prospects and limitations of its citizens. Until recently each country believed it was the center of the world or universe because it was unaware of countries which challenged that universality.[59] Now all this has changed because the West has made its presence felt and imposed its point of view, which reflects that of a culture that regards itself as universal. The West has made known

---

[59] See Arnold J. Toynbee, *A Study of History* (London, 1934-1961).

the existence of history, that is, its own history as world history. It is a history in which the development of other nations and cultures is a mere accident. Such marginal and accidental histories are important only for what they may have contributed to world history, or for what they may become in an uncertain future.

These are the countries that have shown an awareness of their position with respect to the existing world order. It is an awareness of their marginal position vis-à-vis the central position occupied by the Western countries, which have imposed their outlook or, better still, their interests. And this has happened because they were assigned the role of subordinates. Why were they cast in this role and not another? This in fact is the question that these marginal countries have asked and continue to ask themselves. How can this situation be changed? How can the roles be changed? Or at least how can we attain the standard of those countries that are the focus of the world? By adopting their culture, their points of view and values; this is generally the answer which the marginal countries have given to their questions. Until recently these countries were still living in the past, but as a result of the West's impact they have now left it behind, and the same can be said of countries which were still living in a state of natural innocence. Now, all of them, those who lived in the past or were simply a promise, try to integrate themselves into the present established by the West under conditions very different from those imposed on them. There no longer exists a place on earth that has remained untouched by the impact of the West and an awareness of what is universal. No longer is there the awareness that a given place is only "a corner of the world," a province vis-à-vis the rest of the universe. The Western world extends beyond the limited boundaries of nations. From that world beyond have come the people who with their new ideas and new techniques made of their own countries key nations, leaders, and pioneers of civilization and progress.

When the West expanded it gave rise to a new concept of the universal which was detrimental in the long run. Today, even the West, the nations of the West, ask themselves what their place is in a world whose universality made the expansion of the West felt. The philosophy on which the West based its expansion from a moral point of view has helped and is helping the non-Western countries to slow this expansion by invoking ideas whose universality has been accepted by all countries without question. The two great contributions of the West to universal culture, industrialization and democratic institutions, have been and continue to be the goals of countries that have experienced their impact, but now adopt their original meaning. Nature must be harnessed, but for the good of all mankind. Responsible, representative government must be established in independent sovereign states, at the same time recognizing the right of any country on earth to opt for this type of government. For this reason, the non-Western countries demand the universal validity of values which the West claimed for itself alone. "The ideal of our modern Western Democracy," says Toynbee, "has been to apply in practical politics the Christian intuition of the fraternity of all mankind." This ideal, however, was not achieved when the West expanded into other countries. "But the practical politics," continues Toynbee, "which this new democratic ideal found in operation in the Western World, were not ecumenical and humanitarian but were tribal and militant." The West has not known how to grant other countries the rights it claims for itself; it has not been able to see in them the humanity of which it considers itself a proponent. In effect, its nationalism is the obstacle which disturbs the universality of its vision. Beyond the universal there is always the limited point of view of its interests, the spirit of nationality which, says Toynbee, "may be defined as a spirit which makes people feel and act and think about a part of any given society as though it were the whole of that society."[60] Therefore, the countries which have suffered the consequences of this Western outlook are the ones now asking for its extension, that is to say, for their own incorporation into a world which, in its beginnings, was the standard-bearer of the idea of human brotherhood. These countries are already aware that they are a part of mankind, which does not end with the West.

All non-Western countries in the East, Middle East, Africa, and Latin America have reacted to the impact of the West with the weapons the West provided. One of these is nationalism but one that does not adopt the limited outlook of its Western counterpart. It is a nationalism that does not start out with the idea that a part represents the whole, but, on the contrary, begins with the assumption that there are already countries and people that form parts of the whole, a whole in which some are accepted and others not. Parts of a larger world within which an ideology that does not make sense refuses to

---

[60] Ibid., Vol. I, p. 9.

recognize, in the name of universality, the majority of mankind in favor of a minority.   Today there are two types of nationalism opposing each other in several of the West's colonies throughout the world: the nationalism of the so-called "colonists," who try to keep their privileges and rights, which in turn are a denial of the rights and privileges of the so-called "natives"; and the nationalism of the latter, who try to obtain rights similar to those claimed by the "colonists." The first type of nationalism makes of the people in the non-Western countries a "proletariat," and the second type is the nationalism of countries which have become aware of the role they play in the West and now claim their rights in that world.   One nationalism subordinates other countries under a variety of pretexts, and the other demands the right of the people to self-determination. One nationalism, in the name of its preeminence, has imposed its interests on other countries; the other merely claims for itself the same respect that the first demands for what it calls its sovereignty.

This second type of nationalism is not as much a reaction against Western culture as it is a desire to make Western culture authentically universal.   Countries no longer desire to isolate themselves, to reject Western culture, because they know that this is no longer possible and that modern technology makes their isolation impossible.   From the technical point of view, Western culture has also put an end to cultural archipelagos.   The West has imposed its technology on the world in the same way that it imposed its economy and politics, and it is this method which makes the isolation of nations an impossibility.   Western technology in all its aspects is bringing the world closer together and thereby establishing a hitherto unknown unity.   The non-Western people, far from opposing technology, are trying to acquire it because they know that through it they will acquire material strength that will enable them to demand the equality which the West advocates, and to reach the responsible position they feel they can claim in an undertaking in which all people and all nations must participate.   The complex "system of mechanical communications which modern Western ingenuity has conjured up: steamships, railways, telegraphs, telephones, aeroplanes, motorcars, newspapers and the rest," says Toynbee, referring to a non-Western part of the world, the Islamic world, is used by Islamic countries, "not in captaining a 'Holy War' against the West, but in reorganizing their own life on a Western pattern." Among the Islamic countries, Turkey initiated this westernization, hoping to be looked upon as a country responsible enough to share the tasks imposed by Western culture, with which it has identified. Nowadays there are many other countries, such as India, China, Indonesia, Egypt and several others, that are trying hard to become westernized in order to change their situation as subordinates in a culture that incorporated them by force. These countries seem to say yes to westernization but want it in a form that rules out subjection. According to Toynbee, the Turks seem to say, "'we are determined to work out our own salvation'," and we may add, with the Turks all countries of the non-Western world. "And this salvation . . . lies in learning how to stand on our own feet in the posture of an economically self-sufficient and politically independent sovereign state on the Western model . . . The Arabs and the Persians are already on the move. Even the remote Afghans . . . have set their feet on this course, and they will not be the last.   In fact, nationalism, and not Pan-Islamism, is the formation into which the Islamic peoples are falling; and for the majority of Muslims the inevitable, though undesired, outcome of nationalism will be submergence in the cosmopolitan proletariat of the Western world."[61]

The merger, until recently forced upon them, and now a conscious one, gives the non-Western countries an awareness of the role they play in the Western world.   Their role is that of a "cosmopolitan proletariat," as Toynbee calls it.   It is the awareness of the slave facing the master, of which Hegel speaks in his *Phenomenology of the Spirit*; and the coming of age of the proletariat to which Marx alludes.   And with it comes an awareness of the important role that these countries have played in the implementation of Western culture, a culture that is what it is thanks to the obligatory collaboration it has received from the non-Western countries, a culture which grew out of the sacrifice of countless people and nations.   But it is also a culture which prides itself on the highest concepts of human dignity.   It is in the name of that dignity that the victimized people and nations demand a change of status.

---

[61] Arnold J. Toynbee, *Civilization on Trial* (New York, 1948), pp. 210, 211.

16. Nationalism and the Universalizing Influence of the West

Nationalism which, as already stated, had been created by the West, therefore became the most efficient instrument for the non-Western world's merger with Western culture. The nationalism of non-Western countries, far from being an instrument of opposition to Western culture, is on the contrary the best means of furthering the westernization of those countries. "In the struggle for existence," says Toynbee, "the West has driven its contemporaries to the wall and has entangled them in the meshes of its economic and political ascendancy, but it has not yet disarmed them of their distinctive cultures. Hard pressed though they are, they can still call their souls their own, and this means that the mental strife has not yet reached a decision." However, the net has done something more than enmesh the existing nations of the Western world economically and politically; in order to break the net or better still, in order to assume within it a position other than the inferior role assigned to them, the non-Western countries have gradually adopted the best that Western culture has to offer, the Christian ideal of brotherhood. Therefore, people in those countries now ask themselves what justification there is for an inequality which denies the spirit of universal brotherhood of which the West speaks. Awareness of what is human, which according to Hegel did not exist in the non-Western countries, has been awakened and has prompted the people in those countries to ask questions: Who am I? If I am a person, what is my position among my fellow people? Why am I in this place and not in another? "The representatives of the non-Western societies might find relief for their feelings," says Toynbee, "in addressing us in the language in which Job replies to his comforters: 'No doubt but ye are the people, and wisdom shall die with you. But I have understanding as well as you; I am not inferior to you: yea, who knoweth not such things as these?' (Job xii.2-3)."[62]

The nationalism of non-Western countries is based on just such a claim. It is the claim of people and nations that demand a different kind of participation from that of mere subordinates in the development of a culture which they regard as their own. These

---

[62] Arnold J. Toynbee, *A Study of History*, op. cit., Vol. I, pp. 35, 36 (footnote 1).

countries are not against the West, but against the idea the West has of them and its consequences; in other words they are against their inferior position. They are against colonialism, as they have stated, but not against the values of Western culture; on the contrary, they opposed colonialism in the name of those values. Nationalism does not mean to these countries what it meant to the West: a pretext for justifying the inferior position of other countries. No, nationalism for these countries is merely a way of expressing their maturity, a maturity which demands a role in an undertaking they do not consider the exclusive domain of certain countries. "I know that nationalism is today in many circles a suspect word," says President Sukarno of Indonesia, "and that it conveys ideas of chauvinism, of racial supremacy, and a dozen other ideologies that we reject. Those evil things are not nationalism, but distortions of nationalism. Do not confuse the distortions with the sound fruit. How foolish it would be to reject democracy because in some places and at some times democracy has been bent into shapes which are a perversion of the democratic ideal. Equally, how foolish it is to reject nationalism because it has sometimes been perverted." In this way, an Asian, a non-Western man, criticizes the West for corrupting the ideas of democracy and nationalism and acting as if it were the whole of humanity rather than only a part of it.

For this reason nationalism, an invention of the West, is criticized by Westerners once it has been adopted by non-Western countries. Replying to this criticism Sukarno says: "We of Asia are told that the troubles of our continent are due to nationalism. That is as wrong as saying that the world's troubles are due to atomic energy. It is true that there is turbulence in Asia, but that turbulence is the result and aftermath of colonialism and is not due to the liberating effects of nationalism. I say, 'liberating effects of nationalism.' I do not mean only that nations are again free of colonial bonds, but I mean that men feel themselves free." Is not this awareness of freedom which in Hegel's opinion characterized the European or Western countries and made intellectual leaders of them? Today we find that the non-Western countries are the ones which speak of freedom and in its name claim the right, not as Westerners claimed, but rather to become collaborators in an undertaking which is the ultimate fulfillment of man.

How did the non-Western countries acquire an awareness of freedom? Through the West and its impact. "You who have never known colonialism can never appreciate what it does to man. The agrarian effects, the economic effects, the political effects can be measured. The effect on man's mind and spirit cannot. Regard it only in this simple light. For generations the political leaders of colonies work and aim for the destruction of the colonial governments . . . To understand Asia and Africa, we must understand nationalism." Nationalism is a Western idea which has served these countries as a means of becoming westernized in a way different from that imposed on them. It is an idea previously unknown in these countries that has been accepted by them with an enthusiasm never imagined by the West. Such nationalism, instead of separating them from the West, acted as a lever to break the barriers that made the non-Western peoples marginal countries within the Western world. Sukarno describes what this nationalism meant to non-Western countries when he states: "We of Indonesia and the citizens of many countries of Asia and Africa have seen our dearest and best suffer and die, struggle and fail, and rise again to struggle and fail again, and again be resurrected from the very earth and finally achieve their goal. Something burned in them; something inspired them. They called it nationalism. We, who have followed and have seen what they built, but also what they destroyed themselves in building, we, too, call their inspiration, and our inspiration, nationalism . . . For us, there is nothing ignoble in that word. On the contrary, it contains for us all that is best in mankind . . . Therefore I say: do not denigrate our nationalism . . . It is at least a positive creed, an active belief, and has none of the cynicism and lassitude of less virile outlooks."

Is this movement anti-West? No, as we have pointed out already, it is merely a movement which sets out to change the situation to which the Western world had relegated the non-Western countries. It is therefore a movement directed against colonialism and all that makes it unjust in a society that speaks of freedom, democracy, sovereignty, and human dignity. "One misunderstanding should be eliminated immediately. We are not anti-West. We may, in fact we do, sometimes oppose what is called the West. But that is not dictated by a feeling of being anti-West . . . It is true that there is one manifestation of the West which we and all of Asia completely reject and will continue to reject. That manifestation is colonialism." Are these countries opposed to a world order? No, what they oppose is an order based on certain inequalities. They are willing to accept an international order that can no longer be avoided, but it must be based on equal rights for all countries. "Perhaps the future belongs to greater organizations than mere nations," Sukarno continues, ". . . that may be so. In any case, those bodies cannot be built until nations are built first. You cannot establish international bodies until nations have established their national identities."

And none of this can be realized unless we first put an end to injustice, to inequality implicit in colonialism. "We are told that colonialism is dead, . . ." Sukarno continues, "my reply to that is a simple one. Come to Asia and see for yourselves. Travel to Africa and see for yourselves. Colonialism, even in its classical form, is not dead so long as one nation is unfree, so long as the United Nations Charter is not applied to one territory, so long as brother is divided from brother by a colonial barrier . . . Colonialism will not be dead until nations, including my nation, are reunited in that freedom which is the birthright of all men."[63] Resistance is, therefore, directed not against the spirit of Western culture but against a situation that denies its loftiest ideals. The non-Western countries, by using the kind of language quoted here, are showing how westernized they actually are. Their indebtedness to the West is apparent in their adoption of the more positive Western values and by an elimination of the negative ones, namely those which, far from spreading the universalizing influence of the West, hindered it. Nevertheless, there are negative values which under various pretexts are trying to resist the universalizing influence of the West. These are narrow points of view which in time might pose a threat to that influence.

---

[63] "Address to the National Press Club, Washington, D.C., May 18, 1956." U.S. Department of State *Bulletin*, XXXIV (June 4, 1956), pp. 936, 935, 935-936, 936, 937, 936, 937.

17. The Return of Kenyatta

Even if the non-Western countries are hard pressed by the impact of the West, states Toynbee, they may still consider themselves masters of their own souls: "And this means that the ideological contest has not been decided as yet." That is, countries which have accepted the Western world in many of its aspects, countries whose peoples are ready to Westernize their very soul if in return their universal quality as human beings is recognized, could significantly oppose the West if it insists on bargaining with them for the recognition they seek. Toynbee fears that perhaps one of these distinctive cultures, such as Islam, or any other, might serve those countries as a means of rebelling against a control the West does not want to relinquish. "Pan-Islamism," says Toynbee, "is dormant, yet we have to reckon with the possibility that the sleeper may awake if ever the cosmopolitan proletariat of a 'Westernized' world revolts against Western domination and cries out for anti-Western leadership."[64]

But does such a threat exist? And if it exists, where does it originate? In recent years there has been talk in Western circles, particularly in Europe, of apparent threats to that culture. There is talk of a North American threat through the economic and political expansion of the United States in European countries, of the Communist threat posed by Russia and its policy of displacing European influence in Asia and Africa, and of the threat of Afro-Asian countries that are fighting to emancipate themselves from Western colonialism. All these things are indeed threatened; but they are threats not to Western civilization but to the political and economic influence of European imperialism in the world. It is a struggle for world supremacy, but within the sphere of Western culture. At present there is no culture opposing Western culture as in the past Islam opposed Christianity. European culture is not threatened by another culture. The United States and the U.S.S.R., the two great powers now disputing the world, do not represent cultures different from Western culture; on the contrary, both are expressions of that culture in its growth and development. Both the United States and the U.S.S.R. are standard-bearers of Western

---

[64] Arnold J. Toynbee, *Civilization on Trial* (New York, 1948), p. 212.

principles and banners; both are trying to carry to their utmost limit
the values of Western culture. The two republics, one liberal and the
other Communist, do nothing but vie with each other for the
leadership of Western culture by putting the emphasis on "freedom"
or "social justice." These are ideas and values that belong to the
West, expressions of an awareness of the developing world.
Expressions of a culture which have turned into threats for lack of
the agreement that is indispensable if culture is to achieve unity. It
could be said that as Western culture developed, it entered into an
internal conflict, a dialectical conflict without the inevitable
synthesis of which Hegel spoke. On the one hand, the United States
tries to maintain, in the name of freedom, the kind of liberalism we
have analyzed already and which only injures the interests of groups,
classes, or nations that are outside the interests of groups, classes,
or nations that consider themselves beneficiaries of freedom. The
U.S.S.R., on the other hand, limits and violates the freedom of the
individual in the name of so-called community interests. In one
country social justice is amputated in the name of freedom and in the
other freedom is amputated in the name of social justice. In both
countries these amputations are presented as necessary, though
temporary; necessary and temporary measures which always end by
being a denial, not only of the values that are negated but also of
those in whose name the refusal is made. Actually, both pose a
threat to Western culture; but these are threats that have an internal
rather than an external cause and they might result in a fatal
disagreement.

But what is the other threat to Western culture? The colonial
peoples, who are casting off the chains in which Western imperialism
has held them? Do Algiers, Morocco, Egypt, the Arab countries, and
Southern Africa, Indochina, China, etc. pose a threat to Western
culture? Do they oppose the West in the way that Islam fought
against Christianity several centuries ago? Does Buddhism,
Brahmanism, or Confucius pose a threat to Western culture? It does
not seem so. Because, as we have already seen, these countries,
independent in their religion and cultural pattern, and in their
apparent rebellion, do not ask for the enthronement of their
respective religions or cultures, but rather for the fulfillment of the
principles which the West has introduced into the non-Western
world. When the West expanded, it taught other countries values
which they now claim for themselves. Perhaps without desiring it,
the West has become the master of the world, which it has taught

values it had not known before. The educational process has been hard, even violent, but the non-Western countries have acquired through many sacrifices values which were inaccessible before. It can be said that it was the West which taught the world the right to be the master of its own destiny. The West westernized the non-Western countries and awakened in them aspirations formerly alien to them.[65] Now these countries are claiming rights for themselves and the recognition that Westerners demanded and imposed on other countries in their relations with them. In realistic terms they demand respect for their sovereignty or the right of all people and nations to guide their own destiny. According to Raghavan N. Iyer, the British Empire was the most efficient vehicle for the dissemination of European culture in India. "It was true that the racial principle was paramount in the minds of the British leaders but they also emphasized the preservation of the Empire at any price, based on the exploitation of the subjected or inferior races either by force or by granting them small material advantages." However, if it was true that "the liberal principle was the predominant one, it was equally true that the emphasis was placed on the notion of the Commonwealth, on the development of free institutions and the establishment of the highest standards of education." On the one hand they were looking for cheap labor; on the other they were looking for a moral justification of exploitation, offering educational opportunities to the exploited or pretending to make certain concessions on their behalf. Another major preoccupation was the teaching of English to the natives because this best suited England's interests. For the Hindus, education opened up the world of Western culture along with its highest values. According to Iyer, "English opened the doors to European knowledge in India . . . Knowledge of subject matter, discipline in social intercourse, research . . . the desire for institutional reform, to disregard the traditional ritual . . . and the demand for autonomy."[66] The Hindu soon assimilated the spirit of Western culture with all its values and began to act accordingly. Gandhi and Nehru, the most outstanding leaders of Indian emancipation, were educated in accordance with the highest ideals of Western culture. And in conformity with these ideals they demanded that the West grant them their political freedom and the

---

[65] See "L'Empire Britannique, problème de Civilisation." *Comprendre*, Revue de la Société Européenne de Culture. Venice, Nos. 13-14, 1956.
[66] Ibid., p. 75.

right to collaborate in the affairs of the West, which India and all colonial countries considered their birthright.

Where is the threat? We affirm once again that the threat to Western culture does not come from outside. It is an internal threat. And what is threatened is simply the old spirit of exclusiveness of Western culture. Western culture is no longer the concern of Westerners or Europeans alone; it has become the work of all mankind. The Western world has expanded not only in a political and economic sense, but also from a cultural point of view. Those souls of whom Toynbee spoke are Western in the highest sense; for this very reason they demand a place in the Western world. The threat exists but this threat is posed by narrow-minded individuals; people who still consider Western civilization the prerequisite of a privileged class; people who are still bargaining with other people or nations for the right to take an active part in the permanent shaping of that culture; people who still refuse to recognize values in other nations or people, because these are rights which these same individuals claim as their exclusive property; people who still try to justify unjust material advantages obtained by sacrificing the majority on the grounds that they are the spokesmen, the representatives of culture, civilization, or mankind. It is a narrow and limited culture, civilization, and mankind reduced to small groups of people and interests that continue to say with somewhat simulated seriousness that there still "exist uncivilized racial and ethnic groups, poor and backward, who are in need of a guiding hand," and that they are that guiding hand. They justify their permanent exploitation by calling it a civilizing influence, in the name of which they refuse to grant the freedoms they have always demanded for themselves. They refuse to grant freedom to their colonies since it would mean abandoning them to barbarism. "We feel the need," they say, "to guide these less fortunate countries through constitutional phases toward their own form of government and a better standard of living: "The final phase will depend not on the subjected people but on those who subordinate them, who will be the ones to decide when and how the final so-called constitutional phase will be initiated, since the colonies are not considered able to reach that stage on their own initiative, because that, they say, would mean "abandoning them to their own fate," would "expose them to anarchy and would risk their destruction."[67]

It is this point of view that actually endangers Western culture because of the reaction it can provoke in countries which demand for themselves access to the highest values of that culture. It is a point of view whose main fault is the exclusiveness with which it looks upon the validity of those values, an exclusiveness which manifests itself by denying what is human, and this decision is made by one group of people against another. It is an outlook that still prevails in England with regard to some of its colonies or possessions which it refuses to grant autonomy upon the pretext that these are strategic positions necessary to defend not only England's interests but also those of civilization in general. Similar exclusiveness on the part of the French colonists in Algeria toward the natives of that colony was also claimed to be in defense of civilization. The same narrow and exclusive spirit on the part of the Dutch descendants of the Boers prevailed in South Africa against the indigenous people. Similarly, there is the exclusiveness of North American interests vis-à-vis the Latin American countries. This same exclusiveness is found in citizens of those countries who continue to call themselves "criollos" in order to distinguish themselves from the indigenous population. All these attitudes are merely a denial of the highest values of Western culture; values these very people and nations are disseminating but refuse to recognize in the case of other people and nations.

We are dealing here with a spirit of exclusiveness intent on isolating itself from other countries and people. It is an outlook that does not seek to extend and expand Western civilization, but rather, advocates establishing limits and having its exclusiveness apply to a certain group of people and nations. The people and nations that adhere to this spirit of exclusiveness, instead of helping culture to become the universalizing influence of which they claim to be the sponsors, collaborate in setting limits to it and in fact threaten it with destruction. They are looking for ways to limit the scope of this culture, so that it will not extend to people and countries other than those from which it sprang. This is the attitude that prevails in, among other places South Africa, where the descendants of the Boers

---

[67] From a speech by Sir Pierson Dixon given in Mexico City in February of 1956.

do not want Western culture to spread to the natives, whose social status must thus remain unchanged. In South Africa, as in other places, the Westernization of the natives is seen as a danger for Western civilization, paradoxical as that may seem. In other words, this applies to the people who have accepted Western culture as a basis for justifying their superiority. Therefore, in order to avoid Westernizing the natives, South Africa enacted an educational law which left control of the education for its black population in the hands of the Department for Native Affairs.[68] What was the intention? Simply to prevent schools for natives from continuing under the auspices and influence of the Christian missionaries. These schools had taught the natives the Christian doctrine, which proclaims the equality of all people over and above racial and economic differences. As Peter Abrahams observed it is a philosophy which speaks of "the unity of all men and all races." In opposition to this philosophy are the declarations made by the Minister for Native Affairs who, in explaining why the law which put an end to these schools was enacted, said: "There is no place for the black man in the European community, unless it is in certain types of work." The black man can only get the kind of education which corresponds to his inferior role in society. This is what the missionary schools had changed, teaching the natives ideas that went against justifying the inequality with which they were treated. These schools had brought to the African tribes ideas about justice and the equality of all people which were hitherto unknown to them and through these ideas native Africa became acquainted with the highest values of Western culture, the great liberal traditions and the loftiest ideals of a universal character, valid for all mankind. From these schools graduated black men who had a new attitude toward the colonists and demanded responsibility in establishing an Africa which they regarded and rightly so, as their own. From these schools emerged men capable of helping in the transformation, the Westernization of South Africa. These were schools that had put an end to the absurd relationship "between those who were civilized and those who were not."

The black man educated in these schools was already showing his ability to adopt, and adapt to the new techniques and the new Western institutions. All he needed to be efficient was an adequate education, the same kind of education that was available to the white

---

[68] By the law of April 1, 1955.

man. In recent years, says Abrahams, one was surprised to meet
young blacks, true intellectuals, sometimes as sophisticated as
Europeans and in no way different from persons one might find in
Western intellectual circles. Many of them had had the opportunity
to be educated in England or in other centers of Western culture.
These young men were already questioning the rights given to the
black man, because there was no reason why these should be inferior
to those granted to other men. These young men not only spoke up
but began to claim their rights by saying that they should not be
inferior to the descendants of the Boers, just because the latter were
white in a country where 170,000 white men exercised an absolute
control over six million black people. It was decided, therefore, to
put an end to all those questions and demands by prohibiting the
black man from acquiring a type of education not suited to his class
as determined by the colonizer. "Henceforth there would be no more
doctors of philosophy, surgeons, lawyers, writers, musicians or
anything similar" among black men who would no longer be
permitted to attend Oxford or Cambridge or any other university or
center of Western culture. The black man's place was his barbaric
tribe, which would make the civilized white man stand out by
comparison; or in the most menial jobs in the cities, where the only
master was the white Westerner.

What, then, is or could be the reaction of the non-Westerner as
he faces the gathering storm inspired by some Westerners? In South
Africa there has been a reaction already, and the same can happen in
many other countries whose incorporation into the Western world has
been denied: there has been violence, the Mau Mau, a revolt in the
name of another ideology, perhaps, as Toynbee believes, following
another cultural philosophy dormant at present but which might
appear. The first reaction, violence, is a return to barbarism in a
world which refuses to extend civilization, and preserves barbarism
for the benefit of civilization's so-called champions. According to
Abrahams, Jomo Kenyatta is the symbol of this state of affairs in
South Africa. Kenyatta is the former chief of an African tribe who
has been able to overcome his uncivilized state and has educated
himself as a Westerner in the world's foremost centers of learning.
He is the man who has returned to his native land armed with the
best tools civilization can provide, and he knows the significance of
the highest liberal and democratic values. He has returned prepared
to join, and to have his tribes become a part of, the civilized world
of which he is a product. But he is also a man who finds that none

of the things he has learned are relevant for him and for all in his particular situation.   Although black by race, he feels that he is one more among the men who consider themselves representatives of Africa's culture and civilization; like them, he wants to collaborate in Westernizing Africa, but he realizes that this is not feasible for him, or for his kind.   The Western world with all its values is removed from them.   White men reject them, expel them from their centers and want to have nothing to do with them.   They do not accept Kenyatta and still less his ideas of joining that world with his tribe and all other tribes in South Africa.   According to Abrahams, Kenyatta, "who has been nourished by the culture of the white man, feels closer to their world than to the tribal world into which he was born"; but it is useless, because the white man represents Western culture and merely for reasons of color Kenyatta is not and will not be able to represent anything but African barbarism, that barbarism which justifies the domineering attitude of the white man.   The white man represents Western culture in such a way that there is no room for the black man within it, or if by chance there were, it would be the most inferior of all places.   For this reason the least educated, the least cultured of white men must always be superior to the black man.   Even if this black man happens to be Kenyatta, who has returned to his world after assimilating the best that Western culture has to offer.

What happens in such a case?   What is the African Kenyatta, and along with him all those rejected by Western culture going to do? "Lucifer," says Abrahams, "even if the place he occupies is the worst in the world, will always prefer being in charge of Hell to being the least of the angels in heaven."   The same thing happens to the native African; to be a black native, a person of color, disqualifies him from occupying a position in the Western world that is not that of an inferior.   Whatever he may do, he will always represent barbarism of which he will be the symbol, and will stand for whatever is cut off from culture and civilization, which are the privilege of other countries and people.   In spite of all his efforts and achievements, Kenyatta will be condemned to remain outside Paradise, outside culture and civilization.   There only remains for him to take on barbarism and to see in the representatives of Western culture the occupants of his country, the exploiters of his brothers, and to fight against them with all the means at his disposal, to be the barbarian they say he is against a civilization which refuses to assimilate him. Kenyatta is, therefore, the symbol of the man who, having acquired

Western culture, is forced to fight against it, to work for its destruction, because he cannot acquire the color of the people who have made it their exclusive property.[69]

18. A New Interpretation of the History of the West

What has happened to the Western world? As we have said already, it is simply that civilization has expanded, extended to the rest of the world and broken the narrow mold in which it was originally formed. Western man, particularly the European, has been the first to recognize this fact. That very man now finds himself in a world broader than that of the culture in which he grew up, a world which is trying to adapt to this culture, to make it its own, with the inevitable changes in the meaning it used to have for Western man. Today, Western man is aware of the problem this has created. He has inherited a culture now understood beyond the limits of the world in which it originated. Western man also knows that whether this heritage will endure now depends on his ability to create conditions that would help to make it available to countries demanding it as rightfully theirs; on this ability now depends the life of Western culture in societies where it was hitherto not important.

As a direct result of Western man's activities in the world, the circumstances which determined the scope of his culture have expanded and grown in such a way that they have exceeded the limits envisaged by those who created it. Therefore, Western man is now forced to make a readjustment between his actual goals and those established by the culture he represents, since his goals are no longer consonant with those of a world his ever-expanding culture has created. New circumstances have made it necessary for him to adjust himself to goals he formerly thought belonged to the whole world merely because they were his. Is, therefore, this growth, this transformation of Western culture in order to adapt to ever-widening

---

[69] Peter Abrahams, "L'Afrique et l'Occident." *Comprendre*, op. cit., pp. 11-16.

spheres of influence a sign of its decline? Or, is it on the contrary, an expression of its renewal, its natural growth? Many opinions expressed about Western culture in recent years tend to give the impression that the signs point in a downward direction; they interpreted as a decline something that was nothing of the sort but actually meant a broadening, a greater impact of Western culture. One of the first manifestations of the exclusivist spirit which, instead of seeing something positive in the ever-widening sphere of Western culture, interpreted it as a symbol of decadence, is to be found in Spengler's interpretation of history appropriately entitled *The Decline of the West*. It can be said that with Spengler a new interpretation of history begins, whose basis is no longer the history of the Western world as history par excellence, which has become instead the history of just another culture, or one among many, of a culture about to disappear as many others have done before. Spengler, in his *Decisive Years*, not only saw the death of the West but pointed to its assassins, invariably other countries shaped by people whose heritage was an inferior culture or none at all. Culture was threatened, among other dangers, by nonwhites. No one, however, saw the real significance of this threat; which, far from destroying Western culture, enhanced it and made it universal. The non-Western countries, far from posing a threat to Western culture, offered it the chance to achieve universal acceptance.

This is what philosophers of contemporary history have stated after abandoning Spengler's pessimistic thesis. The problem for these philosophers is to make the West understand the need for its readjustment to a world which its actions have created. Upon this readjustment the growth and permanence of the cultural world it established depends. The non-Western world, now Westernized, has forced the Western world to take stock of its position as the educating culture of the world. It is a position of great responsibility in the eyes of the world, which has learned its lesson and demands its rights in accordance with the education it has received. It can be said that Western culture has overstepped its material boundaries, its physical and geographical frontiers, and along with these has surpassed the justification for the well-defined interests of the West. For this reason countries that until recently were subordinated to such interests now demand, in the name of those values with which their subordination has been morally justified, the universal acceptance of those values as a basis for recognition by all countries and all mankind. The non-Western countries react toward the West with arguments of Western origin.

It is this reaction which has forced Western man in recent years to assess his true place in the world within an order originally created by him. This has been pointed out in the interpretations of history of which we spoke. From now on, history has a truly universal character. It has stopped being what is was before, the history of the West, in order to become world history, a history of which Western history forms a part, perhaps the most important part because of its world-wide consequences, but nevertheless a part of the world or universal history. That lineal interpretation of history whereby the West justified its expansion has been abandoned and has been superseded by a cyclical view of history in which other countries and cultures have intervened, are intervening, and may in the future intervene. It is a history in which all mankind, all nations and all cultures play a role.

The West has realized, or has been given to understand by its most outstanding intellectuals, that its culture is no longer exclusive, but belongs to the whole world. It is increasingly aware how universal it has become and how this universality is shown in the demands the world makes. The last two world wars, which were fought for great universal principles of Western origin, were an indication of the relation of the West to the rest of the world. It was a relation that revealed the existence of one world, in which the problems and solutions of each part directly affect the whole picture. This is what philosophers of Western history have seen with great clarity, and they are in direct opposition to those philosophers of history who saw the universal only in relation to Western culture. Toynbee, Berdiaeff, Schweitzer, Sorokin, Marrou and Northrop among others, illustrate this new interpretation of history in which the pessimism which began with Spengler has been abandoned. It is an interpretation which no longer belittles the humanity of other countries, but recognizes in other countries and people those values and rights that the West has claimed for itself and its people. There are now clear-sighted intellectuals in the West who are searching for a way to understand and be understood by people of other countries.[70] It is an attitude which in recent years, and particularly

---

[70] The Société Européenne de Culture, with headquarters in Venice, is an excellent example of this endeavor initiated by European intellectuals, in which citizens of Western and Eastern Europe, North and South America have

since the end of World War II, has become noticeable in the international policies of some European powers such as England, which, during Atlee's Labor Government granted independence to several of its colonies, among them India (and once free, that country became England's close collaborator), while at the same time speeding up the process of Westernization. This attitude also prevailed in France, among political figures such as Mendès-France. Such attitudes of comprehension and understanding toward other nations unfortunately have been curbed recently, as a result of old interests that once promoted the economic expansion of the West, but could now put an end to the finest product of that expansion, namely, the universalizing influence of Western culture.

What does the new interpretation of history at present adopted by the West show? It will be seen that this interpretation is in agreement with the pessimistic views already noted in Spengler, but goes beyond them by revealing the magnificent role Western culture has played in the world it has created. Spengler's pessimistic interpretation is based on awareness of the approaching end of the political and economic superiority of the West's material interests, a kind of superiority other countries and cultures had lost in the past. Looked at in this way, it is not so much Western culture that is in jeopardy, but the West that is in crisis and looking to the experiences of other cultures for the reason and origin of its decline in order to conclude, with Spengler, that such a decline is inevitable and necessary, as it is in the physical world. It is a fatality, necessity, that holds a kind of consolation. Sooner or later all cultures die, like all living organisms die; it would be not at all strange therefore, if one day Western culture were also to die. This interpretation merely reflects the pessimistic expression of that same Western individualism which, at its height, adopted an optimistic attitude. That optimism has been lost because the West no longer rules the world. The death of Western culture is not only its own, as in the case of many cultures in the past, but something much more serious, something that did not happen with those cultures, because it signifies the death of culture as such. Beside it, there is no other culture worthy of the name that bears contemplating. With the death of the protagonist of history, history ceases and along with it all human values. In Spengler, and in all those who like him speak of

---

joined forces for the purpose of achieving a better understanding of the problems of Western culture in relation to other cultures, peoples, or nations.

the death of Western culture, there is no future worth contemplating. Nothing will come after it, as there was nothing before, that merited that name. In Hegel's words, it could be said that the intellect, far from widening its conscious hold, is returning to its unconscious state, its natural state.

This pessimism has been abandoned by the new interpreters of history, who have carefully analyzed the role the West has played in the world. Their point of departure is Spengler's: Western culture is in crisis, is threatened with extinction, the death that many other cultures have experienced. But the difference lies in the fact that this death, so far from being a natural, biological, necessary death, is one that could be avoided, if the people who created and maintained civilization had a genuine awareness of their situation in relation to other people and other nations. History, according to its new interpreters, shows us that cultures or civilizations have died because, placed at the juncture in which Western civilization now finds itself, where it has to fight to keep its material interests or make its spiritual values universal, they have opted for the former. The civilizations and cultures of which history speaks have disappeared because they tried to maintain their political and economic superiority over countries which had already emerged as a force in the world these civilizations and cultures had created. For this reason the emerging countries, in their turn, while fighting to establish their political and economic autonomy, continued the struggle until they displaced the nations that had sought to subordinate them to their own interests. History also shows that in this struggle only those values were saved which, because they pertained to the dignity of man, the best he had to offer, could be adopted by countries that were also aware of their human condition. That is what was saved, and remains, of the great cultures and civilizations which have appeared throughout history. Those values, instead of being the exclusive heritage of the countries which originated them, the nations which first recognized them, are now the universal inheritance, the heritage of all people and all nations.

Therefore, what dies of those civilizations and cultures was their material body, with its shell of concrete and egotistical interests. That is the death which threatens Western culture. But if the West already knows this, why does it not marshall all its strength and all its institutions while it still has power, for a task which instead of signifying its death would mean its continuity? Other nations, other cultures, continue to play a role in the history of man in spite of themselves; why does the West not consciously play that role? Athens, for example, was the teacher of Hellas and became the teacher of the Western world; as in turn the West is today for the whole world. Why not consciously accept this role, with all the vigor it demands and pursue it with like energy, as other cultures and civilizations did in the past, in order to safeguard interests which in the long run did not last? This had not happened before. History provides us with no examples of the kind. But what does that matter? History is the product of freedom and by no means the sum total of a natural need, as Spengler saw it, to justify an egotistic West. The future does not have to be like the past, because history is not ruled by fatalism; history is made by free human beings, capable of choice, even under the most limited circumstances. People who can either elect to follow the ways of their ancestors or choose a new direction. If the reason for the decline and death of other cultures and civilizations was their endeavor to maintain a material superiority over the interests of other people and other countries, then people of Western culture will have to yield in this area and look for a way to reconcile their own interests with those of the rest of the world in order to preserve at all costs the highest values Western culture has created. Among these are first and foremost the ones that concern the dignity of man, values that for their true realization and universal acceptance must be subscribed to by all countries, all mankind, without racial, political, religious, social, or geographical discrimination.

Toynbee, among others, mentions this necessity when he says that there is nothing to prevent Western civilization from following the road that led other civilizations to disaster, but this would be equivalent to committing suicide. "But we are not doomed to make history repeat itself; it is open to us through our own efforts, to give history, in our case, some new and unprecedented turn. As human beings, we are endowed with this freedom of choice, and we cannot shuffle off our responsibility upon the shoulders of God or nature. We must shoulder it ourselves. It is up to us . . . our future largely depends upon ourselves. We are not just at the mercy of an inexorable fate." What direction should we take? We should abandon intolerance with respect to the rights of other countries to organize themselves politically and economically as their physical needs demand, since that is what the Western countries have claimed for themselves. For this reason, the direction to be taken cannot be that of a peace imposed by military means, but rather must be based on an understanding of the needs of other countries. The West has shown these countries that they are not alone, that they are not isolated, that they are a part of a larger community. The impact of the West destroyed all the Chinese Walls of the world, making it possible for all countries to view the universal panorama of mankind. Nevertheless, and here we come upon the great paradox of the Western world, the West, which has broken down all the parochialisms, has been unable to overcome or break down her own. She did not learn the lesson which she taught other countries. "The paradox of our generation," says Toynbee, "is that all the world has now profited by an education which the West has provided, except the West herself. The West today is still looking at history from the old parochial self-centered standpoint which the other living societies have now been compelled to transcend. Yet, sooner or later, the West, in her turn, is bound to receive the re-education which the other civilizations have obtained already from the unification of the world by Western action."[71] This is the lesson that might enable the West to save its highest values and its true universality.

As a result of this lesson people of Western culture have seen with greater clarity the role the West plays in world culture, as an expression of that great culture. History made by the West in accordance with its view of the world, is therefore, not only the history of the West, but a part of world history. "The other societies have not ceased to exist simply because we have ceased to be aware of their existence," says Toynbee, "and we can hardly advance further in our search for an 'intelligible field of study' without reviving or inventing some name to decide our society as a whole and to distinguish it from other representatives of the species." A parochial, egotistical point of view had made that society a society par excellence. And this happened, says Toynbee, "because we are no longer conscious of the presence in the world of other societies of equal standing; and that we now regard our society as being identical with 'civilized' mankind, and the peoples outside of it pale as being mere 'Natives' of territories which they inhabit on sufferance, but which are morally as well as practically at our disposal, by the higher right of our assumed monopoly of civilization, whenever we choose to take possession. Conversely, we regard the internal divisions of our society, the national parts into which this society

---

[71] Arnold J. Toynbee, *Civilization on Trial*, pp. 39, 41, 83-84.

has come to be articulated, as the grand divisions of Mankind, and classify the members of the human race as Frenchmen, Englishmen, Germans, and so on, without remembering that these are merely subdivisions of a single group within the human family."[72]

Ortega y Gasset expresses this same point of view when he says: "During the last few centuries the European has claimed to make history in a way that was objectively universal. In fact, it will always seem to man that his horizon is *the* horizon and that beyond it there is nothing . . . This is actually what has happened to European historical science for three centuries: it has specifically claimed a universal outlook, but strictly speaking, it has only devised European history . . . Gigantic portions of human life in the past and even in the present, were unknown to it, and the non-European destinies that came to its attention were treated as marginal human life, as accidents of secondary value, merely to stress even more its own substantial character, central to European development." But now, says Ortega, "we are beginning to notice how limited this parochial point of view is."[73] History, real history which all people and all countries make, has taught Western man what his real situation is, a situation of which he has perforce been made bitterly aware, for instance through the last wars, which make toys of Westerners as it did of other people in the world. A bitter and tragic awareness which is expressed by another Western mind, the Frenchman Jean-Paul Sartre, when he says: "It has always been so natural to be French, the simplest, the most economical way in the world to feel that one is universal. One did not have to explain things: It was left for the others . . . to explain by what piece of ill-luck, by what fault, it had come about that they were none of them quite human. And now France is lying on her back, and we can take a good look at her, can see her like a piece of large, broken down machinery. And we think, was this an accident of locality, an accident of history? We are still French, but it no longer seems natural. It took no more than an accident to make us realize that we were merely accidental."[74]

Now the awareness of the accidental, of the true humanity of Western man, who is merely a man among other men, is now

---

[72] Arnold J. Toynbee, *A Study of History*, Vol. I, pp. 34, 33.
[73] *Las Atlántidas* (Madrid, 1924).
[74] Jean-Paul Sartre, *Iron on the Soul*, trans. Gerard Hopkins (London, 1950), p. 55.

becoming clear, as is the role he has played and continues to play in the community of mankind. For one thing, he has made other people aware of their humanity and this in turn has promoted his own. There are no people who are any more or less human, except in their inhumanity toward others, because in the last resort they are simply human beings. The origin of this awareness is Western, and it is this outlook that has helped to give the West its universal influence. Consequently, whenever the West fails to honor, in general or in particular the values she recognizes for herself, what she does is to go against her own nature, by denying, by contradicting herself. We may say, therefore, that today the West is in open conflict with herself as an embodiment of the highest values, as these relate to the dignity of the person, and with that part of her which seeks to make these values an exclusive right. The West no longer faces a world that is trying to impose values contrary to those of Western culture, but rather one that is demanding the universalization of Western values. The tragedy of this absurd struggle of the West against herself is shown by the French philosopher Henri Marrou, when he refers to his own country in discussing the Algerian problem: "I already see our sons, soldiers of the Republic, forced to fight against men who invoke words that are sacred to us, liberty, fatherland, equality and honor. Those words are not found in the Koran . . . they come from the lessons which our teachers taught them . . .We call them rebels, but we try to stop them by force, we who proclaim the idea that government must rest on the consent of the governed. We fight against them with methods that are the negation of all that is French, French reality, Frenchness, all that we stand for . . . This is an absurd, godless, useless war because we are fighting ourselves. Yes, more than a civil war, *plus quam civile bellum* . . ."[75] A civil war, a war that the West is fighting against herself, against that aggregate of values and ideals whose teachings she has given to the world.

   What is important, however, is the growing consciousness of the West, through her most eminent people, of her situation and what she means to the world of which she is a part. This consciousness is the most positive result of the awareness which in turn grips the non-Western world in its relations with the West that enables it to see that such relations are inevitable in a world that can no longer go on

---

[75] Henri Marrou, "Sommes-nous sans avenir?" *L'Express*, September 14, 1956.

being divided into great spheres of interests, but must rather become a single great sphere in which interests are counterbalanced, in such a way as to lead to the happiness of people in general and not to that of a single group at the expense of the rest.

CHAPTER V

RUSSIA ON THE FRINGE OF THE WEST

19. Bastion Nations of the West

Outside of history, on the fringe of Western culture and what she symbolizes for modern times remain countries that consider themselves Western although their claims in that direction have been rejected. These countries are of particular interest to our study because of the similarity of their situation with that of America in its relation to the Western world. We are referring here to border countries that are situated on the fringe of the so-called West. These countries, however, feel that they are a part of the Western world, or rather, are her outposts in the non-Western world and her bastions against attacks on the West.

These are border countries where Western habits and customs are blurred and mingle with non-Western ones. These are countries that played an important role in the defense of Christianity when it was threatened by peoples of a different cultural background, countries that felt and still feel they are an integral part not only of the history of the West but of history in general. Their role in the past was that of defensive bastions against the repeated attacks of non-Western peoples who threatened the Christian West. These bastion nations were able to guarantee the frontiers of the West by sacrificing themselves, and from these same borders the West launched her conquest of the world. These countries, because of their close contact with non-Western people, a contact not possible for other Western nations, had acquired many of the habits and characteristics of those countries, although Westerners might think they had become corrupted. These habits and customs enabled them to triumph in their difficult struggle and made it possible for them to live alongside nations that struck at the frontiers of the West. Russia to the East and Spain in the extreme South of the Western world are countries which in the past served as a frontier and defense for the West. On different occasions both of them stopped attacks launched by countries of Eastern origin. On their territory battles were fought that were decisive for Christianity and for the future of the West. Mongols, Tartars, Turks, Arabs, and Moors were stopped and expelled from the frontiers of the West thanks to the tenacity of Russia and Spain in defending them. These countries in spite of being so different from the nations of Western Europe felt that they were a part of that continent and of that Christian and Western world. While defending with such ardor the Christian world to which they felt they belonged, these countries in fact represented an orthodox faction within it: Orthodoxy vis-à-vis Rome and vis-à-vis Protestantism. Russian orthodoxy and Spanish orthodoxy are an expression of those countries' desire and concern for belonging to European history, the history of the West, as defenders and champions of her culture, defending her at home and abroad against European heterodoxy.

Russia because of her Byzantine orthodoxy and Spain because of her Catholicism did not take the path pursued by the West, when she began to follow a new trend, renouncing her Christian past as an experience she had undergone but had no desire to repeat. During this phase Russia had to readjust to the new trend, become Westernized, and abandon that part of the past which no longer had any meaning for Western man. Spain, on the other hand, tried to hold on to a world which the West had already assimilated, and by insisting on this she became an anachronism, thus remaining outside of history, when in fact she had wanted to play an important role in championing a world that had once been European, but was now merely a part of the West's past.

For their part, the leading Western nations refused to accept as full members of their cultural and historical community countries which they felt were different and more like those that had attacked or were attacking their frontiers, or were simply anachronistic. For leaders of countries that felt they were the center of Western culture, Russia and Spain simply did not belong. For them the East began at the Russian border and Africa at the Pyrenees. Russia and Spain were regarded as countries on the fringe of what might be called the European or Western community. Instead of accepting them in this community, provocations were countenanced as a means of containing them within their own borders, from which they were not to move, neither toward the West nor toward the non-Western world once the incorporation of the latter had been decided upon by the West. Moreover Russia and Spain were accorded the same treatment the West gave to non-Western countries. It was a question either of subjecting them to the West's influence or of neutralizing them as happened in the case of Russia.

As the West extended its hold on the world, Russia and Spain were subjected to different kinds of aggression in order to eliminate them as political forces in a world whose control the West did not wish to share. "The Russians," says Toynbee, "will remind the West that their country has been invaded by Western armies overland in 1941, 1915, 1812, 1709, and 1610."[76] As regards Spain, that country had played a role at the beginning of modern times (we are referring to the Western world during the sixteenth century) that might have been decisive for Western history, but once she had been removed from the scene of that world's interests and forgotten behind the frontier of the Pyrenees, she was also attacked by the West, by Napoleon in 1810, by North America in 1898, and in 1936 by Germany and Italy with the complicity of the rest of the Western world. In spite of all the difficulties, Russia and Spain insisted on participating in a history and a world to which they felt they belonged. Their determination was similar to that of the Latin American countries, as we shall see later. It is the same determination that we see today in the rest of the non-Western world, which knows that it was originally Western, heir to a culture whose sum total is the Western world.

---

[76] Arnold J. Toynbee, *The World and the West* (New York and London, 1953), p. 2.

20. Russia and the West

Toynbee, in accordance with the theory that the West has been able to entrap the world in her economic and political net, but not its soul (that is to say, its different cultures) also sees in Russia, a world that culturally speaking is different from the West, a world which, in order to save its cultural soul, has been forced to Westernize in a way that is partial and relative. According to the English philosopher of history the great preoccupation of the Russians has been to keep that inherited cultural spirit, defending it from its possible destruction by the concerted action of the West. "For nearly a thousand years past," as he sees it, "the Russians have been members, not of our Western civilization, but of the Byzantine, a sister society, of the same Greco-Roman parentage as ours, but a distinct and different civilization from our own, nevertheless. The Russian members of this Byzantine family have always put up a strong resistance against threats of being overwhelmed by our Western world, and they are keeping up this resistance today. In order to save themselves from being conquered and forcibly assimilated by the West, they have repeatedly been constrained to make themselves masters of our Western technology. This *tour de force* has been achieved at least twice over in Russian history: first by Peter the Great, and then again by the Bolsheviks."[77]

Toynbee emphasizes this in order to place Russia in the non-Western world, as what we have called an anachronism of the so-called Byzantine civilization, independent of the common genealogical tree to which it belongs. A world that exists apart from the Western world, but without the same degree of anachronism, and here a case could be made for Christianity, even though the West is its historical continuation. Catholic Spain, too, is an anachronism vis-á-vis the Western world viewed as a manifestation of the modernity that defeated her and relegated her to the past and to history. However, as will be seen later, both Russia and Spain, once they became aware that they were anachronisms tried to master not only technology, but also the Western outlook in order to participate in a world of which they knew they are an integral part. Their great concern has been not so much to defend an inherited culture as to overcome their anachronism in order to be in step with

---

[77] Arnold J. Toynbee, *Civilization on Trial*, p. 166.

the times. But even if they were to break with that heritage or renounce it, their reconciliation with Western culture as it stands would not be possible. This is what Russia, Spain, and Latin America have attempted: to break with a past that seems anachronistic and prevents their participation in the historical progress of the West. Of course, that past, anachronistic as it is cannot be erased, or eliminated just like that, but continues to be a part of those countries, and their personality, characterizing and distinguishing them from other nations; as one individual is distinguished from another, without thereby causing his expulsion from a given community. Toynbee starts with this fact in mind when he says: "The present regime in Russia claims to have made a clean cut with Russia's past, not, perhaps, in all minor externals, but at any rate in most things that matter. And the West has taken it from the Bolsheviks that they have done what they say. We have believed and trembled. Yet reflection suggests that it is not so easy to repudiate one's heritage. When we do try to repudiate the past, it has, as Horace knew, a sly way of coming back on us in a thinly disguised form."[78]

Actually in contemporary Russia, as in Spain, which struggles to become Westernized, and in the countries of Latin America that try to do the same, that past surfaces, that heritage which has not yet been assimilated as the West has assimilated its past, although it is the same heritage. The problem for those countries will be to bridge the historical gap in a flash, within a few years, when it has taken the West several centuries to accomplish this. They have to realize by means of revolution what the West has done by what might be called normal development. We are dealing here with countries on the fringe of the West which, for one reason or another, were forced to withdraw from the normal development of Western Christianity into a simply Western or modern culture, and established themselves at a tangent to it, while at the same time defending some of its manifestations which in the long run tended to become anachronistic. But this backwardness, this anachronism in relation to the progress of Western civilization or culture, is not peculiar to these countries, although it is more obvious because they represent the extremities of that culture. The European countries in which the so-called modern or Western culture originated, England, France, Germany, and Italy, have not developed evenly, either. Of the four countries, England

---

[78] Ibid., p. 164.

has best reflected the development of that culture; it is the one that has best expressed that Western world, while the others have seen themselves fall behind or have lagged behind in their development. The same lagging behind is now experienced by England and all of Western Europe in relation to Anglo-Saxon America or North America, the present leader of the Western world and the highest expression and development of Western culture.   In this world Europe itself now seems anachronistic, consciously so in her desire to maintain and defend what she calls European culture, which is no longer what is truly understood by Western culture. A culture which now turns its eyes on that Christian past which modernity was believed to have left behind.[79] A European world which now, like the rest of the world, is caught in the political and economic net of the West, of which it is the past and of which North America is now the present.[80]

     According to Toynbee, when we speak of Russia we are not trying to accept a kind of Westernization in order to save the soul of Russian culture from being completely Westernized. "In order to save themselves from being completely Westernized by force they have to Westernize themselves partially, and in this they have to take the initiative if they are to make sure of both Westernizing in time and of keeping the repugnant process within bounds . . . Can one manage to adopt an alien civilization partially without being drawn on," asks Toynbee, "step by step, into adopting it as a whole?" But we might answer him: Isn't this what Russia has been trying to do? Isn't this what countries in a situation similar to Russia's, like Spain and Latin America, have also tried to do? Their major problem has been precisely to join that culture by various means, actually through education or by force. The political and cultural leaders of these countries have insisted on complete Westernization by all the means at their disposal, even violence, violence that they consider necessary as a means to an end, which ultimately will have the opposite effect.   Terror or dictatorship as a tool for the democratization of a country which, for reasons beyond its control, has remained an anachronism in the face of an evolution which has led other countries to democracy.[81]   There is an awareness of this

---

[79] See *Comprendre*, Nos. 10-11 (Venice, 1954) on "Puissance et Culture: Le Nouveau Continent."

[80] Refer to chapter VIII where this situation is analyzed in detail.

[81] At a meeting in the United Nations, the Russian Minister Vishinsky declared that the U.S.S.R. was a democracy, a declaration to which Mrs.

anachronism by an active minority, who decided that their country must span in a few years the distance traveled by the West in centuries. The goal of such Westernization is not to defend an already anachronistic past, but to place itself in a present which should have been attained through normal development. There is no question, as in the case of Eastern countries with a culture different from that of the West, of obstinately holding on to a given culture, even if in order to do so it is necessary to adopt Western technology, as has happened in Japan. Neither is there any question of renouncing one culture in favor of another, as might happen in countries like China, India, and Burma. What does matter, however, is to be up to date in the culture to which they belong, although they know they are backward.

Not only is that same backwardness condoned in countries controlled by the West, but it has even been encouraged by the West as a means of subjection. The West, says Toynbee, in its relation with Russia, has always tried to subject her to its interests, although the opposite appears to be true when looked at through Western eyes. "In the West we have a notion that Russia is the aggressor, as indeed she has all the appearance of being when looked at through Western eyes . . . To Russian eyes, appearances are just the contrary. The Russians see themselves as the perpetual victims of aggression from the West, and, on a longer historical perspective, there is perhaps greater justification than we might suppose for the Russian point of view." The West has invaded Russian territory at various times in history. "It is true that, during the eighteenth and nineteenth centuries, Russian armies also marched and fought on Western ground, but they came in always as allies of one Western power against another in some Western family quarrel. In the annals of the centuries-long warfare between the two Christendoms, it would seem to be the fact that the Russians have been the victims of aggression, and the Westerners the aggressors, more often than not." What is the reason for this permanent aggression? Toynbee, in accordance with his idea about the struggle between civilizations, even if they are Christian, believes that this hostility is due to Russian

---

Roosevelt, the North American representative, objected. The Russian Minister asked Mrs. Roosevelt for a definition of what she understood by democracy; whereupon she gave the classic definition of "the greatest good for the greatest number." To this Vishinsky replied by saying that it was the same idea the U.S.S.R. supported with respect to democracy, but with one addition: "The greatest good for the greatest number, whether they like it or not."

stubbornness in a civilization that seems alien to the West. "The Russians have incurred the hostility of the West through being obstinate adherents," he says, "of an alien civilization, and, down to the Bolshevik revolution of 1917, this Russian 'mark of the beast' was the Byzantine civilization of Eastern Orthodox Christendom." Does the hostility perhaps spring from the fear that Russia is right with respect to matters that the West considers strictly her own? Russia has been a rebellious country toward the West but in addition has felt in the past, and still feels that she has a right in the future to discuss matters pertaining to the West, in particular those European problems which she considers more her own than those of Asia, for example. And when she intervenes in the East, or in other parts of the world, she does so because she wants to have a say in issues that concern the West. It is not so much a question of the struggle of one civilization against another, but rather, of a domestic struggle which perhaps, as Toynbee also believes, has its roots in the division within the Christian Church. A problem of orthodoxy and heterodoxy, of people who believe they are right as against those who do not think along the same lines. And in this struggle, as we mentioned before, Russia, like Spain, has taken the side of what she considers orthodoxy, of what she regards as legitimate and right in a matter of common interest for both Russia and the West. It is not so much a question of imposing a civilization, or of making it prevail over another (as happened in the struggle between Islam and Christianity), but rather of being in the right and of siding with whatever seems right at the time.

Being in the right about what? In the right concerning problems and issues which affect Europe or the West, issues on which only Frenchmen or Englishmen and perhaps some other Europeans as well feel they are entitled to act or express themselves, since they are the so-called heirs of Western civilization. These are the issues in which Russia, as another of the so-called heirs, has tried to intervene. The struggle is not so much to impose a given civilization as to compete for supremacy, the birthright. It used to be Rome or Moscow, now it is Washington or Moscow. Toynbee, although doubting Russia's right, does not fail to recognize the basis for this struggle when he says: "We 'Franks' (as the Byzantines and the Muslims call us) sincerely believe that we are the chosen heirs of Israel, Greece and Rome, the Heirs of the Promise, with whom, in consequence, the future lies . . . The Byzantines do just the same, except that they award themselves the improbable birthright that, on our Western scheme, is ours. The Heirs of the Promise, the people with the unique future, are not the Franks but the Byzantines . . . When Byzantium and the West are at odds, Byzantium is always right and the West is always wrong. "

"It will be evident that this sense of orthodoxy and sense of destiny, which have been taken over by the Russians from the Byzantine Greeks, are just as characteristic of the present Communist regime in Russia as they were of the previous Eastern Orthodox Christian dispensation there.   Marxism is, no doubt, a Western creed, but it is a Western creed which puts Western civilization 'on the spot'. . . A creed which allows the Russian people to preserve this   traditional   Russian   government   as   an   instrument   for industrializing Russia in order to save her from being conquered by an   already   industrialized   West,   is   one   of   those   providentially convenient gifts of the gods that naturally fall into the lap of the Chosen People. "[82]

Is it only a question of defense against conquest by the West, or is there something else? Russia wants to do something more than defend herself, and contemporary history shows this: she wants to be the world's leading representative of Western civilization or culture. The problems she discusses are those of the Western world rather than her own.   In our day, these are problems created by Western industrialization and expansionism.   Russia, precisely, presents herself to the world as the nation that has solved these problems, as the nation that has found an adequate solution to the class struggle that originated with industrialism and nationalism, which in turn created the need for Western expansion. The struggle is therefore a struggle for rights, a struggle for "justification," a struggle to establish who has better right and better justification to intervene in world affairs in a world created by the West. Formerly, during the period of the Tzars and the supremacy of England and France, the aim of the struggle was to gain influence in Europe; now it is to gain influence in a world that almost everywhere has been Westernized and Europeanized.   And now, as before, the West continues to deny Russia the right and justification to intervene in a world which the West considers her exclusive domain.[83]

---

[82] Arnold J. Toynbee, *Civilization on Trial*, pp. 167, 169, 171-173.

[83] At present it is the United States, as leader of the West, who opposes Russia's world expansion. The most recent opposition was in the Middle East, in countries that border on Russia and not on the United States. President

21. Slavism as Opposed to the Ideology of the West

What point of view does Russia adopt in her struggle with the West? Where does the heterodoxy of the West stand in relation to Russia's orthodoxy in the modern world? Russia agrees, accepts and assimilates the values of the modern world, its institutions and Western technology, but there is one aspect of the West that she does not accept. This is an aspect that she singles out as a great defect in the West, as a misguided interpretation, a heresy. "For the Russian Marxian, Russian Slavophil, and Russian Orthodox Christian alike, Russia is 'Holy Russia'," says Toynbee, "and the Western world of The Borgias and Queen Victoria, Smiles' Self-Help and Tammany Hall, is uniformly heretical, corrupt and decadent."[84] What constitutes this heresy, corruption and decadence of the West? The Russians will answer: the abandonment of man. In the West, technology does not serve man or the human race, but only a few privileged individuals. And this is a sin against God and mankind, and will spell the end of that technology of which the Westerner is so proud. Here we have the root of the heresy; it is a part of the individualism that justifies it all.

Alexander Herzen, who knew Europe around the middle of the nineteenth century, spoke of his experience in that world and pointed out its shortcomings which were those of an individualism bordering on the inhuman. Herzen admired that world, admired its technology and its success, but he was against the way this technology was employed and the use to which that success was applied. "The chivalrous behavior, the charm of aristocratic manners, the austere principles of Protestantism, the proud self-reliance of Englishmen, the luxurious life of Italian artists, the sparkling intellect of the Encyclopedists, the gloomy energy of the terrorists, all these have dissolved and been transformed into a whole complex of totally different ruling conventions: those of the bourgeoisie. All parties and shades of opinion in this bourgeois world have gradually divided

---

Eisenhower, in the text justifying North American intervention in the Middle East, links the attitude of his country towards Rusia with that of Europe when he says: "The Russian leaders have long tried to control the Middle East. The Tzars had the same desires that the Bolsheviks now have." Then, as the United States is doing now, Europe opposed Russian control and kept it herself, leaving the present "vacuum," and the West's need for it to be filled by a Western nation.

[84] Arnold J. Toynbee, *Civilization on Trial*, p. 172.

into two principal camps: on one side the property-owning bourgeoisie, obstinately refusing to part with its monopolies; on the other side the bourgeoisie without property, who want to seize it from those who have it, but lack the strength to do so; that is to say, on the one side avarice, on the other, envy . . . The atmosphere of European life is heaviest and most intolerable in those parts where these prevailing conditions are highly developed, which are the richest, most industrialized. That is why it is less stifling to live somewhere in Italy or Spain than in France or England."[85]

Western Europe, which learned how to control nature, and discovered the supreme benefits of freedom and democracy, forgot the Christian spirit that would make these ideals serve all people and not merely a small group. Russia, like Spain, felt that she was the guardian of that spirit, which Western Europe had forgotten, and she tried to reconcile it with the new values. That was the point of view from which Russia confronted Europe and accused her. Western Europe had moved away from man's natural development, and this was reflected in the common man. The common man had been forgotten by Western Europe. He knew nothing of the great technological progress that was being made, nor of the great achievements of genuine freedom and democracy. Russia did not forget them and for this reason felt called upon to fulfill a great destiny. Russia had to do for the world what Western Europe had forgotten in spite of her great contributions to progress. That accounts for the appearance of the Slavophile movement, a combination of humanistic universality and nationalism, which believed that Russia was the nation called upon to achieve that humanism.

The Slavophile was anti-Western but not anti-European, because he considered himself a European. He was anti-Western because Western Europe had forgotten its genuine European roots in Christianity, but he was European in the sense that he considered himself the truest representative of Europe, of that Europe from whose values the West had moved away.[86] In opposition to Russian

[85] Richard Hare, *Russian Literature from Pushkin to the Present Day* (London, 1947), p. 4.
[86] It is a situation similar to the one existing at present among people of European background in their relations with the United States, a country that has inherited Western culture and brought it to its highest level, to the point of controlling Europe economically and politically, just as Europe had once

Slavism appeared Westernism, which had the same goals but began
incorporating the technology invented by Western Europe, a
technology that was to enable Russia to become stronger
economically and thus play a decisive role in shaping Europe's
destiny.   That was the policy of Peter the Great, and also the
direction the Communists were to take later.   The goal was the same
but it was approached from different angles.   One approach was
religious, the other rational, and the goal in its highest expression
was the discovery of the common man.   This expression was Russian
orthodoxy as opposed to Western heterodoxy, which had forgotten
man.   In discussing the Slavophiles, Alexander Herzen spoke of
"Slavophilism, . . . not as theory or doctrine, but as an indignant
national feeling, as a dark memory and an instinct of the masses."[87]
Of the Westerners he said: "Foreigners at home, foreigners abroad,
idle spectators, spoilt for Russia by Western prejudices, spoilt for
Europe by Russian habits, they were intelligent but useless, and
wasted themselves in an artificial life, in gratifying their senses and
in an intolerable parade of egotism."[88]

Russia's great concern then was to take the lead in the
progress first of Europe and then of the West.   To that leadership the
nations of Western Europe had forfeited their right, since they had
forgotten their humanistic mission when they made man into a mere
instrument of other men.   This Russian philosophy was revealed by
Dostoevski in his oration on the death of Pushkin: "We took into our
soul the genius of foreign nations and thus showed our readiness and
predilection for the universal human unification, of all branches of
the great Aryan race.   Yes, the destiny of the Russian is to be super-
European and universal.   To be a real Russian, a complete Russian,
it may only be necessary to become the brother of all men.   All this
is called Slavophilism; and what we call Westernism, is only a great,
though a historical and inevitable, misunderstanding.   To the
Russian, Europe and the affairs of the great Aryan race are as dear as
the affairs of his native country, because our affairs are those of the
whole world.   This may sound arrogant.   We are destined to speak a

---

controlled the non-Western world.   Now people of European background are
indicting North America and its culture as unsuited to Europe and a potential
threat to the old European culture, which they now link to its Christian and
Greco-Roman past.   See *Comprendre,* op. cit.
    [87] Richard Hare, *Russian Literature from Pushkin to the Present Day,*
p. 1.
    [88] Ibid., p. 3.

new word in human history." What was that mark? What was the
mission Dostoevski envisaged for "Holy Russia"? World supremacy,
the harnessing of nature as carried out by Western Europe? No, said
the great Russian writer: "I am not speaking of economic prowess, of
the power of the sword, or of science. I speak only of the
brotherhood of human beings. It is absurd to affirm that our poor
and disorderly land cannot foster such a high mission until it has
adopted the economic and social structure of Europe. The genuine
moral treasures of the soul, in their essence at least, do not depend
on economic power."[89] The latter is the main reason for the
difference between Slavophiles and adherents of the West; a
difference the Communists were to solve in the same way that Peter
the Great once tried to solve it; by making Russia a European,
Western, and world power, capable of making its weight felt in the
progress of a Europeanized or Westernized world. An economic,
political, and military power, but with a goal that would transcend
the national interests which always characterized the Western
powers, so that it could adopt aims that were supra-national, supra-
European, supra-Western, and global. A Universalism that more
closely resembles the European past which the West abandoned than
what she supported when her world expansion began. Communism
as opposed to individualism, these are the two types of humanism
arraigned against each other. One emphasizes the relationship of
man with other men and with the community, and the other places a
value on the individual, his personality and freedom. Orthodoxy as
opposed to heterodoxy? Or are these simply manifestations of man
locked in self-combat? It is a part of herself that the West forgot in
her growth, which is facing her now, forcing her to take a new
approach and make a readjustment in a situation for which she
herself is responsible.

22. The Struggle for Western Leadership

Russia's efforts, like those of Spain and the Latin American
countries, to join the Western world encountered, as we have seen,
great obstacles placed in their way by a world that was willing

---

[89] As quoted by Richard Hare in ibid., pp. 18-19.

neither to permit unfavorable competition, as in the case of Russia, nor to be displaced from a world leadership which she regarded as her own achievement. In 1869, during the Tzarist regime, the Russian historian Danilevsky wrote a book entitled *Russia and Europe* in which he described the efforts made by his country to join the European community of nations to which she felt she belonged, and Europe's efforts to exclude Russia from European history, namely the history made by Western nations in Europe and the world.

"Europe," says Danilevsky, "does not consider Russia its own part. Europe sees in Russia and in Slavs generally something quite alien to itself and at the same time something that cannot be used as mere material to be exploited for Europe's profit as Europe exploits China and India, Africa and the greater part of the Americas, a material which Europe can fashion in its own image and pattern . . . Europe sees in Russia and in Slavhood not only something foreign, but an inimical force, a principle that is in opposition to her own ideology." Therefore, Russia and Slavhood have always been hated by all European parties, conservative and liberal alike, because all see in her the enemy, the possible competitor. "No matter what interests divide Europe," continues Danilevsky, "all its parties unite together in their animosity toward Russia. In this animosity, European clericals shake hands with liberals, Catholics with Protestants, conservatives with progressives, aristocrats with democrats, monarchists with anarchists, the reds with the whites, the legitimists and the Orleanists with the Bonapartists." Why? Russia has done nothing to provoke this ill-will. On the contrary, Russia, instead of foisting her expansion on Europe, as Europe repeatedly did to her, has merely defended Europe's interests when these were threatened from within; and vis-à-vis Europe all she has done is defend herself. "Thus the composition of the Russian state, the wars which it carried on, the objectives it pursued, and especially the most favorable situation, so often repeated, which Russia could use for its aggrandizement and did not, all go to show that Russia is not an ambitious power bent on conquest. In the recent period especially, Russia sacrificed many of her obvious, most just and legitimate interests in favor of European interests, often acting intentionally and dutifully not as a self-sufficient organism, leaving itself a justification for all its strivings, but as a mere instrument of European interests." Therefore, she asks herself, why this hatred? Why this distrust of Russia? Why does Europe reject us?

The reason, according to Danilevsky, is to be found in old and subconscious tribal prejudices struggling for control. "However long we search for the reasons of this hatred of Europe toward Russia we cannot find them either in this or that action of Russia, or in other rationally comprehensible facts. There is nothing conscious in this hatred for which Europe can account in rational terms. The real cause lies deeper. It lies in those unfathomed depths of tribal sympathies and antipathies which are a sort of historical instinct of peoples and lead them (regardless of, though not contrary to, their will and consciousness) toward a goal unknown to them." What happens is that the whole has become confused with a particular part. Russia, like the countries of Western Europe, is part of a larger whole and of a culture that is universal, "an area of Germano-Romanic civilization . . . or Europe is the Germano-Romanic civilization itself . . . Russia fortunately or unfortunately," says Danilevsky, "also does not belong to Europe or to the Germano-Romanic civilization."[90] Russia did not belong to Charlemagne's Holy Roman Empire, nor did she accept Catholicism or Protestantism. Russia was not subjected to the oppression of Scholasticism, nor did she know the freedom of thought which created modern science. She is somewhat further removed from European culture, which is another manifestation of that common past. She is an expression of something that has been neither contaminated nor corrupted. Something that might return to the whole Westernized world when corruption has ended. This can be seen in Russia's continual struggle for the leadership of Europe, the West, and the world, and is reflected in the spirit of Mayakovsky's poem about the Russian Revolution:

"Beat on the street the march of rebellion,
Sweeping over the heads of the proud,
We, the flood of a second deluge,
Shall wash the world like a bursting cloud."[91]

---

[90] As quoted by Pitirim A. Sorokin in his book, *Modern Historical and Social Philosophies* (New York, 1963), pp. 51, 51-52, 52, 53.
[91] B.H. Sumner, *A Short History of Russia* (New York, 1949), p. 304.

Thus Russia was in spite of herself a country on the fringe of history and European and Western culture, a country which, like others in her situation, tried and went on trying to be an active element in and of that culture. On several occasions she was the bastion or shock-absorber of European defense against forces of Oriental origin, but she was never permitted to be a representative of European culture in the non-Western world, like England, France, Holland, and Germany. Neither was she permitted to intervene in European affairs, nor in the world-wide expansion of the West. Moreover, when Russia tried to represent the West in the Western world, and to expand her sphere of influence as the English, French, Dutch, Portuguese, and North Americans, she was stopped immediately. Pitirim Sorokin, a Russian sociologist and philosopher of history and a professor at Harvard University says, "The whole history of Europe's politics toward Russia does not indicate any kindred attitudes or feelings. Europe does not even allow Russia to play the role of an agent of European civilization in the Orient or anywhere else. As soon as Russia tries to play this role, whether it be in Turkey, Persia, the Caucasus, India, China or wherever, Europe at once vetoes such an action and begins a cold or hot war against Russia in alliance with blatantly non-European and non-Christian nations, like Turkey, Persia, and China, or even with pre-literate groups and savages."[92]

In spite of this opposition, Russia has made various attempts to join the world that rejects her, in order to contribute to its destiny. The most noteworthy of these attempts have already been mentioned: the one made by Peter the Great between the seventeenth and eighteenth centuries, and the Communist Revolution of 1917. In order to transform Russia into a European power, capable of making her weight felt in Europe's destiny and of establishing her right to be a representative of the West in the non-Western world, Peter the Great adopted Western technology and the irreligion of which the Europe of his time was proud. He also established and initiated something which Europe was to take as a model, "enlightened despotism," which was to force the Russian people to adapt to the new Western customs and technology. His goal was, as we have

---

[92] See Pitirim A. Sorokin, op. cit., p. 54. Here the West has followed the same policy which she pursued in world expansion, when she looked for an alliance with feudal and reactionary forces that opposed change. Also refer to chapter III of this book.

already pointed out, to participate as a Western power on Europe's political stage and in its history.

As regards the Communist Revolution of 1917, it is well known that this was based on a doctrine of Western origin. Marxism is a doctrine which evolved in relation to problems that beset Europe around the middle of the nineteenth century, and to their future development. It took account of problems that arose as a consequence of the new technology and of industrialization in Europe. Those problems did not exist in Russia even during the twentieth century with the acuteness that they were being felt in Western Europe. From the point of view of industrialization, Russia was lagging behind when the Revolution, which should have had a Western cradle like Germany, broke out. In spite of this, the leaders of the Russian Revolution adopted Marxism as a revolutionary doctrine appropriate to their situation and gave it an ideological thrust. With the Revolution, Russia, which was still an agricultural country, entered a period which even put her ahead of Europe. Russia not only became industrialized, but in addition, gave the world an example of a society which has solved the problems that industrialism and capitalism have created for the West.

It may be said that Russia is not only trying to become a part of the Western world and her history, but is ahead of history. She has anticipated the solution, which, in accordance with Marxism, must be given to the problems of the Western world. In this way, Russia is presented as the leader of a new Europe, as a leader of the West in its march toward progress. Progress that can no longer travel the old liberal road. The Russian leaders insist on turning their country, a country which is still in the agrarian state, into a nation that will be a model for the countries of the future; a society with all the advantages of Western technology, but without the social problems technology has created in the West. Capitalism without capitalists, but capitalism for the community. Soviet Russia's admiration for the United States, the present leader of the Western world, which is struggling for the control of an already Westernized universe, is well known. This admiration is shown in Josef Stalin's words when he states: "The best antidote to revolutionary fantasy is practical work imbued with the American spirit. Such a businesslike, practical endeavor is an unquenchable force, one which recognizes no obstacles, one which, by sheer common sense, thrusts aside everything which might impede progress, one which invariably carries a thing once embarked upon to completion (even though the affair may seem a puny one), one without which any genuine work of construction is impossible." But here appears the orthodox remembering the true meaning of practical work in relation to the change it has undergone in the West. "The practical, businesslike American spirit is liable to degenerate into narrow-minded, unprincipled commercialism, if it not be allied with revolutionary zeal." In other words, unless it is associated with the idea of converting its efforts into an instrument of service to the community, the nation, in short, the majority of the people. "A combination of revolutionary zeal with the practical spirit constitutes the essence of Leninism,"[93] concludes Stalin. With the use of atomic energy, this admiration has changed in our time into a rivalry for the control of technology, which holds the key to war and peace. It is a competitive race whose final goal is the leadership of Western culture, which has extended to all parts of the globe.

---

[93] Josef Stalin, "Foundations of Leninism." In *Leninism* (New York, 1928), pp. 176, 177.

CHAPTER VI

SPAIN ON THE FRINGE OF THE WEST

23. Spain, Bastion of Western Christendom

With the advent of Modernity, the Iberian Peninsula, like Russia, remained outside the European sphere. Spain, which had banished Islam, the perennial enemy of Christianity from the peninsula, remained outside European history. Like Russia, Spain was looked upon by Europe as a country alien to Western European culture as regarded that continent's emerging culture. However, when the new European culture began, Spain, for a number of historical reasons, was a world power. During the sixteenth century, Spain, owing to her laws and because of a series of political alliances, was one of the principal protagonists of European history. Spain's incorporation into the Habsburg empire under Charles V, then King of Spain, made her a decisive power in controlling Europe's destiny and in shaping her cultural development.[94] Moreover, both Spain and Portugal started the expansionist movement that encompassed the non-Western world and was to be

---

[94] For a discussion of this point, refer to chapter X.

decisive for the history of the West. Spain discovered and conquered almost all of the new American continent and began her expansion into Asia. Portugal did something similar in a large segment of America and Asia. Nevertheless, there was something about those countries that made them foreign in the eyes of the Western European. There was something about the people from the other side of the Pyrenees that made them more like the nations against whom they had fought than those they had defended by their resistance. There was something "barbarian" which sat them apart from Western Europe. In fact, Spain was a warlike nation more accustomed to arms than to letters and the intellect as understood by the European. Spain had produced her share of great geniuses and personalities during that brilliant period, the European Renaissance, and they in turn had something which distinguished them from all the other Europeans. They also had a special quality which made them fight, go to war and combat for what they believed was right. Spain's mystics, poets, dramatists, and novelists seemed to be perpetually in arms to fight for an idea, in the hope that it might triumph over any kind of reasoning.

Reasoning, the kind of reasoning so dear to the new Europe which was emerging. The only kind of reasoning the Iberians understood was imposed by their will and their strength. The spirit of continual warfare which had formed the inhabitants of the peninsula was shown by her expansion all over the world, and in the way she tried to participate in matters affecting Europe. She was a nation that strove with all the means at her disposal to belong to an emerging Europe. She studied and endeavored to assimilate Europe's philosophy in order to belong, but that individuality which is so typical of her made the best European minds distrust her. In the Peninsula, as in Western Europe, there appeared a humanism whose principal mentor was Erasmus of Rotterdam, but it was different from the rational humanism that was emerging in Europe. According to Bataillon: "Spain was another kind of mankind" for Erasmus. "Seen through Western eyes, Spain was one of those strange countries where Christendom made contact with Semites opposed to Christianity and mixed with them."[95] Far from attracting him, Spain, with which he was not familiar at all, rather disgusted him. It was perhaps a matter of instinct. Spain seemed to him more

---

[95] Marcel Bataillon, *Erasmo y España* (Mexico City, 1950), Vol. I, p. 91.

Semitic than European, closer to that world of Jews and Mohammedans with which she was in contact than with the humanistic Christianity and the new Europe about to emerge which Erasmus represented. "In Spain," he says, "there are hardly any Christians."

And yet, if Spain had done anything, it was to defend Christianity, and if at that time there was something she was trying to do, it was to continue guarding it against attack. She had defended Christianity against Jews and Mahommedans, now she hoped to protect it against heresy or whatever heterodoxy might appear in Europe. Like Russia when she chose the Byzantine Church, Spain during the sixteenth century saw herself as the defender of Christian orthodoxy, of Catholicism in Europe against the new heterodoxies that appeared with Modernity. Her warlike spirit, tempered in innumerable battles against Paganism, was now directed against the heretics. Spain considered herself the standard-bearer of a great mission: to Christianize the pagan world and to Christianize anew a heretical Europe. It was that acceptance of what she felt as her mission, that faithfulness to the new Christian orthodoxy, which provoked the reaction of a Europe that had set its sights on a different goal. That reaction would ultimately place Spain on the fringe of the Western world. During the Religious Wars which devastated Europe in the seventeenth century, Spain became the leader of the side that was trying to uphold Christian orthodoxy at all costs, in a struggle in which she would be defeated and confined to the Peninsula and her colonies, only to be driven out later by the very spirit she had fought against. Cromwell, regarded as the symbol of the heresy of the emerging West, justified his struggle against Spain by saying: "We are at war with Spain. We began it out of necessity. Spain is our greatest enemy, our natural enemy, an enemy foreordained by God since she symbolizes Papism."[96] In other words, she was a symbol of Europe's past, the personification of backwardness and of everything that was contrary to civilization in a world that was beginning to make progress the center of its existence. She was an anachronistic nation that belonged to the past, and for the same reason no longer had to go on being the power she once was.

---

[96] See *Histoire de la Diplomatie*, edited by Vladimir Potiemkine (Paris, 1953).

Spain's stubbornness in her struggle to defend the Christian values which she considered her heritage had turned her into a backward nation on the fringe of history. In the new Europe other interests were already at play; these no longer favored that Christian spirit which Spain had tried to represent. Feudalism had passed into history already and along with it its economic, political, and social manifestations. The Church was no longer the spiritual and material bond of Europe's union. The world about to emerge was based on other principles, which were no longer those that Spain continued to hold in esteem. By strongly supporting what she recognized as Christian orthodoxy she opposed the beginnings of Modernity in Europe and the Peninsula. Spanish orthodoxy would nullify at home the efforts of a group of her citizens to reconcile the heritage they had defended with the new values that were emerging, or in other words, to reconcile Christianity with Modernity. The voices of the Vives brothers, Vitoria, Valdés, and other Spanish humanists who tried to bring about this reconciliation of Spain and Europe, of Spanish orthodoxy with the new heterodoxy, were silenced. With the same stubbornness and insistence with which she had stopped and expelled the Oriental invaders threatening Europe, Spain stopped, persecuted and drove out any idea that might present a danger to her orthodoxy. The new ideas which appeared in Western Europe, ideas which had contributed to the greatness and strength of her new enemy, England, were opposed by Spain at a moment in her history when future progress depended on her goodwill.[97] During that period of her history Spain was closed to new ideas and the technology these had developed. Unable to Christianize Europe anew, or to compete with its world-wide expansion, Spain retreated within her borders, withdrew from Western Europe and the Western world, and accepted the Pyrenees as her boundary. Henceforth, she would be content to dream about her past glories, remembering that period which might have been decisive for her history as the leader of a Europe now following its own course, a new course where there was no longer any room for Spain. Western Europe would now try to avoid the resurrection of a Spain that might return to play a role on the stage of European and world politics. It was not with Spain that the world Europe had discovered and expanded would be shared. On the contrary, the West was trying to find a way to expel her from the world it had succeeded in controlling by encouraging the obvious desire of Spain's colonies to escape oppression, although oppression

---

[97] See chapter X.

from another quarter was already in the offing. Spain and her colonies had merely become a part of the non-Western world, spoils of war to be conquered as Asia, Africa, and Oceania had been before.

24. Recognition of Spain's Anachronism

Spain, in spite of a series of internal and external difficulties, the firm opposition of the feudal spirit which still inspired her and Europe's opposition, which had removed her from the political stage, recognized her anachronism, the falseness of her situation in a world that was following a different course and yet she persisted in her attempt to belong. Spain's first efforts to modernize, to adapt to the new technology and spirit which had made possible the greatness and might of Western Europe, were made during the eighteenth century. Various reasons and historical events were responsible for this new Renaissance, but we shall consider only the spirit that inspired it. Spain's new outlook became apparent in her renewed desire to regain a place of importance in Europe's destiny, by adopting European institutions and ways of life.

During the eighteenth century, Spain was animated by the same ideas that gave fresh vigor to the new Europe, the same ideology that in a combative era destroys theocracies and despotism. The virus of Modernity seemed to have infiltrated the last bastion of theocracy. Even the Spanish kings, scions of Western Europe, encouraged the Spanish Renaissance to follow in the footsteps of "enlightened despotism," a system originated by Peter the Great of Russia, which forced the Spanish people to follow the new trend of history. When Spain clashed with the new ideas that originated in Western Europe she realized her backwardness, analyzed her marginal position in the new history that was unfolding, and persisted in adopting an outlook that would enable her to regain her role in history. Certainly not a decisive role, but one she felt was incumbent upon her as a European nation.

Reacting against the decline of which they had become aware, and inspired by a desire for intellectual renewal, a group of

Spaniards introduced the seed of European Modernism into Spain. A
desire for clarity, for greater illumination of the darkness left by a
theocratic Spain, permeated all disciplines of eighteenth-century
Spanish culture. It was necessary to illuminate, enlighten, clarify,
and distinguish in accordance with the rational philosophy which was
beginning to permeate the modern world. On the one hand there was
the world of reason, and on the other the world of faith. Spain's
mistake had been to confuse the two. Those worlds were not at
variance with each other, provided they kept to their natural
boundaries. Politics and science belonged to the world of reason,
and not to that of faith and the divine, as the Spanish theocratic
philosophy had claimed. Politics and science as expressions of
man's rational ability had created the great symbols of the modern
world in Western Europe: democratic institutions and physics, the
mother of technology which was making nature the servant of man.
Europe's only mistake had been to apply this rational spirit to the
field of religion, thus creating the atheism which appeared in her
philosophy and attitude toward life. In Spain, it was not necessary
to take this step, since the world of man and the world of the divine
were clearly differentiated.

There appeared a new eclecticism, a new insistence on
reconciling Christianity, whose champion Spain was with Modernity,
which had been responsible for the material wealth of the nations that
had espoused it. The same attempt had been made earlier by Spanish
Erasmians to reconcile worlds that seemed poles apart. The new
philosophy, rationalism and empiricism, took hold of the minds of
Spain's foremost intellectuals.

The defenders of the new philosophy were members of the
Spanish nobility and the clergy. It was the same philosophy that
threatened the European nobility and eventually hastened their
downfall; the same philosophy that cast doubt on the right of the
Church to intervene in national politics. Nevertheless, Charles III
disseminated these ideas in Spain and in her American colonies. The
clergy produced some of the most brilliant propagandists of the new
ideas. Alongside the Benedictine Feijóo appeared the Jesuits
Exímenos, Andrés and Isla, vigorously attacking an anachronistic
scholasticism which had prevented the Spaniards from establishing
science in Spain as it had been established in other European
countries. Royalty, for its part, spoke of a policy to ensure the
happiness of all its subjects. The old topics of classical metaphysics

were abandoned and in their place the real world, nature, and the Spaniard's conviviality were studied. Man and his natural surroundings became focal themes for study and observation by the new men of Spanish culture. Historians, writers, geographers, astronomers, and mathematicians were the people now striving to save Spain from what they felt was her decline. All of them fought for the honor of saving her from the backwardness which was her sad lot.

Spain thus made a new effort to become Westernized again. It was a vain attempt so far as the West was concerned. Western Europe was not ready to share its influence in the world with any other power. Here too, Europe was to align herself with the forces that represented the theocratic and feudal spirit of Spain. At the beginning of the nineteenth century, liberal Spanish factions which were among the most persistent in desiring Spain's participation in the new European political movements, were attached and oppressed by the France of Napoleon I, the very country that in Europe posed as the leader of the new ideas and political freedoms. Regardless of her leaders, Spain was for Western Europe merely a pawn in the game. Henceforth and right up to the present time, the Western powers of Europe and America would always find good pretexts for hindering the Westernization of Spain, for preventing her from joining the West in a role other than subordinate. Gradually, little by little, Spain was pushed off the stage of Western history. By nurturing the same spirit Spain had bequeathed to them, her descendants in America achieved their political emancipation, but without being able to avoid an economic subjection from which was to derive another form of Spanish America's political subjugation to the West.

Spain's efforts to Westernize were met by opposition from internal theocratic forces unwilling to give up their privileged position, and from the modern powers of the West, which did not wish to lose the status they enjoyed in a colonized Spain. These opposing forces worked together by common consent in the West's policies of world-wide expansion. In Spain, as in Russia and Latin America, the nineteenth century saw an attempt to overcome the backwardness which had been her lot. Her efforts were always in vain because in the end the forces that tried to stop her were victorious. During the twentieth century, one last effort was the Spanish Republic, as we shall see later. Yet another attempt to

Westernize was largely due to Spain's new awareness of her backwardness produced by her defeat in 1898 by the United States, the youngest representative of the Western world. Again, the best Spanish minds attempted to rejoin Europe by erasing the physical and spiritual boundary of the Pyrenees. The result was that, once again, not only Europe but the West would oppose Spain's desire to rejoin that community of nations. Once again the West, in its most totalitarian manner, attacked Spain and imposed on her the most reactionary and backward forces in the country, while democratic Europe, the Western world of freedom and democracy, let a nation die upon the pretext that the policy of Non-Intervention had never been a reality. That policy was merely another form of intervention in the destiny of Spain, which had become aware of her backwardness and tried to escape in vain. The West once again rejected participation in its history by one of the nations that had done the most to protect its frontiers and implement its values.

25. Liberalism as a Tool in Westernization

As we have already pointed out, the nineteenth century was a period in Spain's history when she tried to Westernize, to become Europeanized, as the Spaniards called it. This enormous effort manifested itself in liberalism, a liberalism which, like its Spanish American counterpart would try to erase a past that had been so ominous in Spain's history. The spirit of conciliation so much in evidence in the Erasmians and eclectics was gradually disappearing. The Spanish liberal realized that the feudal theocratic past was one of the main stumbling blocks in his way. Therefore, without being opposed to religion, he was anti-clerical. But, like his Spanish American counterpart, he found himself in the minority in a nation shaped by the old Spanish theocratic philosophy which at one time had represented the highest values in her history. In order to succeed, liberalism needed to activate the power of the people but there was no social class or popular group that stood behind liberalism. It was a movement that represented the future, but not the past, not the present, of Spain. The first great liberal effort was made by the group of Spaniards who, together with the ordinary people, resisted French intervention under Napoleon. According to

Oliveira Martins, "that was the awakening of a benumbed nation faced with the shock of a terrible war. Impressions accumulated, ideas whirled around crazily in minds weakened by centuries of atrophy." The establishment of the famous Cortes of Cádiz seemed to indicate that Spain was beginning to follow the line of progress set by the West. It was a sincere aspiration, that unfortunately came to nothing. Ferdinand VII, the Spanish king in whom the liberals thought they had found a leader ready to guide them on this new road, retracted, dissolved the Cortes and thus restored the values of old theocratic Spain. The same forces which had seemed to triumph in the Europe of the Holy Alliance, over the Modernity of Western Europe, reinstated a Spanish monarch who would have nothing to do with liberalism. Napoleon had been defeated, and along with him the liberal spirit that had fought against him in Spain. "Those fantastic and naive Cortes," says Oliveira, "disappeared atomized and like an event without precedent or meaning in the midst of languor and the worship of the common people, to whom their old and cherished symbols were restored. Between one dream and the next, the troubled peninsula stretched her limbs, and, half asleep, threw out the French and scattered the seed of future revolutions"[98] in the Peninsula and her colonies.

The first half of the nineteenth century witnessed a constant struggle for liberalism in Spain, which, though repressed again and again, sought to change her into a modern nation. It was a liberalism perpetually battling the forces of theocratic Spain and the interests of Western Europe which were turning Spain into a new economic colony for the profit of the West. The liberals struggled in vain to establish a national bourgeoisie, a middle class which, as in Western Europe, would contribute to the greatness of the new Spanish nation. The most they accomplished was disentailment of the property of the clergy, and they were able to do this because it benefited the wealthier classes, which saw in it an opportunity to acquire land formerly belonging to the Church. What liberalism could no longer do was to carry out the necessary social, political, and economic reforms to transform Spain into a modern nation. In Spain, as in Spanish America during the same period, old privileges remained in force and prevented the establishment of a middle class that might have acted as a springboard for the nation's progress. All that was achieved was the appearance of a semi-feudal group made up of old

---

98 Antonio Ramos-Oliveira, *Historia de España* (Mexico City, 1952).

landowners and the new ones that appeared when the Church lands were apportioned, and these were joined by military men who had fought in the long civil war and by officials returning from Spanish America. Thus was formed an oligarchy similar to the many others which have appeared in Spanish America. Like them, the Spanish oligarchy was interested in establishing peace, since that would enable the new class to enjoy all possible advantages. These were new struggles, new bargaining with respect to Spain's future, in which the partisans of an order that left the narrow interests of the oligarchy alone invariable triumphed. The realization of the liberals' dream of a liberal, Europeanized, and Westernized Spain was thus postponed.

Tradition, a return to the past, became the program of a class that did not want its interests to be touched. Consequently, peace and order appeared as the motto of government.[99] Spain had no need to follow trends that were not her own, nor those of her past, nor in line with her traditions. Her backwardness, far from being a shortcoming, was an advantage to be preserved. "And in order to keep public order inviolate," says Ortega y Gasset, "one refrains from attacking any of Spain's vital issues because, if a visceral problem is dealt with, the Spaniard if not stone dead, reacts by charging with both arms raised in readiness for a strong, healthy struggle."[100] Unable to get popular support, liberalism merely represented a class that was useful in certain situations for furthering the interests of an oligarchy determined to maintain the peace and order which served their own ends. Spain, despite all her efforts, continued to live in the past. She was a backward nation of no importance whatever in the history of Western Europe and America. However, she was soon to become aware of her backwardness and awaken from the dream to which she had once more surrendered. Her last possessions in America and Asia, the Antilles and the Philippines, were clamoring for independence, and behind them, waiting for their liberation, was North America, the youngest member of the West, the world which Spain had tried in vain to join.

---

[99] Something similar happens in almost all Latin American nations, where oligarchies appear which, in the name of peace and order establish dictatorial regimes that bolster their interests. Refer to my books *Positivism in Mexico* and *The Latin American Mind.*

[100] José Ortega y Gasset, *Obras completas* (Madrid, 1947), Vol. I, p. 281. Also see Fernando Salmerón, *Las mocedades de Ortega y Gasset* (Mexico City, 1959) where this period and the reaction of Ortega's generation is analyzed.

The defeat of 1898 was to promote a new awareness of her backwardness, and along with it a renewed effort to escape, and join the world of Modernity, Europe and the West. Again, Spain asked what her chances were of becoming a modern nation, of making a Spanish contribution to science, of joining Europe. To achieve those aims, she must alter her ways, strengthen and remodel herself, and that could be done only if she became Europeanized. In view of the most recent national catastrophe, it was the goal of that generation to Europeanize Spain.

The generation in question, however, was to have an exceptional model, that of a group of intellectuals educated in the difficult environment which had shattered Spanish liberalism. They, too, were liberals, but with a clearer understanding of the nature of the Spanish problem. They knew that it was not sufficient to import a particular philosophy in order to turn Spain into a European nation. The important thing was to assimilate the spirit that had made Europe what she was: the modern world. And that spirit was rationalism. Spain could become truly liberal and European, indeed Western, if only she would be more ready to listen to reason. This was the main worry of the group responsible for "Spanish Krausism." "These men were impelled by the desire to break the thick wall of rustic distrust which, by isolating Spain from European thought, had caused her to sink into an intellectual apathy and poverty. But the contemplation of contemporary Spain, ignorant and garrulous, indigent and bleeding, made them see the need to break with the Old Spain that had emerged with the Counter-Reformation and had reinforced the arm of Catholic imperialism, a Spain at once military and priestlike, which rightly or wrongly they blamed for the misery of the present. For this task of historical scrutiny, inherited ideas, traditional beliefs, the platitudes and the obligatory trivialities of 'casticismo' were no longer of any use." What was important was to assimilate the rationalism that characterized the culture of Western Europe. To accept or reject Europe was tantamount to accepting or rejecting the rational outlook that had started Europe on her march toward progress during the seventeenth century. Therefore, according to López Morillas, the attempt to Europeanize Spain was an entirely logical development. "Among the attempts at Europeanization that had begun in Spain in the eighteenth century, Krausism was the first movement that clearly perceived the essential problem. Other movements had been content to advocate that adoption of foreign principles and customs, even of political ideas, foreign economic doctrines, social practices, literary styles, and fashions in art, without realizing that such principles and customs were the normal outgrowth of a particular attitude toward life that was unknown in Spain." Therefore, if "one accepts the proposition that Spain should be Europeanized, one has to conclude that the Krausists dealt with the question in a more logical manner than their predecessors." They longed to introduce into Spain something more than isolated forms of European culture, because they wanted to assimilate the spirit that had created it.

To Europeanize Spain was thus an old desire which hitherto had never been realized. Attempts to achieve it had been made during the sixteenth century by the Spanish Erasmians, during the eighteenth by the eclectics and the disciples of the Enlightenment, and during the first half of the nineteenth century by the liberals. Now it was the Krausists' turn to attempt it. The novelty of their approach, according to López Morillas, was that they "equated Europe with the rational view of the world, and accordingly tried to guide Spanish culture in the direction of rationalism." As Menéndez Pelayo had foreseen, a new heterodoxy appeared. Spanish orthodoxy seemed to these new intellectuals to be an anachronism that had to be overcome if Spain was to get out of the fringe position to which she had been relegated. It was this feeling of being on the fringe, of being anachronistic, that once more roused the Spaniard. The failure of liberalism was one sign of the backwardness that had to be overcome. Around the middle of the last century, says López Morillas, the Spaniard "saw himself bypassed, left in an obscure corner of the stage of Europe, whence he observed avidly and not without humiliation that the star roles were being played by actors not of Spanish blood."[101] The defeat of 1898 accentuated this impression. Consequently, a new, and until now the last effort to Westernize Spain was undertaken.

---

[101] José López Morillas, *El krausismo español* (Mexico City, 1956).

26. Europeanizing Spain

Does Spain have a history? Does she belong to history? No, answered the generation that made the most recent effort to Westernize or Europeanize Spain. "Spain," says Joaquín Xirau, "is a nation without a history. She lacks the continuity of a sober and critical judgment of the reason for her presence and transitory development in the Western world. Spain's history is determined either by the patient accumulation of meaningless facts or by the casual handling of important topics without exploring them in depth . . . topics designed to sing her glories or to insult her abjection."[102] According to the new generation, Spain, in her relations with a world of which she knew she was a part, was not aware of her position in world history and in that of the West. Moreover, Spain was not only ignorant of her position in history, but had acted in an anachronistic manner that had hindered her progress. Spain, said Ortega y Gasset, had taken upon herself missions that were not her concern, while Europe channeled its progress elsewhere. Spain had carried out missions not properly hers, such as the expulsion of the Jews, the conquest of America, the control of Flanders and Italy, opposition to the Reformation, and the strengthening of the power of the Popes. Ortega, therefore, suggested a revision of Spanish history through the application of a different standard, "a philosophic spirit that is scientific and not merely scholarly." Such a history would show the physiognomy of a race that has lived upside down in opposition to history.[103]

The great problem now was to live with history, to become a part of history, a genuine part of the West or more precisely Europe, which was the part of the world where history was being made. Not the Europe of the past which, just because it belonged to the past had no further reason to go on existing. Not the feudal Europe of the Holy Roman Empire, but rather modern Europe, which had taken its culture to the confines of the world. Not credulous, emotional, religious Europe, but rational, sober and practical Europe. Not the Europe of saints and miracles, but the Europe of scientists and technology that control nature. How could change be brought about

---

[102] Joaquín Xirau, "Humanismo español." In *Cuadernos americanos* (Mexico City, January/February 1942).
[103] See Fernando Salmerón, op. cit.

in Spain? How could she be encouraged to embark on a new course? How could she be Westernized? How could she be Europeanized? In order to achieve this, it was not enough to copy institutions for which Spain was not ready. That was the mistake liberals and republicans had made when they insisted on bringing to the Peninsula institutions and simple ways without previously changing the Spanish character. The conflicts between Republicans and Monarchists during the nineteenth century had revealed the immaturity of Spain's desire to become Westernized. In these conflicts, irreconcilable ideals and ideas had been arraigned against each other and could survive only by totally eliminating their opponents. Spain had lacked the dialectic of logic of which Hegel spoke. She had lacked that rationalizing spirit which, by knowing and understanding itself, assimilated a past that, because it had existed, no longer had any reason to exist or to go on existing. The new European institutions were merely the genuine product of Europe's ability to assimilate and rationalize. Europe symbolized the assumption of all affirmations and denials, and this had acted as an incentive. Europe had renounced her past, in the most acceptable manner, by assimilation. "The European," says Ortega y Gasset, "has been a democrat, liberal, absolutist and feudalist, but he no longer is strictly speaking. Does this mean that has ceased to be like that? Of course not. The European continues to be all those things, but in the sense that he has experienced them all."[104] What had happened to the Spaniard? The exact opposite. He had either stubbornly held on to the past as if it still existed, or had tried to clear in one jump the distance that separated feudalism from liberalism. It was important, therefore, to become aware of the past and to assimilate it. That was what the new Spanish generation of which Ortega y Gasset was one of the leaders tried to do.

To revise Spanish history in relation to world history or that of the West was one of the major concerns of Ortega's generation. It was Spain's assessment of herself that would allow her to become a part of the universality represented by the Western world. Spain must come to know herself not as a unique and isolated entity, but rather as part of a larger whole: she must know her place in world culture. "We must try to find for our circumstance, such as it is," said Ortega, "and precisely in its very limitation and peculiarity, its

---

[104] José Ortega y Gasset, "Historia como sistema" in *Obras completas*, Vol. VI (Madrid, 1947).

appropriate place in the immense perspective of the world. We must not stop in perpetual ecstasy before hieratic values, but conquer the right place among them for our individual life.   In short, the reabsorption of circumstance is the concrete destiny of man."

"My natural exit toward the universe is through the mountain passes of the Guadarrama or the plain of Ontígola. This sector of circumstantial reality forms the other half of my person; only through it can I integrate myself and be fully myself . . . I am myself and my circumstance, and if I do not save my circumstance, I cannot save myself. To assimilate Spain's past, to take hold of it, is the best way to overcome it, since it places so many obstacles in the way of the future. Spain has been referred to as the 'land of ancestors'. Therefore, it is not ours, not the free property of present-day Spaniards. Those who have gone before continue to rule us and form an oligarchy of the dead, which oppresses us." How could this be overcome? By treating it for what it was, an experience that was over and for which there was no need to continue. "The death of what is dead is life." The past is only a way of life, but not life itself. What the reactionary cannot see is how to "treat the past as a form of life." Therefore, "he pulls it out of the sphere of vitality, and, thoroughly dead as it is, he places it on its throne so that it may rule over souls." Consequently, in order to save Spain one must renounce, assimilate her past by making it what it really is, an experience to benefit her future, but no longer the only possible course for her to take. What the new generation attempted was to deny the existence of a weak Spain. But that carried with it an obligation: to uphold another Spain. "Having denied one Spain, honor bids us find another and will not let us rest until we do so."[105]

Beginning with this appraisal of Spain's situation in European culture, the new generation tried to understand that culture in order to make it their own. What distinguishes a European from other people? His scientific ability, they answered, that enabled him to transform nature and place it at his service. And the basis of his ability was his rationalism, the rationalism that Spain so sorely lacked. Not an abstract, imitative rationalism, but rather one that was a part of life and therefore at its service. Reason and life, "vital reason." This is the proper combination that the new generation has

---

[105] José Ortega y Gassett, *Meditations on Quixote*. Trans. Evelyn Rugg and Diego Marín (New York, 1961), pp. 45, 48, 49, 53.

found. That was the best way to Europeanize Spain, to make her join the world to which she belonged. Thus a reconciliation between Europe and Spain was achieved. The latter without ceasing to be Spanish, could also be European, indeed universal. Therefore, the second quarter of our century was marked in Spain by the new generation's efforts in that direction. New deeds and new ideas. The most modern philosophies, ideas that created a stir on the contemporary scene, were disseminated through Ortega's *Revista de Occidente*, one of Spain's best cultural tools in her desire to Europeanize. The review's two main themes were: Spaniards must learn to appreciate their own country, and must develop an understanding of Western culture. Ortega considered German culture the focal point of Western culture. Therefore, the program of the new generation was to introduce German ideas into Spain as one of the best ways to Westernize her outlook. These hopes and desires were shattered by a new and violent rejection on the part of the Western world that Spain had admired so much. Once more, Spain, like other countries in similar circumstances, was to be rejected by Western history; once more she was to be placed on the fringe and relegated to that past which, encouraged by the West, resisted repudiation and assimilation.

CHAPTER VII

EUROPE ON THE FRINGE OF THE WEST

27. Is Europe a North American Colony?

In one of Europe's most successful novels of recent times, *The Mandarins* by Simone de Beauvoir, the characters firmly state: "We are going to be annexed by Russia or colonized by America." What is voiced in that novel is the feeling in Western Europe, which is revealed in various ways. La Société Européenne de Culture, already mentioned in another context, and one of the institutions most aware of the problems of the intellectual, has considered the two superpowers with respect to the influence either may have on the future of European culture.[106] Here, as well as in the international forums of São Paulo and Geneva organized by UNESCO in 1954, on the cultural and moral relations between the Old and the New World, it was shown that a feeling existed that Europe was being colonized

---

[106] See "Puissance et Culture: le Nouveau Continent." In *Comprendre* (Venice), Nos. 10-11 (1954) and "Puissance Soviétique, Communisme et Culture." In *Comprendre* (Venice), No. 12 (1955).

by the United States.[107] This feeling arises from confrontation with the inescapable fact, one of the most important realities of contemporary world history, of the rapid growth of America, or, more precisely, of one of the Americas: Anglo-Saxon America, North America, the United States of America.

The growth of the United States began with the First World War, at the end of which, instead of being Europe's debtor, she became its creditor. The Second World War strengthened the foothold secured during the First World War. The United States became one of the foremost powers, a supremacy challenged only by the Soviet Union. During the interval between the two World Wars, the nations which until then had been regarded as the major powers, England, France, and Germany, became second-class nations and more recently pawns in the complicated game in which the United States and Russia are engaged for world supremacy. This was borne out when England and France, in their designs on Egypt, could no longer act as they used to do as major powers, when they employed any kind of pretext to further their interests in countries weaker than themselves. At that time, the United States was interested in these same countries for the purpose of expanding her sphere of influence, and this was one of the factors ultimately responsible for Western Europe's failure in the Middle East. That fiasco has elicited from European politicians and journalists uninhibited views similar to those expressed by intellectuals, to the effect that Europe is a colony of the West, a West now represented by the United States in all its might. A West in which her two great contributions, liberal institutions and industrial technology, have reached their highest point of development, with all the problems which that entails and may still entail.

Europe is at present divided into two major spheres of political and economic influence: Western and Eastern. Within the former are nations that have played a key role in the history of what is known as Western culture, nations in which the great cultural movements that marked the beginning of the so-called modern world originated, that same culture which today is passing through a most pathetic crisis. England, France, Germany, and Italy, cradle of the great intellectual movements which gave meaning to modern or Western culture, are

---

[107] See *The Old and the New World. Their Cultural and Moral Relations.* UNESCO (Paris, 1956).

now caught in the train of the offspring of their own culture developed to the highest degree by North America, the nation engendered by Western Europe during the initial stages of her expansion over the rest of the world. The same spirit that made possible the colonization of the non-Western world by the West is now turning against Europe and subordinating her to its interests. Western Europe ends her role as colonizer in order to accept the status of a colony in a world which she created. From the economic and political points of view, the United States is making Europe a tool of her interests, a relationship similar to that of European nations with non-Western countries. The role that Europe used to play in the world devolves on the United States. In this case we are not dealing with a revolt of a non-Western country against the West, as might happen with China, India, or any other Asian or African country. We are simply dealing with a country, a nation, shaped by Europe, created by Europeans, that has outgrown the mother country and has turned Europe into a world situated on the fringe of its own expansion.

In this sense, and I insist, the United States is the highest expression of the Western spirit. It is also one of the expressions adopted by Western Europe in her modern development. The philosophy of "clarity and precision," of "order and planning," so dear to the modern world is a philosophy at present expressed in what Europeans call the United States' "simplistic" policy toward European affairs, a policy which in its desire to simplify problems avoids issues that are more complex and consequently more difficult to solve. It is this simplistic approach to European affairs that makes the United States appear more like a threat than an ally. A simplicity at the core of which are always clear-cut and obvious economic interests. A simplicity which to the European mind is bound to clash with the complex European reality rooted in centuries of tradition and history. Only by taking into account this tradition and history, already alien to the United States, can one begin to solve the manifold problems which Europe's reality poses. And it is America's inability to see those difficulties as evidenced by the simple solutions it offers in answer to Europe's problems, that has caused alarm about the future of European culture. Is America capable of discharging her new responsibilities? Indeed, Europeans ask themselves, is America capable of being the leader of Western culture? America, or rather the United States, has attained at present complete economic and political superiority over the world, but can she give the world a new way of life? Is she capable of directing the creative spirit which has characterized Western Europe? Or, on the contrary, will she obstruct this spirit and, instead, give the world a simplistic meaning and thereby make it mechanical and inhuman? Many of Europe's foremost intellectuals are alarmed at the prospect facing their culture, indeed, European culture, and are asking America to realize her position and the responsibility it carries with it.

28. Western Culture and European Culture

What is it that is threatened by the simplicity of America's outlook in her relations with Europe? Does this simplicity pose a threat to Western culture or European culture? American lack of sophistication with respect to the world at large is, as already pointed out, merely the expression of so-called modern culture in its desire to see the world as something easy and accessible to man, and to turn the world into something useful and easy to handle. This philosophy is typical of one aspect of European culture as it developed, but not of that culture in general. It is typical of so-called Western culture but not, for example, of Western Christian culture. It is not typical of America's disputed past, even though she is at present Western culture's major exponent and its leader. Therefore, it is not Western culture that is threatened by America's simplistic approach, but rather the segment of that culture still alive in Europe. Europe vindicates her past vis-à-vis the United States. A past revealed in its culture, which can still be seen in her museums and cities, and in the philosophy of her people; a past that Modernity tried in vain to discard. It is just this past of European culture that is in danger and not the past of Western culture, of which North America is also a manifestation. It is a past that the philosophy of Western culture, seeking a new way of life puts in a marginal position, a past now in arms against the world it engendered, but to which it no longer belongs. Europe, like Spain and Russia, regards this past as the focal point of her orthodoxy. At present, America has political and economic control of the Western world. She is its leader. But Europe is and will remain the center of true culture, universal culture par excellence, that European culture of which

Western culture, now represented by America, is only one manifestation. Europe will continue to set the standards for genuine culture as she has done in the past and does at present, although she no longer has political and economic control of the world. Her culture is not confined to technology, the control of nature, but instead is based on the creative spirit of man. Permanent reliance on technology for controlling nature can only lead to heresy in respect of what, from an orthodox point of view, culture ought to be.

The United States has carried the material achievement of which Western culture was an expression to its highest level, yet it has been unable to produce the other kinds of creative work characteristic of modern and contemporary European Christian culture. "North America," says Paul Rivet, "has produced a number of eminent technicians, builders of skyscrapers, dams, bridges, roads, up-to-date machinery, etc., whose equals are not, I think, to be found anywhere else in the world. The material side of its civilization has thus been developed to an unprecedented extent. But this exceptional wealth of engineering talent has been accompanied by a surprising poverty in the field of discovery and invention, in philosophy, literature, and the arts. Men of world-wide fame who hold North American passports were in many cases trained abroad, they are imported plants bedded out in American soil . . . A visit to the Museum of Modern Art in New York reveals the lack of individuality of the works it contains, beautiful as many of them undoubtedly are. Inspiration is drawn chiefly from the great masters of the Old World. There are few really original creations in which no European echoes are perceived. The only aesthetic canon proper to America seems to be that of the grandiose, or rather the gigantic." Is this because we are dealing with a new country? "Fifteenth-century France gave birth to Rabelais, sixteenth-century Spain produced Cervantes, seventeenth-century England brought forth Shakespeare; were these old peoples? Were the Greeks of Homer's day an old people already? I have often asked this question, and on many occasions the reply has been 'yes.' This reply brings us nearer to the core of the problem. I gained the impression that those to whom I spoke regarded a people as 'old' if it had behind it a traditional, uninterrupted civilization of its own, or if its civilization had been enriched by drawing upon earlier civilizations, with no break in continuity."[108] America is therefore outside the tradition of European culture, although representing the highest expression of one of its phases. In pursuing this point of view it may be said that America is an expression of Western culture, which originated in Europe, but not an expression of European culture.

Both genuine culture and cultural orthodoxy are European. Europe has lost political and economic control of the Western world, which has shifted more to the West, but she has not lost her cultural control, according to the European who refuses to be displaced in this area and resists being relegated to the edge of the cultural sphere. "America," says Antony Babel, " has too long believed that, henceforth, Europe's role in the world would be that of Greece: to serve as a museum or a library whose resources other parts of the world could tap at will, but which would have no longer any activity of its own. That is a role which Europe has never accepted. Now, America is gradually beginning to realize that its judgment was at fault; in reality, the Old World, politically and materially weakened though it may be, is more active than ever in the intellectual sphere."[109] Europe has created culture and will continue to shape it regardless of the fact that she has lost her political and economic control of the world. In Europe there is the great past of a culture that serves as a permanent guarantee for a culture ever renewed. That great past, which America does not have, is found in the classical world and in Christianity. Europe is regaining possession of this world, which is the world that strengthens her orthodoxy, and she rejects the practical, utilitarian, and materialistic spirit she attributes to America. Europe, now displaced in the political and economic sphere, opposes with all the power at her command the spirit that has brought this about in the Western world, thus taking the lead from America. Europe regards herself as classical and Christian, confronted by capitalism and the bourgeoisie at present prevailing in America. According to Guido Piovene, "it seems . . . that the European objections to American ways of life are in the last resort based on two main grounds: one Christian, the other Humanist . . . An important aspect of Europe's self-appraisement in the face of America is certainly its revolutionary reliance on its

---

[108] Paul Rivet, "The Background and Task of the Ibero-American Peoples." *In The Old and the New World. Their Cultural and Moral Relations*, op. cit., pp. 44-45, 46.
[109] Antony Babel, "Two Worlds Face to Face." In *The Old and the New World. Their Cultural and Moral Relations*, op. cit., p. 152.

Christian spirit . . . Many prominent people are convinced that the crisis in modern society points toward the need for putting the Gospel message into practice wholeheartedly."

However, this message, this return to a kind of Christian community encounters difficulties in a bourgeois and capitalist society. Europeans therefore fear the victory of American society and civilization in the world, because it would perpetuate that capitalist and bourgeois society. This attitude, continues Piovene, has led Europe into a double opposition, "its essential mission being, in this view, to oppose American civilization, because it is bourgeois-capitalist, and to oppose Soviet civilization because it is not Christian. But, at bottom, some proponents of these views ask themselves whether it might not be well to aim at an agreement with Soviet civilization, not immediately perhaps, but in some indeterminable future. It would be Soviet's civilization's task to clear the ground of the bourgeois-capitalist superstructures, which stand in the way of the realization of the Christian Gospel . . . The Christian Gospel could then be preached under more propitious circumstances, the worst obstacles to it having been cleared away . . . The other objection is a humanist one . . . a protest against the prominence given to monetary values in assessing the merits of a human individual . . . it means the end of that . . . humanist world to which we are emotionally attached by our traditions. Even in a society like the American . . . individuals are grouped not by classes but by economic levels" as a determining factor of human achievement. "'Money value' dominates and constricts the mind; the will to possess is the chief and constant motive for action." As against America, Russia appears to offer a way once more into that humanistic and classical world. According to Guido Piovene, "thus in Europe we face, so it seems to me, a paradox. Many cultivated, anti-Communist Europeans feel attracted to Soviet society, not because they see in it 'the world of the future,' but because through it they see a hope for a more 'ancient,' more classical world. That is why the Soviet world seduces many artists and many educated men versed in the humanistic disciplines and the study of past civilizations."[110]

---

[110] Guido Piovene, "Europe and the Civilization of America." In *The Old and the New World. Their Cultural and Moral Relations*, op. cit., pp. 27, 28, 29.

Thus Europe, once considered the center of the Western world, which regarded countries like Russia, Spain, and Latin American countries as marginal, now begins to feel remote or on the fringe in relation to that world, whose focal point has shifted to the United States, and closer to the countries that once were marginal. In those countries she begins to see the manifestation of a world which she recognizes as her true domain: the humanistic and Christian world. A world of which Europe was the center, a position she could regain. A world already far away from the heterodoxy that Modernity represents. Russia and the Iberian world are, in her opinion, closer to human and Christian orthodoxy than is America, the highest expression of heterodox Modernity and the Western world. Europe, therefore, is beginning to show an interest in the Latin American countries and their political and economic relations with the United States, which are similar to her own. They also serve Europe as an example in her new relationship of political and economic inferiority with respect to America.

Europe therefore continues to base her superiority on her culture, a culture which is no longer simply what is generally called Western culture. Although Europe created this culture she no longer regards its present manifestation and development as her own. Moreover, any culture rests on a past, in this case the humanistic and Christian past which Europe feels America has forgotten. That same past which clashed with modern times, is in turn responsible for Western culture. A humanistic-Christian past whose values were contrary to those created by Modernity, which insisted on establishing a society where the best and most able elements would rise to the top. These Christian and humanistic values the European of today finds reflected in forms of society founded on ideals, such as Socialism and Communism. European philosophers of history like Toynbee, Berdiaeff, Schweitzer, and many others have clamored and continue to clamor for the adoption and return of these values because they feel that this might offer a solution to the crisis of the West. With these values, which only lately have begun to preoccupy America, Europe now confronts the values of so-called Western culture. European orthodoxy is pitted against Western heterodoxy.

29. American Frustration and Disillusionment

Confronting European cultural orthodoxy is the strangeness and disillusionment of America; the alienation and disillusionment of a nation that had persisted in being Europe's faithful disciple and had carried to its highest realization values that originally came from Europe; alienation and disillusionment at being faced with condemnation by a culture whose leading representative she wanted to be. A feeling of disappointment, great disillusionment, which the tremendous political and economic success of the United States in the world fails to erase. A disappointment revealed in the complaints of several American intellectuals about the European's lack of understanding. The North American, says George N. Shuster, "sees that his best slogans do not kindle fire in the disheveled world abroad.   His desire to be popular, to shoulder his world responsibilities, to help establish peace upon the earth, is thwarted less by hostile Russian propaganda, than by what, for him, is the amazing indifference of those who should be his friends. And in the end he asks himself whether his people may not be after all, akin to one of his well-remembered characters, Diamond Jim Brady, with a priceless gem in his necktie, an uncanny instinct for distinguishing good cuisine from bad, and a certain yawning emptiness which must be filled if all the rest is to have meaning." An indifference that is incomprehensible because this man feels he is a model of efficiency in the cultural field of which he is a devoted disciple.

In developing the inherited modern culture or Western culture, the North American has succeeded in wresting nature's secrets from her on behalf of man's happiness. Why then is he criticized and censured for the know-how that has enabled him to do this, an achievement which is considered of doubtful value? "The North American," continues Shuster, "is conscious of his ability to establish a social order which, despite its need for improvement and for modification in detail, is fundamentally satisfying to the vast majority of those who live within it. The average citizen, for instance, has money to spend. His wife can be emancipated from grueling physical labor. His children enjoy a larger measure of security, perhaps, than young people have known anywhere since the dawn of time. The advantages of steadily pursued scientific research are his, so that he can, for instance, view with equanimity the growth of population because he knows that the sources of food and supply of energy are being steadily increased. Within the lifetime of an older citizen, the yield per acre of corn and wheat has been doubled. New sources of energy have been discovered, some of them revolutionary. Medicine has made unprecedented strides. It is possible to say that conundrums have therewith been solved which in the past, seemed far beyond human conjuring. All this is a reason for pride in an achievement and gratitude for all it has been possible to learn. It may be concluded that the American is therefore inclined to consider the outlook for progress in all that might conceivably affect the mundane lot of man as being very good indeed."

The North American knows that he is the heir of European culture and civilization, but he is an heir who knows how to increase the inheritance he has received by ensuring that it yields maximum returns and attains its most extraordinary development. However, this development and progress, far from pleasing the world, far from eliciting the warm approval of a Europe which bestowed that heritage, produces coldness, or what is worse, hostility. Instead of being applauded for its contribution to culture, America is criticized. "One of the most keen-witted and perceptive of American observers, Mary McCarthy," continues Shuster, "recently stated the matter in terms of English-American relationship, no doubt with that grace of over-statement which so often attends a fresh perception of the truth. There has, she thinks, never been 'a period in the history of our two countries when England was so prized'; and she thinks this is due in large measure to the feeling that the English have done so many things well that we have done badly. Therefore, she concludes, it is weirdly ironical that at precisely this time Americans should have grown so unpopular in Britain. Something comparable could no doubt be said of France, though it would have to be differently phrased." Something, therefore, has gone wrong. Somebody has deceived the Americans. Somebody has given them an underhanded blow. "One might, from the point of view of the United States, attribute this development to the sense of frustrated insecurity which arises from the fact that the soul of the American has been knifed at its most sensitive spot." This nation is already under the impression that she has been deceived, that she "has been taken for a ride, politically and diplomatically has been led to commit staggering blunders of judgment, for which she can blame no one but herself." The American, who is a faithful disciple of the Western world and of its highest manifestations, finds that in spite of himself he is living in a heterodox culture; that his faithfulness, instead of engendering a feeling of pride in his progenitor and mentor, has produced the opposite effect, rather as if he were someone who has stepped out of line. Something or someone has deceived him. Something has gone wrong with him, leading him to the failure of success. From this follows, adds Shuster, "the witch-hunting," the praise for the methods of Senator McCarthy, "because he finds satisfaction, sometimes avowed and yet again often secret, in the fact that they can presumably be relied upon to deliver punitive blows. It is true that such attitudes reveal a deplorable impatience and a failure to examine his own conscience."

In this way, once success has been attained, the greatest and best material triumphs that the North American has achieved, far from satisfying him, leave him with an empty feeling. What he does is neither recognized nor approved. No country has ever attained greater material progress than the United States, yet it seems that this success is not considered of any importance. Praise is avoided, and the recognition which has always been bestowed on the greatest nation in history is withheld. America's success is a triumph divested of its significance. In vain does the American in modern times hoist the highest ideals like a banner, ideals like "freedom" and "democracy." He tries in vain to have his conception of freedom and democracy accepted enthusiastically by other countries. He is the spokesman of those ideals, yet, the recognition of his leadership is withheld. The nations he helps, instead of looking upon him with kindness, view him with mistrust and hostility. His banners, his highest ideals, if he is the one who proclaims them, seem to lack meaning and attraction. According to Shuster, "it becomes fashionable in some parts of Europe to believe that, disreputable and bloodcurdling though the social system imposed upon Russia by its masters might be, the American cultural alternative was almost equally frightening: jazz blared out from dawn to midnight, a certain type of motion picture, anti-intellectualism, an infantile, purely quantitative sex mania . . ." What would America not give to gain for its culture the recognition the European culture has won! If it were possible, the American people "would acquire, on loan if need be, the inner life which so far has lent meaning to the abiding definitions of European civilization, just as he has already purchased its art and its manuscripts, or has continued to subsidize them through the lavish benefactions which constitute the tourist trade." But she knows that none of this is possible, that she cannot do anything of the kind. "Perhaps, one may say in conclusion," continues Shuster, "that what is particularly tragic about the present

world situation, so heartrendingly ominous in nearly every sense, is
this: while unprecedented American technological achievement has
made possible the discovery of weapons of destruction, which if
employed, might well render the continued existence of the human
race impossible, general world-wide regard for the generosity,
idealism, and restraint of the American people has most unfortunately
reached a low ebb."[111]

30. Europe's Objection to America

What is the reason for Europe's apparent lack of understanding
of America? What is it that Europe objects to in America? We have
already given one answer: separation from what Europe considers
genuine culture, and America's apparent surrender to materialism.
But there is something more, something to which the non-Western
world objects, with respect not only to America, but to the West in
general, and this includes the Europe that established colonialism in
the world. That something is the refusal of the Western world to
recognize in other countries the same values which she claims for
herself and demands that other nations acknowledge. Europe
recognizes the great value of America's contributions to culture,
particularly in the field of technology, which has given man greater
control over nature, and in respect of her liberal institutions, which
are a model, regardless of some minor flaws common to all
countries. In fact, she does not allow other countries to expand
materially as she is doing, and to enjoy the same democratic
freedoms because of American expansion, and raises her voice in
protest against the restrictions imposed by the United States. This
protest makes the European feel he is a brother of people in other
countries as he opposes their oppression by America. Granted that
America is a living symbol of democracy and human freedom, she
should not therefore try to become the leader, impose her way of life
and her interests on other countries. She may indeed be an example
of freedom and democracy, but she must learn to recognize that same

---

[111] George N. Shuster, "The Culture of the United States of America."
In *The Old and the New World. Their Cultural and Moral Relations*, op. cit.,
pp. 64, 63, 56, 56-57, 57, 56, 64.

freedom and democracy in other countries. "It is not by preaching
the civic virtues but by exemplifying them that America will be able
to exercise and influence," says André Maurois. "So long as it does
believe that it has a mission to spread the American way of life
throughout the world; so long as it becomes once more the America
of the great Americanism which won its freedom; so long as it is the
America of Lincoln and Franklin Roosevelt; so long as it proves its
ability to solve the problems of men and women in a free economy;
and so long as it can be seen to be the America of our dreams and, at
the same time, is strong, it will be respected."[112]

Paul Rivet also alluded to the relations between the United
States and Latin America, where this desire of America to impose its
own point of view and interests on the world has been in evidence:
"'Independence' is a word which makes a strong appeal everywhere
at the present moment," says Rivet, "and the idea it conveys is
expressed by all statesmen, from Mexico to Chile, Brazil and
Argentina, in differing language perhaps, but with unanimity of
meaning. This will to independence, to emancipation, is the common
factor of their action." However, this desire has met with the
hostility of the United States, a country proud of her material
development and of the liberal ideals which have made this possible.
"What chances of success has this urge for independence, which is
now being expressed in some countries by measures stigmatized as
revolutionary?" The pressure exerted by the United States on these
countries is enormous, up to the point of causing the failure of those
countries' domestic policies, as has happened in Guatemala and in
other countries as well. "It is possible, if not probable," says Paul
Rivet, "that the United States of America will bring pressure to bear
upon those governments which are now introducing large-scale
Socialist and national reforms, and will try to paralyze their
efforts."[113]

The trouble here, therefore, is not failure to understand the
values of American civilization, or to recognize their great
contribution to Western culture. It is rather that the values and
ideals Americans proclaim, such as freedom, national sovereignty,
and material happiness, are incompatible with the attitude they adopt

---

[112] André Maurois, "The American Mentality." In *The Old and the New
World. Their Cultural and Moral Relations*, op. cit., pp. 324-325.
[113] Paul Rivet, op. cit., pp. 43, 44.

toward countries desiring to attain these same goals, or that try to emulate their example. American democracy is not compatible with the American support of dictatorships in Latin America in order to defend the financial interests of United States' companies and trusts in those countries. Such political and economic pressures have been exerted by the United States not only in Latin America and Asia, but also in Europe. The European countries acknowledge the help America gave them during the war and the period of reconstruction, but they also know the political and economic concessions that had to be made in return for that assistance. They were reminded of that assistance whenever one of them objected to the interests the United States' Government was defending, a reminder invariably accompanied by a threat to suspend aid. Looking at it from this point of view, it is not astonishing that some Europeans prefer other influences, namely Russia's. Some Europeans even feel that the brutal German control during the last war was preferable to that of the United States today. Against the former, they say, the rebellion of those who did not accept conquest, or the submissiveness of the collaborators, was to be expected; against the Americans, neither is appropriate, because moral justification is based on a superiority which, in the last analysis, is as materialistic as was that of the Germans. In this case there are no bayonets, bullets, or concentration camps, because Europe's own bullets, and concentration camps, ensure the maintenance of an order best suited to the interests of the new master. In this case, people and countries cannot rebel against a country and people for whom they must feel gratitude. Gratitude toward people whose country helped them to break their chains when they were enslaved by Nazi-Fascist totalitarianism, gratitude toward a country that offered asylum to their best scientists and intellectuals; protected their wives and children and many of their most precious works of art; a country that helped them rebuild their cities and artistic monuments; a country that also helped to feed and clothe them when hunger and lack of clothing were the rule in Europe. It is the same country that today offers them weapons and money to defend democracy and freedom threatened by new doctrines. For that democracy and freedom both Europeans and Americans have died. How can one oppose their ideas and the business interests that accompany them? American expansion in Europe, as in the rest of the world, is accompanied by the highest moral justification, although these values are not recognized as such in other countries.

Europeans, and peoples in the same situation, are thus aware of the meaning of America's attitude toward the world. It is the attitude of a nation that, because she has the highest ideals, feels entitled to use them to strengthen her own interests, which are no longer those of countries once in agreement with that principle. It is the attitude of a nation that considers herself called upon to bring to the world ideals of freedom and democracy, but makes their dissemination dependent on the expansion of her own interests. The destiny of America seems to her to be to bring to the world, not so much the ideals of freedom and democracy as those of American freedom and democracy, created by Americans for Americans. A nation that thinks herself predestined, chosen to bring to the world "the American way of life" and not the freedom and democracy appropriate to each country.[114] Europeans, in pointing out that attitude in Americans, justify without embarrassment a similar attitude on the part of their own nations toward countries dependent upon them. Indeed, many of the Europeans who condemn American imperialism do not hesitate to justify French or British imperialism or even that of other nations.

The main European objection with respect to America is in the cultural sphere. The American way of life is not the course European culture is going to take, even though it is one of the manifestations of that culture. The American way of life cannot be that of the European nations. The Europeanization of America is a fact, but there should be no Americanization of Europe, except for an aberration. Such a development, moreover, would be neither valid nor acceptable, because the control of the Westernizing influence has shifted more toward the West, a West that is no longer in Europe. From this point of view, and confronted with the fear of complete Westernization or Americanization of Europe, several Europeans look toward Latin America as a continent capable of preserving those values that are considered truly universal or European. What Michele Federico Sciacca says when he speaks of the future of philosophy, and of European philosophy in particular is symptomatic. "Latin America," he says, "shows a truly philosophical sensibility . . . From this point of view, Latin America then is closer than North America to European culture . . ." and "it is not unlikely that the young countries of Latin America will be able to continue the best philosophical tradition of Europe . . . " What is it

---

[114] See chapter IX, "Puritanism as a Component of the American Mind."

that the United States lacks in order to be at the level of genuine culture and philosophy, at the intellectual level of European culture? Sciacca does not reject the possibility that North America attain this intellectual climate, a maturity that Latin America seems to be reaching more rapidly; he does not lose hope that one day America will abandon what we have called the heterodoxy of Western culture and will return to her true path, that course whose only guide has been, is, and will continue to be Europe. "We do not exclude," he says, "the possibility that even the United States of America may be able to perform this task . . . and, in any event, attain such a maturity as to be able to 'understand' philosophy, that is, the problem of the spirit and the meaning of the words 'truth,' 'idea,' 'being,' 'intellect,' and others. But, as things stand at the present, the latter possibility seems to us to be uncertain for two main reasons: one is that unless Europe finds itself once more, its metaphysical and cultural 'soul' . . . will end by being either 'Americanized' or by becoming entirely 'Marxist'; and the other reason is that, on account of its political and military power, the United States will inevitably believe itself to be a 'superior' people and will mistake power for 'wisdom' and its superiority in means for intellectual and cultural maturity. In such a case, its people will be inclined to consider themselves more as teachers than as pupils, so that they will wish to spread, with their characteristic, missionary ardor, their 'philosophy' or conception of life as the most advanced one. Success and riches should be accompanied by a corresponding intellectual and spiritual advancement and by a tradition that has stood for centuries, a tradition that gives a fine sense of detachment and, with it, the ability to look at them in perspective, so as to see their limits and understand the true domain of man over things; if this is not so, then they turn one's head and create the illusion of an unconditional superiority, the offspring of a naive conviction according to which everything can be bought or built with money, even a head philosophically well made and a spirit culturally well educated and mature."

But what is that genuinely European spirit which persists in Latin America? What is it that properly belongs to European or universal culture? What is understood by genuine European cultural orthodoxy? It revealed itself already in Christianity and in the so-called Western culture. It is the spirit which now seems to have been supported tenaciously by Spain, the Spain that separated from the Western world of Europe when the latter was the hub of Western culture. Because of her Spanish, Christian, and Catholic origin, Latin America seems to be called upon to continue preserving truly European culture, something that the United States cannot do. On the other hand, says Sciacca, the dangers that we see in the United States are not evident in Latin America, even if it becomes a power equal or superior to the United States, "because it would be safeguarded by the fact that such attainment would be accompanied by a philosophical and cultural maturity of its own . . . In all these considerations, it must not be forgotten that the United States was colonized by England, and Latin America by Spain, that is, a nation whose culture represents one of the essential dimensions in the authentic spirit of Europe. Moreover, this signifies something highly important, that is to say, the United States of America, which until some decades ago was not really receptive to other cultures, was molded by an ideology that was made up of elements coming from the Puritan tradition, the 1688 English revolution, and the culture of the Enlightenment,"[115] that is to say, movements which represent a denial of religious truths (Catholic and Christian) and of man's spiritual values. America is, therefore, the embodiment of modern Western values, values that originated in Europe but were exceeded in the United States. Nevertheless, Europe symbolizes something more than those values.

[115] Michele Federico Sciacca, *Philosophical Trends in the Contemporary World*. Trans. Attilio Salerno. (Notre Dame, 1964), pp. 640, 641, 642. This is the first book on the history of philosophy written by a European in which a chapter on "Philosophy in Latin America" is included.

CHAPTER VIII

LATIN AMERICA ON THE FRINGE OF THE WEST

31. An Old American Experience

What saddens Europe at present is an old American problem, namely America's past preoccupation with Europe, coupled with Latin America's constant preoccupation with the United States. It is an old problem for all nations below the Rio Bravo and extends all the way to Tierra del Fuego. The questions that Europe is asking at present about the United States are those that Latin America has raised from the very moment when independence from Spain and Portugal was achieved and her republics came into being. Once their political independence had been secured, these nations found that they were caught in the net of yet another dependence imposed on them at first by Western Europe, England and France in particular, and somewhat later by the United States. Several of the most distinguished Latin American statesmen soon became aware of their dangerous neighbor to the north. They soon realized that they had to defend themselves not only against the aggression of Western Europe but also against aggression from that part of North America which had been shaped by Western Europe.

The United States was not a nation close to the rest of the American Republics, to which they could appeal when faced with foreign aggression. The Monroe Doctrine, established by the United States, was in no way intended to defend the interests of the American continent as a whole, but rather to safeguard those of an expanding United States. Shortly before Latin America began her emancipation movements, Spain was already aware of her dangerous neighbor who was going to act as an agent of the West that had displaced the Iberian nation from the modern world. An apocryphal brief attributed to the Count of Aranda stated, with reference to the recently emancipated United States, "We can say this republic was born dwarfish and in order to achieve independence has needed the help of two powerful nations, Spain and France. But the day will come when that nation will be a giant, a real colossus to be feared in that part of the world and then she will forget the favors she has received while thinking only of her own interests and progress." Once the Latin American countries' struggle for independence had begun and the famous Monroe Doctrine had been proclaimed, supposedly for the defense of America by Americans, the intelligent and astute Chilean dictator Diego Portales commented on that Doctrine in a letter to his friend José M. Cea in 1822: "My dear Cea, the newspapers report favorably on the progress of revolution in the Americas. It seems almost confirmed that the United States recognizes the independence of Latin America. Although I have not discussed it with anyone, I shall tell you what I think about the matter. Mr. Monroe, the President of the North American Federation has stated: 'It is a recognized fact that America is for Americans.' Let us be careful not to escape one domination only to fall under another! We must distrust those people who wholeheartedly approve the struggle of our freedom fighters without having helped us at all. This is precisely the reason for my fear. Why the haste with which the United States accredits ministers and delegates, and recognizes Latin American independence without having done anything to further it? This is indeed a strange way of doing things, my friend! I believe that all this is in accordance with a preconceived plan to conquer the Americas not by means of military intervention, but by exerting influence in all spheres. It may not happen now but it will surely happen in the not too distant future. Let us not be enticed by sweets as children are, without thinking that they might be poisoned."[116]

---

[116] Feliú Cruz, *Epistolario de Don Diego Portales* (Santiago, 1937).

Simón Bolívar, the great liberator, knew from experience that he could not expect any help from Western Europe or the United States in his struggle for the independence of the Latin American countries unless it were geared to the West and her interests rather that those he sought. "How vain has been that hope!" he wrote in his famous Jamaica letter. "Not only the Europeans, but even our brothers of the North have been apathetic bystanders in this struggle which, by its very essence, is the most just, and its consequences the most noble and vital of any which have been raised in ancient or in modern times. Indeed, can the far-reaching effects of freedom for the hemisphere which Columbus discovered ever be calculated?"[117] How and why do England and the United States help or how can they help Spanish America? Only in the way which best suits and advances their own interests. England, according to Bolívar, "fears revolution in Europe but welcomes it in America, as the one brings her endless cares, while the other gives her inexhaustible resources." With respect to the United States he wrote: "North America in accordance with her business-like conduct of affairs, will avail herself of the opportunity to take the Floridas, to gain our friendship, and to secure a wider field for her commerce."[118] For this very reason Bolívar was afraid to strain relations with either country. He feared England, the leader of Western Europe, and the United States, which already saw themselves as the managers of the West's expansion. Therefore, in a letter to Bernardo de Monteagudo in which Bolívar mentioned the reasons why he felt that neither England nor the United States should be invited to the meeting that he wanted to take place in Panama in order to bring together all the Spanish-speaking countries, the Liberator stated: "After England places herself at the head of such a league, we shall be her humble servants; for, in making a pact with the strong, the weak assume an eternal obligation. All things considered we shall have guardians during our youth, masters during our maturity, and freedom in our old age."[119] With respect to the United States, he wrote to General Santander: "I then find that a very rich and powerful nation, extremely warlike and capable of anything is at the head of this

[117] "Reply of a South American to a gentleman of this island, Kingston, Jamaica, September 6, 1815." In *Selected Writings of Bolívar*. Ed. Harold A. Bierck and trans. Lewis Bertrand (New York, 1951), Vol. I, p. 108.
[118] "To Guillermo White, Merchant of Trinidad, San Cristobal, May 1, 1820." In ibid., Vol. I, p. 224.
[119] "To Bernardo Monteagudo, Guayaquil, August 5, 1823." In ibid., Vol. II, pp. 388-389.

continent. This nation is unfriendly to Europe, and it is also opposed to the powerful English, who desire to lay down the law to us and who, moreover, ultimately will."[120] Latin America could not hope for anything from such dangerous allies who would help her only in order to force her into a new subjection. The Latin American nations must determine their own freedom and future. No nation would help them. The nations that offered their help did so only out of self-interest. "The United States," according to Bolívar, "is both the worst and the most powerful."[121] The United States, which loved its own freedom so much, did not feel the same about the freedom of other countries. On the contrary, it had used this very freedom as a tool to bring unhappiness to other countries. "The United States," wrote Bolívar, "seem destined by Providence to plague America with torments in the name of freedom."[122] A freedom desired by Spanish America but haggled over by the countries that most loudly championed it.

The fears of the Liberator and of other Latin American statesmen were soon to be confirmed. Latin America was to be the victim of several aggressive acts by Western Europe and the United States. The Monroe Doctrine would become an instrument to defend the interests of the United States alone, which was why it did not work in the case of aggression of Western Europe in Latin America where those interests were not affected. It was merely a notice delivered by the United States that Europe was not to attack United States' interests. Provided these were respected, Europe and the United States, or the West, could spread their influence to Latin America. Therefore, in spite of the Monroe Doctrine and with the knowledge of the United States, Europe could attack Latin America with impunity in order to enlarge and defend its own interests. Mexico was attacked by Spain in 1829, in an attempt to regain her colony; the British occupied the Falkland Islands in 1833 with the help of the United States. In 1835 England took over Belize despite Guatemala's request for help from the United States by invoking the Monroe Doctrine. In 1838 and 1849, England and France landed

---

[120] "To General Francisco de Paula Santander, Ibarra, December 23, 1822." In ibid., Vol. I, p. 307.
[121] "To Estanislao Vergara, Guayaquil, September 20, 1829." In Simón Bolívar, *Obras completas* (Havana, 1947).
[122] "To Col. Patrick Campbell, British chargé d'affaires, Bogotá, Guayaquil, August 5, 1829." In *Selected Writings of Bolívar*, op. cit., Vol. II, p. 732.

troops to commit hostilities against dictator Rosas in the River Plate. In 1847 the English landed in Nicaragua and, with the consent of the United States, established the Protectorate of La Mosquitia. In 1848 the English, again helped by the United States, extended the boundaries of La Guyana, at the expense of Venezuela. In 1852 England created in the Caribbean Bay of Amatique a new colony: The Honduras Islands of the Bay. In 1862 Spain regained control of Santo Domingo. That same year, France invaded Mexico to establish an empire there. In 1864 a Spanish squadron took over the Peruvian Islands of Chinchas and bombed the port cities of Callao and Valparaiso. In all those cases the Monroe Doctrine was conspicuous by its absence. During the same period the United States was involved in armed intervention in Latin America. In Mexico beginning in 1831 and that same year also in the Falkland Islands. In Texas and northern Mexico from 1831 to 1847, when Mexico had her largest territorial losses. In Valparaiso in 1891, Puerto Rico in 1898, Cuba in 1902 and 1933; in Panama beginning in 1903, La Guyana in 1908; Nicaragua in 1855, 1909, 1912 and 1924, Haiti and Veracruz in 1914, Santo Domingo in 1916, Honduras in 1860 and 1924, Guatemala in 1953 and at other times in a more or less scandalous manner. The West, in its European and American expression, attacked and subjected those American countries which happened to be on the fringe of the Western world.[123]

This is why the problem faced by Western Europe after having lost her position as leader of the West, was actually an old one for Latin America. The Latin American nations have suffered many types of aggression from the Western world, in particular the aggression of a Westernized Anglo-Saxon America, which has mutilated them and imposed its interests on them. Consequently, the history of those countries is now of interest to Western Europe because she finds herself in a similar situation. It is the history and experience of a group of nations which, like Spain and Russia, have their roots in European culture but have been displaced from that culture by one of its representatives. It is the experience of the achievements of a group of nations defending themselves against all odds in order to survive, despite the many pressures to which the West in its European and American forms has subjected them.

---

[123] See Juan José Arévalo, *The Shark and the Sardines* (New York, 1961), pp. 73-74, 106-107.

32. America as the Champion of the West

As we have seen in another part of this study, all America had been placed on the fringe of Western culture by Europe; on the fringe of what was considered to be essential history. The possibility of making America a part of the West was only accepted when efforts in this direction were made by Western people. The Westernizing of America could only be successful if Western people were intent on pursuing it as they were in other parts of the world. Only the total colonization of America in a political, economic, social, and cultural sense would make the process of Westernization possible. This was also De Pauw's point of view. The wise Prussian said in the eighteenth century that America would become integrated with European progress through the work and influence of the settlers, but he felt that it would take three hundred years. Hegel said something similar with respect to the American continent.

However, in spite of such predictions Anglo-Saxon America, or the United States, would gradually come to be accepted thanks to its ability to act in the world that Western Europe had reserved for its own sphere of action. America, after all, was the achievement of European settlers, the solid achievement of European colonization. America was the most genuine achievement of Europe's ability to Westernize the world. In America the most cherished Western ideals were perpetuated and realized. The modern world, better known as the West, achieved here its highest development free of the bonds that had fettered it in the Old World. The war against a non-Western past of Europe was unnecessary in America. America was not only the country of the future but also a land that had no past. In this country the European could forget old ties and begin a common history that would mark the beginning of the cherished road toward progress. In America, man could build in a virgin world and uncompromisingly put into action Utopian dreams and the visions of idealistic philosophers who had been the creators of the West. Soon Anglo-Saxon America would become the promised land for Europe and at the same time, the country where all the dreams of the new Europe could be realized. Within a few years the United States would translate that promise into reality and thus fulfill the dreams of the West. That is the achievement which the United States symbolizes at present as a nation and leader of the West whose greatest creation it was. Historians and philosophers of history, therefore, no longer dispute America's place in the Western world. America is for them a Western nation. Toynbee and other philosophers of history place Russia and Latin America among the non-Western nations and call the people of the United States "American Westerners."

Consequently America, as the present leader and champion of the West, is pitted against the America of Iberian or Latin origin, that America which, like Russia and Spain, has striven to become an integral part of Western history and culture. Latin America, like Anglo-Saxon America, is the result of European expansion in America, but she has been placed on the fringe of history and rejected like her European colonizers.

Latin America began by being rejected, as had also Spain and Portugal because of their culture, shaped by a religious past which was rejected by the leading nations of the West. Latin America, like Spain and Portugal, was to be looked upon as a stronghold of the forces that opposed world progress, as a stronghold of "blind Papists." The Spanish and Portuguese colonies in America were strongholds of obscurantism at a time when reason and enlightenment prevailed. In addition, unlike those in North America, these colonizers had amalgamated their obscurantism with the primitive and superstitious spirit of the natives.[124] They were not only against the march of progress but, in addition, had insisted on lowering themselves as members of a great culture by mixing with inferior races, with people whose human qualities had not been established as yet. Europeans bore the responsibility for creating a type of person who was inferior to the native: the half-breed. Therefore, the Prussian De Pauw, the Frenchman Buffon and a large number of Anglo-Saxon naturalists referred repeatedly to the inferior quality of the people responsible for creating the Latin American nations, people who stubbornly held fast to a culture that already represented

---

[124] Sarmiento and others based Latin America's backwardness on that heritage and amalgam in comparing her with the United States. If we accept that the use of intelligence enlarges the brain, then, he said: "we must believe that the Spaniard has not grown since the XVIth century, before the Inquisition began to function," and with regard to the Latin American we must fear, he added, that "in general it is smaller than that of the Spaniard because of the mixture with races that, as we know, have a smaller brain than that of Europeans." *Conflicto y armonía de las razas en América* (Buenos Aires, 1916).

modern Europe's past and who, in addition, had lowered themselves by mixing with the indigenous element.

None of this had taken place in North America, which was colonized by people faithful to the religious and political ideals of their race and the modern world. These people, instead of mixing with the natives, had avoided any contamination and had introduced civilization into areas where only barbarism had existed before. Therefore, Puritanism, as an expression of religious tolerance and racial and cultural intolerance, would be looked upon as a symbol of progress by comparison with the Iberian colonizer's Catholicism with its expression of religious intolerance but cultural and racial tolerance. America's Western frontier would be determined by the United States' ability to expand on the American continent. The United States, in its struggle against obscurantism and primitivism would be the champion of the West in America. Thus, Latin America remained outside the so-called West, that is to say, outside of history. The "American Westerner" would keep her at bay, subject only to the limits of his expansion, which would at times be in conflict and at other times be with the collaboration of Western Europe. The United States treated the Latin Americans in America exactly as Western Europe had treated the Russians and Iberians in the Old World.

Latin America, as Spain, Portugal, and Russia had done before her in Europe, would try to join the world that rejected her. She made repeated attempts to join the West in order to become one of the nations respected by history, and to participate in an endeavor that she also regarded as her own. It may be said, therefore, that the history of the Latin American people centers on their effort to become Westernized, by adopting Western ideals, philosophy, and technology on the one hand and on the other, by renouncing their Iberian past. In organizing their governments the recently emancipated Latin American nations would model themselves on France, England, and America.

The history of the nineteenth century reveals how those nations strove to free themselves from their Iberian heritage, both politically and culturally. They made a great effort to get rid of habits and customs felt to be in opposition to the new spirit of the West which had made world progress possible. The culture of England and France, and the political institutions of the United

States, were the models for Latin American nations trying to reorganize themselves in order to become an integral part of progress represented by the West. This was the golden dream of Latin America's great intellectual leaders, such as Sarmiento, Mora, Luz y Caballero, Lastarria, and many others throughout the continent.[125] These men were not satisfied merely to adopt Western technology but, in addition, tried to adapt to the philosophy which had made that technology possible. They dreamed of the possibility of establishing the same kind of philosophy that had made progress possible in countries they took as a model. This preoccupation was to show up in the great and bloody struggles that rent Latin America during the first half of the nineteenth century, civil wars springing from the great dilemma those countries faced: either to remain faithful to their origins or to undergo a change. It was a war between those who were trying to maintain the old order inherited from Spain and those who wanted to adhere to the new order modeled on Western Europe and America. It was a struggle between liberals and conservatives, federalists and centralists, civilization and barbarism (as the Argentine Sarmiento called it). Some hoped to introduce into Latin America the freedoms and rights associated with American democracy, the British parliamentary system, and the revolutionary French spirit; whereas others sought to maintain the old colonial order supported by the clergy and the military establishment. "Republicanism or Catholicism," is the American dilemma, said the Chilean Bilbao; "democracy or absolutism," said Sarmiento; "progress or reaction," clamored the Mexican Mora.[126]

In the second half of the nineteenth century, when the liberal parties were winning in Spanish and Portuguese America, there began what could be called the Westernization of Latin America, which started with the adoption of educational and political systems patterned after those of the West. In general, Positivism was adopted as a philosophy and a political order was established that claimed to be democratic by imitating the constitutions of the United States and France, and the English parliamentary system. But something else was also adopted: namely the discriminatory spirit which characterized the Westerner. This led to rejection not only of the Iberian past, but also of the native and natives in general, thus following in the footsteps of Anglo-Saxon America. And if the

---

[125] Refer to my book *The Latin American Mind*.
[126] Ibid.

natives were not repudiated openly, at least it was felt that they were incapable of self-government. This apparent inability made it possible for the leaders of the new social order, *criollos* or half-breeds for the most part, to adopt strange liberal dictatorships and establish order for progress or liberal absolutism. In countries like Argentina, they followed in the footsteps of the American pioneers, and in the name of civilization and against barbarism liquidated all natives from the pampa. In countries where the native population was more numerous, such as Mexico, Peru, Ecuador, Colombia, and several others, dictatorships were established on the principle that "the people were not yet ready for self government. "

33. The West's Reply to Latin America

What was the West's reply to Latin America's eagerness for Westernization? The answer was in no way different from the one the West had given in the case of similar efforts in Europe and other parts of the world: a categorical rejection. We have already mentioned the reasons given by the European and American West for confining the Latin American nations to the sphere assigned to nations regarded as outside of history, civilization, or culture. Latin America's efforts to break with a past that confined her to a world opposed to progress were not recognized; neither were her attempts to acquire Western habits and customs, thereby rejecting her inheritance. Latin America continued to be a sub-continent of barbarism, which could only be redeemed by subjection to the West. In the name of civilization, therefore, the French and British bombarded her harbors, invaded South America and even formed alliances with the forces that opposed Westernization in Latin America. In the name of that same civilization and progress, the United States extended her frontiers, annexing Mexican territory in 1847. In 1863 France, also in the name of civilization, supported conservative Mexican forces in their struggle against the liberals by trying to impose an empire which would have meant the negation of the very progress of which the invaders were the champions. Also in the name of civilization, freedom, and democracy, America, the model for all Latin American countries, supported petty tyrants and dictators who opposed and denied these principles, and did this in order to strengthen by these means the West's real interests in America's expansion.

Much has been said about the lack of understanding that exists between Anglo-Saxon America and Latin America. It is the same lack of understanding that we find existing between the West and the rest of the world. American journalists have often discussed the inability of the Latin American to understand the lofty goals and values embodied in American civilization, which had engendered the highest manifestations of democracy, freedom, and material comfort. Latin Americans have been unable to understand that the importance of these contributions to culture would be held to justify American intervention for the purpose of imposing these same values, if necessary. From that standpoint, many of America's interventions in Latin America were in a sense justified because they were meant to safeguard freedom and democracy when these were threatened. Likewise because freedom and democracy were threatened, dictatorships were imposed that supposedly had as their goal to defend freedom and democracy at least symbolically, but actually these cannot exist under any form of dictatorship, whatever its justification.

The American, Filmer S. Northrop, a philosopher of history, undertook in good faith the task of finding the elements that would allow what he calls the interpenetration of the two Americas, or their mutual understanding. Such an undertaking, in turn, would form the basis for a better understanding between the West and the rest of the world, or what he refers to as the East and the West. According to him, this understanding could be achieved if the Americas were to assimilate their different yet complementary values. Western values could be assimilated by the East and vice versa. A philosophy and a culture "related by the two termed relation of epistemic correlation" would, " remove the traditional opposition between the Orient and the Occident, Soviet Russia and the traditional democracies, the Latin and the Anglo-Saxon cultures. Any culture and society gains greatly and enriches itself when different cultural values that are made to blend harmoniously supplement and reinforce it. Thus, for example, the West can become enormously enriched by taking from the religious and cultural values of the Orient which are rooted in the aesthetic component . . . By the same token the East could benefit immeasurably by acquiring Western science and its more theoretically grounded determinate economic values of a culture that is predominantly scientific."[127] Epistemic correlation of the two worlds could thus be achieved without implying a threat to the dignity or the subjection of either. These ideas stated in good faith were naive, as we shall see later.

There really is no reason why America and the West she represents could not adopt a number of Latin American and Eastern values, as Northrop pointed out in his book significantly entitled: *The Meeting of East and West*. America's intellectual tolerance is indeed a positive factor in the proposed esthetic and religious assimilation: that quality is no longer to be found in Latin America whose philosophy in general is characterized by religious intolerance. It would be difficult to achieve in Latin America the religious freedom that has made the adoption of many faiths and churches possible in the United States. On the other hand, there is one aspect of mutual assimilation that would be accepted easily by Latin America because it is something she has always wanted to achieve, namely, the adoption of the Western values as indicated by Northrop: science, technology, and other theoretical values, that is to say the values that gave the West her material power over the rest of the world. Nevertheless, the adoption of those values has encountered the greatest internal and external difficulties in Latin America, especially the latter. And here Latin America has stumbled upon something more serious than the intolerance coming from within, and that is the intolerance emanating from the West, the very world responsible for creating those values.

Something has been happening here that seems paradoxical because the tolerance shown by the West, and America in particular, in the area of religion, esthetics, etc., becomes an attitude of intolerance in the material realm. America tolerates the appearance of many creeds and respects them, but she cannot tolerate in similar fashion the appearance of material forces that might challenge her world preeminence in that sphere. And what has been said particularly with respect to America could also be applied to the West in general. Generally speaking, America and the West find it difficult to tolerate any competition other than a purely religious one. The West has never been nor is it ready to tolerate the technical, industrial, and commercial competition of other nations, arising as a

---

[127] Filmer S.C. Northrop, *The Meeting of East and West* (New York, 1946), pp. 454, 466, 436, 460, 455.

natural consequence of adopting the Western values of which Northrop spoke. And if there is something that distinguishes Western imperialism from other forms of imperialism, it is the way in which it subjects other nations through its economic policies. The West has never been concerned with subjecting other nations either culturally or intellectually. Economic subjection is all she wants and for that reason there does not have to be military subjection. Once economic subjection has been achieved, the nations concerned are / free to continue thinking along the same lines as their forebears, or as they like. In spite of the West, those nations have developed their own cultural expression in order to claim in its name the rights previously denied. The economic predominance of the West is the basis of its world power. This is an area, therefore, in which she will never voluntarily accept any competition that she can avoid from the very beginning. In this area the tolerant world of the West is transformed into a highly intolerant one. This has been and continues to be the basis for her expansion in the world. As has been shown by the great Western powers England and France, the West is able to respect the culture, religion, habits, and customs of the countries that form her colonies and can even tolerate their relative political independence. The United States likewise tolerates any kind of government in its economic colonies. But what none of these powers can tolerate is the economic emancipation of their colonies, the economic emancipation of the world, although within this world there happens to be Western Europe. This is quite natural and could not be otherwise; it has to be understood because this emancipation would signal the end of the world domination of the West.

With respect to Latin America's relations with the United States, it does not seem that the former shows any lack of understanding for values which she has tried to assimilate from the very beginning of her political independence. As has been pointed out already, Latin America has always tried to achieve those values and to make them flourish in her own nations. Latin America not only has understood the importance of these modern values, but has insisted on achieving them, thereby denying the importance of her own cultural values. Latin America has struggled, therefore, to establish political institutions that were liberal and democratic in character and similar to those of the United States. She has also striven to adopt a technology that would enable her to achieve economic independence and thereby material comforts for her citizens. Like the United States she has fought in the international arena for the recognition of her nations' sovereignty and their right to self-determination. Latin America has tried to belong to the Western block of nations, but as an equal and not as a second-class partner, with equal rights and privileges that must prevail among nations that are equal partners. Latin America has tried to participate in the history of the West and has been saddened by her failure.

All her efforts have been met with failure because instead of receiving help to achieve her goals, obstacles have been placed in her way. The West, as symbolized by the United States, has tried to maintain forms of government in Latin America that are contrary to the liberal and democratic institutions which the West encouraged in its own lands. It has been the Western endeavor to make of Latin America simply a provider of raw materials without any technical ability for their conversion, and into a market for the goods processed from them by means of Western technology. The tremendous tolerance which the West maintains within her orbit for any kind of government would turn into intolerance if a government were to appear whose sole desire was to transform the nation into a Western country with freedom, rights, and the appropriate material comforts. It would be an absolute intolerance directed against the establishment of liberal democratic institutions, not because the West opposes freedom and democracy, but rather because of the economic consequences that their establishment would have on her own financial interests, because the establishment of freedom and democracy as a form of government in such countries would of necessity lead to the demand that their rights be recognized by other nations on the international level. This is why they continue to be considered as fringe nations, as simple purveyors of raw materials or forced consumers of the manufactured goods produced from them. Internal self-determination by the Iberian people also implies external self-determination. This conflict is the cause of a lack of understanding in the relationship between the two Americas and is responsible for a contradiction in certain Western values which up to now, that is to say when the political and economic values were the exclusive property of the West, were in harmony. Thus liberal democracy, which found itself in opposition to the way in which the economic expansion of the West was being carried out, when adopted by non-Western countries denied them the right to that expansion.

One limiting the other and vice versa: economic expansion denying freedom and democracy to the countries concerned.

34. Western Ideals in Crisis

We have stated once before that on the world stage the West sees herself as the champion of the great ideals which she sponsored. Of the Western countries, the United States has proclaimed this the most often. The ideals of liberty and democracy for individuals and nations have only recently come into conflict with the material interests of their advocates. Hitherto, these ideals have not conflicted with the economic policies of Western expansion, because they did not exist in non-Western countries. Up to now these countries have been looked upon as second, third or fourth-class nations: they were relegated to whatever class was necessary to disqualify them from claiming rights in the name of those ideals. But these same ideals of freedom and democracy justified their extension to a world which knew nothing about them, a world whose ideals could only be fulfilled by Westerners in whatever part of the world they chose to stay. It was an ideal conception that justified material expansion. After all, this expansion was merely going to be a means of fulfilling the ideals for which it stood, an achievement that still seemed to lie very much in the future. Unfortunately, it was going to be a rather distant future before all countries could enjoy the privileges of the West. This is what the interpretation of history as a constant pursuit of progress meant. It meant the complete Westernization of the world, even if that implied the liquidation of non-Western natives in countries all over the world, which would then be places similar to those created exclusively by the Westerner in the United States, Canada, Australia, New Zealand, and many other regions. Unfortunately for the West, this kind of Westernization could not be established in places where the native element continued to be a majority difficult to eliminate.

It is in these places, therefore, that Westernization is being carried out, but as adopted by the natives themselves. That is the situation in Latin America, which in many ways has become Westernized by adopting the technology and the political system of the West. It was the West's resistance to acceptance of the Westernization of the world which caused the crisis in Western ideals. The contradiction arose because Latin Americans, Africans, Asians, and others wanted to make those ideals their own. It is the resistance of the West which has placed her values in jeopardy, or at least her claim to be their champion, a claim inconsistent with her policy toward other countries. As we have pointed out already, one thing is the policy she follows within her borders and what she does in other countries quite another. At home she holds on to the liberal democratic institutions and their ideals; outside her borders these same ideals are opposed in order to assert the validity of her economic interests over the world. Consequently, the Latin American countries, in their relations with Western nations like the United States demand the treatment that the West expects from other nations. National sovereignty and self-determination derive from the West's liberal and democratic ideals. Therefore, the Western nations are now faced with an unpleasant choice between the perpetuation of their economic domination, the abandonment of the ideals they championed, or the permanent establishment of those values coupled with an abandonment of their economic monopoly. It is a difficult choice between ideal and material values, since the ones cannot be maintained without denying the others.

In view of this contradiction, also in evidence in non-Western countries, Latin America has become strongly aware of its own identity hitherto denied and unassimilated. For this very reason a new attitude, of which this study is an expression, has developed in Latin America that involves taking stock of herself. The useless endeavor to completely Westernize Latin America is being abandoned and in its place the non-Western cultural origins which are a component of her cultural amalgam are accepted as positive elements. Latin America realizes that history is made by people and nations. She also knows that in this history she plays a part, and that it is unimportant whether she has a leading role or not. She also knows that her cultural rather than her ethnological amalgam can be taken as a point of departure and that this would perhaps give her a special place within the context of history. Many Western philosophers have already predicted this development. They see Latin America as a bridge between conquering and conquered nations, between East and West, and finally between the West and the rest of the world.

Therefore, within the context of history, Latin America's history of cultural and racial amalgam might be very important.[128]

The Latin American nations' new awareness raises questions about their place and their prospects in history, a history whose making is no longer the task of the privileged nations but of all countries. Latin America is thus abandoning an absurd insistence on appearing other than she really is. Her differences with respect to the West are no longer such that she has to feel inferior, but simply different, individualistic and, up to a point, unique in a world where nations like people are individuals. Differences are no longer seen as a sign of inferiority. Thanks to these differences Latin America has become aware of herself and whether she wants to or not she is making history, thus playing a role in world history. With respect to her old pretensions or her desire to become a part of the West, the kind of history she has made, is making and will make will be Western, but without losing its non-Western characteristics. We have already mentioned that in Latin America's history there is a twofold experience: that of conquering nations and of subjugated peoples. That is a twofold experience generally unknown to present-day nations which have known only how to dominate or be dominated.

This experience, if it is to be successful, must lead Latin America to properly assimilate the values of the diverse world for which she acts as a bridge. The experience of trying to Westernize on the one hand, and on the other of the insistence with which she has been denied access to Westernization has been heartbreaking for Latin America. The attempt was doubly contradictory because it involved and still involves many of the so-called liberal and conservative forces of Latin America, In one way, they were trying to create nations similar to a given Western country such as the United States and in another to remain static as if history were not a perennial forward march. These mixed objectives only led to liberal and conservative dictatorships but not to nations capable of choosing the direction in which they wanted to move. Some leaders wanted a future that had nothing in common with the past and others were hanging on to the past as if there were no future to consider. There

---

[128] At present this is the point of view taken by several Latin American philosophers among whom we may count José Vasconcelos, who believes that in this amalgam lies Latin America's future as the melting pot for a new race which he calls the cosmic race.

was intolerance on both sides and this played into the hands of nations not troubled by these contradictory preoccupations. Spiritual and ideological intolerance runs counter to the tolerance that has made the modern world possible, and is also at variance with that other tolerance represented by Christianity and rejected by the West.

Is there something in the Latin American world that might be considered a contribution to the world now being created, a world that can no longer be divided into East and West in the simple way to which we have become accustomed? Perhaps this something will appear if we analyze carefully what we have called the Latin American nations' characteristics. It is an individuality which will become more apparent if we analyze it in juxtaposition with the other America on the reverse side of the mirror in which the Latin American countries have always seen themselves as a reflection: a mirror which made them see only their defects and incompetence. Perhaps this same mirror will now reflect their qualities and abilities. As a point of departure in this confrontation we shall look for the ideals from which both Americas sprang, and which manifested themselves particularly in their religions. We must remember that the modern world was born out of religious conflict: the conflict between Christianity, to which the Iberian world wanted to remain faithful, and Modernity, whose champion was Western Europe with her ideals of religious freedom. It was a conflict between Latin American Catholicism and Anglo-Saxon Puritanism. We shall analyze the latter as a religious expression of the West in America, in order to discuss Catholicism as the religious expression of the Latin American countries, that appear to be a kind of permanent contradiction to the United States.

CHAPTER IX

PURITANISM AS A COMPONENT OF THE AMERICAN MIND

35. The Encounter with America

The new European, tired of a world into which he had been born and in the building of which he had no direct share, would endeavor to find lands where he could begin a new history, one no longer passed on to him by his forebears and in which he already occupied a rigidly assigned place. That new land, that new world where he could begin as if nothing had existed before his arrival, was America. The new continent fulfilled the aspirations of the new man because he saw in it a world that was devoid of social, economic, political, religious, or any other kind of obligation. It was a world that could be built from its very foundations, and on a basis of reason.[129] It could be a planned and uniform world with "well and wealthily ordered" laws, in accordance with a rational order.[130] It was a world where equality based on reason was

---

[129] See René Descartes, op. cit.
[130] See Sir Thomas More, *Utopia* (New York, 1928), p. 78.

common to all people and this would be manifest also in their human relations. It was an equality that foreshadowed another kind of inequality, namely one that would be based on the individual's ability. In short, a world offering opportunities to all people to fulfill their natural destiny and limited only by their ability to fulfill that promise. To what extent a man fulfilled that promise would be seen in his capacity or incapacity for creative action. In that world, privilege based on traditions and customs would no longer count: every man would be responsible for his own well-being and would create his own privileges.

Nevertheless, America was not exempt from obligations and relations as the European had imagined, because he found that other people were living there, people who had obligations and relationships, their own history, the kind of history made by all people and all countries. They were peoples with a different cultural heritage, some extremely advanced, as were the Aztecs in Mexico and the Incas in Peru; or the peoples who were still in a beginning or primitive stage, such as the natives who lived on the plains and in the virgin forests of North America. But all of them were people with a conception of the world and of life that was different from that of the European. These were people who had also had a past, a tradition which in some cases was advanced and in others rudimentary. We might say that their history and traditions were in direct opposition to those represented by their discoverers, conquistadores and colonizers. What course of action should the latter take toward them? Liquidate them by imposing their own interests? The task would not be an easy one, at least not from the moral point of view. The Europeans were Christians, people who in spite of their struggles spoke with respect of their fellow-men. But were these natives fellow-men? One might even ask whether they could be considered men at all? Confronting the Europeans there were other people, at least that is what they seemed to be in appearance. But were they really people? Were they people in spite of their different physical appearance as shown by the color of their skin, eyes, and hair? Were they people in spite of their different customs? And if they were to be considered as such, then how could one explain those differences? And how could the physical and cultural differences be explained without diminishing those of their discoverers and conquerors?

Not all Europeans, however, came to America in order to get rid of their traditions. Some came to extend them as a prolongation of their world, the Christian world. That was one of the main preoccupations of the Iberian conquistadores. The conquistadores, although they were looking for a way to change their social station in lands where class distinctions did not exist, did not renounce the culture whose standard-bearers they were. They aspired only to be the first, equals among equals, an equality that was no longer possible in the Iberian peninsula. For the European who did not want to cast off his Christian tradition, the Catholic represented by those groups who conquered and colonized a part of America in the name of the Catholic Kings of Spain and Portugal, the problem with respect to the natives was how they could best be assimilated within the social and cultural framework of Christian society. How could these people be converted to Christianity and at the same time become tools serving the greatness of their new master? The missionaries were concerned with the former problem and the conquistadores and their descendents with the latter. A new aristocracy, Christian as in Spain, was going to develop in America, an aristocracy that would justify its domination on the ground of racial and cultural differences.

The problem revolved around the kind of people the natives were since they stubbornly resisted integration into a Christian society. What they were like was to be adduced from their strange religion, their moral code and customs so different from those of Christianity.[131] It was this difference that made them appear less than human. Aristotle would have called them barbarians and Sepúlveda called them beasts.[132] They were beasts according to the idea man had of Christianity and barbarians according to the concept the Hellenic world had of man. Men who did not belong to Christian culture, which made a human being of man, were considered beasts in the same way that Aristotle considered barbarians those men who could not speak Greek properly because they were not a part of Greek culture.[133] It was the same kind of bestiality into which any

---

[131] See Edmundo O'Gorman, "Sobre la naturaleza bestial del indio americano." *Filosofía y Letras*. Revista de la Facultad de Filosofía y Letras de la Universidad Nacional Autónoma de México. (Nos. 1-2, 1941).

[132] Juan Ginés de Sepúlveda, *Tratado sobre las justas causas de la guerra contra los indios* (Mexico City, 1949).

[133] José Gallegos Rocafull, *El pensamiento mexicano de los siglos XVI y XVII* (Mexico City, 1951).

Christian would sink if he withdrew from the Church after having violated the social laws and the ethics of Christianity. That bestiality which originated in the sin of violating the Christian order also originated in the abandonment of God by personal choice at the prompting of the Devil. The latter was precisely the case of the American natives. Their bestiality had its origin in the wiles of the Evil One. They were men but they lived as if they were beasts because they had been seduced by the Devil.[134] In this way cultural diversity was explained without considering the physical reality. It was a cultural diversity explained by origin. It was felt that Christian culture was good and the only one to be followed, whereas the other, because it opposed the Christian order, must have its origin in the Devil.[135] God, for reasons known only to Himself, had kept a whole continent outside of his sphere of influence and excluded it from tradition and the Christian order. Its discovery meant that the moment had come to have these people become a part of Christendom, and this was the mission of Spain and Portugal in America. Particularly the missionaries of the various Catholic orders devoted themselves to this task of evangelizing Latin America and many went beyond the Latin American boundaries, for it was the same mission that the French undertook in Canada. Their main concern was to convert the native and assimilate his culture to Christianity. In this endeavor the missionaries knew how to find not only differences which they attributed to a diabolical origin but also similarities that were of divine origin.[136] The natives were people who had the same origin as Christians and were created by God, but had forgotten their Creator through the stratagems of the Devil. Nevertheless, in many of their habits and customs there was evidence that they remembered their true or Christian origin even though it might have been quite lost sight of. The missionaries therefore tried to translate those habits and customs into Christian terms and in this way the native became a part of the Christian world from which he had been diverted. Those aspects of the past and native tradition that did not clash openly with the point of view of the Christian colonizers were thus incorporated into Christian society. On the strong foundation of indigenous culture the missionaries superimposed Catholic culture as represented by Spain and Portugal.

---

[134] See O'Gorman, op. cit.
[135] See Luis Villoro, *Los grandes momentos del indigenismo en México* (Mexico City, 1950).
[136] See Bernardo de Sahagún, *Historia general de las cosas de Nueva España* (Mexico City, 1938).

The Conquistadores were to do something similar when they built their new cities over those built by the natives, placing their churches on top of Indian temples and making use of Indian monasteries, as can still be seen today in Mexico City and the city of Cuzco in Peru.

Here again, the European thought that in America he could divest himself of traditions he no longer accepted and thus make his own history. He was, as we have seen, a man no longer willing to accept the tradition and history of his forebears, and therefore even less interested in accepting the traditions, habits, and customs of the natives with which he had nothing in common. Traditions and customs he did not even have to accept on a provisional basis.[137] However, in order to be consistent with respect to what he considered human, he began by accepting the natives as human beings. They were after all men like himself, endowed with reason like everyone else. But they were people whose rudimentary culture showed that they had not known how to make use of that equalizing gift which is the source of progress.

The Western European found that the natural life was good and free from obligations, but only as a point of departure and not as permanent program for life. The return to nature, to the origins, as advocated by the European, was good as a way to get rid of obligations one no longer had any desire to honor, but would be bad if the situation became permanent. The native whom the European held up to Europe as an example of cultural simplicity by comparison with the complexity of that continent's culture would be a bad model for the new man, the modern European whose spirit was animated by constant action and the desire to dominate.

The native was a human being, a fellow-man by origin, similar in his beginnings, but who ceased to be a fellow creature when the Western European aspired to goals transcending the natural and simple life of the native. The native's only preoccupation was simply to live with nature and use it for his own ends. For the European this was not sufficient, because he also wanted to harness nature. The native identified with nature and the European incorporated it into his own life-style. The European saw that the native identified with nature because he was a man unspoiled by

---

[137] See René Descartes, op. cit.

civilization. But the European did not identify with it because he had the ability to be independent of it. Not only was he unmindful of nature but he turned against it and harnessed it to serve the needs of his culture. Therefore the native, inseparable as he was from nature, finally lost his human quality by becoming a part of that nature that can be dominated just like the local flora and fauna.[138] In this way the man who did not know how to harness his plains, forests, and rivers lowered his status as a human being and became a savage, a native, with all that word implies. When the native was unable to fulfill his potential as a human being by becoming independent of nature he was looked upon merely as a project of man but not as a man. He was someone who could develop into something but as yet had not. A project of man who had neither developed nor progressed. The Westerner who dominated those new lands thought that one became a man by defeating, dominating, and finally becoming independent of nature. That is exactly what the native had not been able to do and therefore he was a primitive. From that primitiveness he could free himself when he acquired the constructive qualities of the modern European or Westerner. Only then and not before could he be looked upon as a fellow-human being; only then could he become a part of mankind and civilization. And this he could only achieve under the protection and in the service of men and nations who have made the harnessing of nature their mission.[139]

36. America and Puritanism

The modern European, like the traditionalist, would see America from the vantage point of whatever religious outlook he had. That outlook would justify him morally vis-à-vis "others," namely the people he would encounter in his expansion toward the West and would spring from a modern interpretation of Christianity, Calvinism, which would appear as Puritanism in America. Puritanism would offer its followers sufficiently ample ideological means to justify their aspirations for expansion and the privileges

---

[138] See Arnold J. Toynbee, *A Study of History*, op. cit., Vol. I, p. 152.
[139] Ibid., pp. 152-153.

derived therefrom. Calvinism would be the doctrine that could best serve the interests and aspirations of the Western man who burst upon history in the middle of the sixteenth century and spread all over the world during the seventeenth. This would be a new Church, a new Christian church, but one whose tradition and history began with the founder from whom it took its name. It was a Church which like others of that period appeared to be questioning the whole organization of the Christian church in its Catholic expression. It began by disavowing traditional authority, that is, any authority that did not have as its basis the individual who submits it to his reasoning. Its adherents were the new Christians who tried to establish what they considered a genuine Christian order. These were Christians who championed the return to the origins of Christianity, the Holy Scriptures or Bible as a primary source of authority. Taking these origins as a point of departure, a new Church, a new Jerusalem would be established, in which the human and the divine would commingle and the faithful would be merely interpreters, tools of God's will and executors of his designs.

The individual, as in all expressions of Modernity, would be the foundation of this new Church, which would fight against any form of ecclesiastical authority for which her followers found no rational justification. There would exist a kind of pact, a direct relationship between God and the faithful, which would be expressed by reading and interpreting the Bible. The elements on which the new Church would be founded were based on the reasoning of the new Christian. He would not accept the existence of an ecclesiastical power capable of saving man; the individual himself must accomplish the salvation of his soul, through his own efforts. But these forces were too weak unless they counted on Divine intervention, an assistance that the individual could receive through humility and by placing his trust in God. Any human being could have a mission to which he must be faithful, because only in this way would salvation be possible. Consequently, a man's faithfulness would be shown by what he accomplished through his labor.

What was man's mission on earth? To glorify God and to establish His kingdom on earth. There was a need therefore, to reshape the world in the image of that kingdom. In addition, there was the desire to maintain a Christian community that was the expression of the "glory of God."[140] The world, instead of being simply a place of exile, would set the stage for Divine action through human action. Therefore, there was no room for pure asceticism in the form of Christianity, as it had existed in primitive Christianity. The world, like man, was God's creation and therefore a manifestation of his glory. It was here that a man's faith as a Christian was put to the test as well as his ability or inability to serve the glory of the Creator. In his ability to influence the world, the Christian would find an answer to his desire for salvation. By harnessing nature, making it work for him, he would glorify God. The evidence of Divine glory depended, therefore, on the ability of man to transform the world. That was the reason why the new Christian claimed the right to systematically take advantage of all the possibilities implied in human action in order to dominate nature. All that might contribute to man's progress, all that implied his growing authority over nature, would contribute to the greater glory of God. There was a need therefore, to improve the lot of the Christian and of his community on earth. His prosperity was a sure sign of his ability to make God's glory known. The Puritan considered his work, therefore, as an activity that would redound to the greater glory to God and thereby bring honor to his community. The harder he worked the more he gained, and the greater the honor and the glory. He did not work merely because it was necessary, but in order to increase that glory and honor in such a way that it would transcend man's needs. It was not enough to have what one needed, it was necessary in addition to accumulate and add interest to the capital held.[141] For man merely to act or just work ceased to be a means to an end and became an end in itself. What had been achieved was merely the capital to be used for a new and larger investment. Therefore, working for the sake of work, doing for the sake of doing, and accumulating for the sake of accumulating had their beginnings in this kind of working, doing, and accumulating for the greater glory of God in this world.

This behavior and the desire to accumulate, which originally were for God's greater glory, finally ended by being for the greater glory and advantage of the individual who worked and earned, as well as for that of his community. "In the 'intra-mundane'

---

[140] See Ernst Troeltsch, *Protestantism and Progress* (Boston, 1958), p. 83.
[141] See R.H. Tawney, *Religion and the Rise of Capitalism* (New York, 1926).

asceticism," said Troeltsch, "the world and heaven were at odds; and in the struggle the world has proved the stronger."[142] Man, who was searching for God in his innermost self ended by confusing Him with himself. The struggle that had begun with the accumulation of wealth in the world, to the detriment of salvation in the next, found a satisfactory solution by making the achievement of the former open up the possibility of success in the latter. Success in this world instead of being an obstacle to salvation, was regarded rather as a sign that one was heading in that direction. In keeping with that new interpretation, the individual who worked and successfully held his own in the world had fulfilled the mission entrusted to him and was therefore doing all that was required for his salvation. Moreover, the man who acted and was successful in the world had become more than a mere mortal, he had become the Creator's tool. God spoke through the work of that man. The accumulation of material wealth was therefore no longer an indication of avarice: on the contrary, it became transformed into a tool for action on a larger and unending divine scale.

What kind of people did this new Christian meet when he stepped onto American soil? He met the so-called natives, who were strangely different. They were men, if one might call them that, who did not understand work in the way the Puritan understood it. They did not know of work or action for its own sake. The native worked simply to achieve what he considered necessary. He did not know how to accumulate, except for what was essential for his survival. He lived, one might say, from day to day; he took only what he needed from nature, and she freely provided for his needs. It was an attitude that aroused displeasure in men who had made work and the accumulation of wealth an end in itself. It seemed to these men that the natives, whose humanity was questioned for this very reason, had forsaken the mission God had entrusted to all people.

The Puritan conquistadores and colonizers of North America would accept merely that they shared a common origin with the natives: original sin. The natives were their fellow-creatures in so far as they were the descendents of Adam and heirs of the first sin committed by man against God. The colonizers felt that they were different from the natives, who had remained in a state of sin, as was clear from their work and their primitive civilization; whereas the

---

[142] Ernst Troeltsch, op. cit., p. 140.

new Christians tried to fight sin with works that honored God. The
Devil had been able to establish his domain in America through those
men. The Boston preacher, Cotton Mather said: "We do not know
how nor when these Indians began to inhabit this great continent, but
it is possible to believe that it was probably the Devil who attracted
these miserable savages in the hope that the Gospel of our Lord
Jesus Christ would never destroy or disturb his absolute power over
them."[143] Latin America's missionaries had thought much the same
but they tried to convert the natives to Catholicism. The mission of
the Puritan colonizers in America was not so much directed at saving
the natives from the clutches of the Devil; rather they wished to make
them a part of nature that they had not made use of, looking upon
them as a profitable element of nature, but not as people. Nature,
not man, was going to be saved from the Devil.[144]

This does not mean that the Puritan colonizer did not try to
assimilate the natives into his new Christian community. He
endeavored to do so but failed.[145] His religious ideas, more rational
than emotional, were the main obstacle to this assimilation. The
Puritan went on the assumption that the inspiration which enabled
him to look upon his work as a collaboration with God was not felt
by all people. Only the chosen few had an awareness of that
collaboration. This grace was granted to certain men only, who then
were able to overcome their animality or natural state. According to
his literature the Puritan was one of mankind's chosen few. Such a
man was aware of his mission. He was chosen by God for a mission
on earth, in this case America. Precisely there his mission would
have as its goal to make that continent a part of Divine glory. With
respect to the men whom he found there, he felt that it was his
obligation to induce them to enter the new community. His mission
was in part to preach among them so that they would join the
Christian community. He was to attract but not lead them, because
this was something only they could do for themselves. His mission
was to give them a chance of salvation, simply a chance that would
make it possible to single out those among them who were
predestined for salvation. Those who came into contact with the men
who brought the Divine message, if indeed they were predestined,

---

[143] Lewis Hanke, *The Spanish Struggle for Justice in the Conquest of
America* (Philadelphia, 1949).
[144] See Luis Villoro, op. cit.
[145] Juan A. Ortega y Medina, *El horizonte de la evangelización
anglosajona en Norteamérica* (soon to be published).

would hear the call and would join the new community by choice. It was a call that only God could make men hear. It could not be given to others, nor could it be heard unless they were called by Divine will. "God," said the first colonizers of America, "has not permitted that a grace such as the inspiration of His word and a knowledge of Him be revealed to the infidels before the proper time has arrived."[146] The colonizers could only make available to the natives certain means whereby grace, if it existed, cold manifest itself. But, above all, what was essential was to make them a part of the Christian order, subjugating them and their possessions if necessary, in order to give them the opportunity to live within the order established by the colonizers. If the colonizers were successful, then the natives were on the right path and it would be a first step toward a possible achievement of grace. "If in return for all their possessions they would only accept conversion to Christianity," the colonizers felt "well rewarded."[147]

Of course, the acceptance of the natives and their possessions into Puritan society was no guarantee that they would attain grace and finally salvation. Grace could be attained only through Divine intervention and revealed itself in the material, physical, and tangible accomplishments of man's labor. Grace could be attained by being successful, but that was hard for the natives to achieve, considering their inferior material situation. The indigenous element was going to achieve little in a competition in which they were defeated at the outset by the colonizers. Even if we accept that the colonizers had the best intentions in their relations with the natives, it would have been difficult for the natives to change in one bound from a natural kind of life to one governed by Calvinism and the social organization it inspired. In the view of the colonizers there was no other choice for the natives than indefinite subjection (and this did not even guarantee their salvation), or not to accept the Calvinist world and to remain in their own, persisting in the natural way of life to which they were accustomed. The Puritan looked upon that situation as a Divine indication that God was not on the side of the native. The native's inability to understand the difficult interpretation of the Puritan religion, to suddenly shift to a kind of life contrary to his own, was interpreted as a sign of his low humanity. The return, the escape to a natural way of life, merely indicated the triumph of the

---

146 Ibid.
147 Ibid.

Devil over the native. It was true that the American native seemed lost to God, civilization, and progress. The colonizers could do nothing to save him; only through his own efforts could he achieve his salvation and make it manifest; his failure as a member of the new order was the best proof that he was shut off from God.

Once this idea was accepted, the right of the Puritan colonizer to dominate America's virgin land was also accepted. God and only God had given him that land so that it could produce the crops that the natives had been unable to make it produce. God's glory was revealed in those crops. Confronting the colonizers was a new and virgin land without history, appropriate for new men ready to make a new sacred history. A history made with their own hands, with the accomplishments of their best efforts. A history in which the natives no longer had a place. Those men, if one could call them that, had done nothing to transform the land which it had been their good fortune to possess; they had done nothing to effect the transformation which was the colonizer's will. On the contrary, wasting that opportunity, the natives had merely placed obstacles in the way of the new community and opposed glory. The native was merely an obstacle, a disturbance, and a danger to the extension of Christianity, civilization, or progress, as the descendents of the Puritan colonizers would say. The Puritan, like his descendants, once he was convinced that it was impossible to assimilate the Indian into the new order, also realized that he himself could be corrupted by the Indian. He could therefore no longer treat the native as an equal. If he did he would run the risk of becoming contaminated and might fall prey to the Devil whom the native served. Besides, the native could draw him away from his mission, vocation, or Divine calling. The native's persistence in continuing to live in natural surroundings made of him something more than an unfortunate being or someone who had simply fallen from grace: it made him a tool of evil, the personification of evil, whereas the Puritan represented all that was virtuous.

Not only was the native himself regarded as the personification of evil; his cultural institutions and his physical appearance met with the same distrust. The color of his skin, which seemed to be the reason for his physical inability to understand the world of the colonizer and adapt to his way of life, also expressed the personification of evil the native symbolized. Whatever made the native different from his white colonizer was viewed as the personification of evil par excellence and as a source of contamination. Physical, moral and cultural contamination was to be avoided at all times. Evil was personified in that race and in the poverty of its men. It was an evil to be avoided. That was how the native, the original American, was turned into a contaminated being and one to be avoided. We might say that the American native was the first to suffer from discrimination for the greater glory of God and the triumph of virtue. The Puritans, unable to culturally incorporate the native into their society, decreed his expulsion from the land which ought to serve the ends of greater Divine glory. They expelled him to avoid any kind of contact that might render impossible the work of the chosen. Intermarriage was prohibited. By contrast with the Catholic colonizers in Latin America, marriage with natives was forbidden and physical relations were punished. They went on to prohibit any kind of relation with natives that might mean the recognition of an equality already prohibited. Puritanism felt called upon to widen the rule of the virtuous by eradicating evil. Therefore, to wrest the American land from the unable and diabolical hands of those monsters of evil was deemed the proper task of the virtuous. The expansion of the frontier, colonization in a steady Westward march, was regarded as a mission of virtue, progress, and civilization.

In this way modern man's ambition and uncontainable desire for material expansion found a religious justification. Whatever did not coincide with his desires was seen as an expression of evil, a point of view that the American colonizer was to extend to other areas of expansion, first to the natives, then to the Latin American countries, and currently to the rest of the world in his struggle against nations that dispute American preeminence. This outlook marked from the very beginning the difficult relationship between the United States and the Latin American countries. Religious difference was the basis of the opinion Americans had formed of the Latin American countries colonized by Spain, the nation responsible for the "Black Legend." They would therefore be placed on the prohibited list. The "Papists" were another expression of the evil that had to be eradicated. Later, other reasons would be advanced that differed very little from those used to justify the expansion into the native territory of the Western plains.

37. Puritanism and Democracy

Puritanism as a religious expression of modern man's ideals
gave to the social and political organization which arose in America
the ideological elements which made the United States the cradle of
modern democracy.   Protestantism in general is founded on the
concept of individuality and symbolizes modern individualism.   It
was the spirit of individualism which opposed religious absolutism
as symbolized by the Catholic Church.   Protestantism developed
freedom of religious inquiry and interpretation. It held that there are
no truths other than those revealed by the individuals who interpret
them.   Individuals have a direct relationship with God, without
intermediaries.   This kind of relationship exists of course also
through the community to which the individual belongs, but it is a
kind of community whose organization corresponds to what Tonnies
calls the society, a community organized in accordance with the
modern ideal of what Rousseau would call the social contract, a city
where the determining factor is the will of the individual who accepts
and makes it possible.

Puritanism is based on the idea of a community supported
freely by the individuals in it, who are the kernel of its organization.
Following Calvin, Puritanism asserts that the role of the state is to
maintain the worship of God, preserve the purity of the religious
doctrine, defend the constitution of the Church, regulate life in
accordance with the needs of society, and customs in accordance
with civil justice, promote harmony and establish peace and social
order.[148] Social organization is not something ready-made. It has to
evolve and be authenticated from day to day.   It is founded on the
individual's obligation to achieve peace, which makes security
possible.   The limits that society imposes are the same that
individuals have established for themselves in order to achieve
greater security.   Puritan communities originated in the will of
individuals, who established them to better guarantee their well-
being in this world and to increase the possibility of salvation in the
hereafter.   Only by living in accordance with the interests of the
community to which one belonged, interests that coincided with
one's own, and by adhering to Divine law could the desired double

---

[148] See Ralph Barton Perry, *Puritanism and Democracy* (New York,
1944).

security be achieved: security in this world and in the next.   By
means of a series of contracts with God and with men bonds were
created that made this double security possible.

In the Puritan communities established in the early American
colonies, civil authority was a part of religious authority and
functioned as its coordinating center.   "Civil authority," said
Angélica Mendoza, "was subordinated to religious and civil
standards and subjected to ecclesiastical rules handing over the
conduct of the citizen's life to the congregations."[149]   The aim of
ecclesiastic authority was to establish the kingdom of God among
men which in turn guaranteed their living together.   This authority
told individuals who belonged to the community that a minimum of
religious and social obligations made double security possible.   Once
those limitations were respected, the individual kept a number of
freedoms, in the economic sphere and in his conscience, which made
free inquiry possible.   Freedom of thought and freedom as to the use
of material wealth acquired by individuals were also guaranteed.   An
equilibrium between freedom and order was established: that
minimum of order which helped to safeguard freedom, a kind of
freedom which tended rather to avoid that minimum of limitations
than to accept it.

The Calvinist order, in spite of its rigidity, thus permitted the
establishment of the first democratic communities in America.   As we
have already mentioned, a kind of social contract was drawn up
showing the individual's desire to accept the restrictions imposed on
him by the community through his church.   The authority established
by the Church had its origin in such a desire and might be considered
an expression of it; of course, this submission could be interpreted
in turn as a good or bad relationship with the Divinity.   To freely
accept the religious and social limitations imposed by the community
was already a sign that one had attained its level and was faithful to
the lofty ideals that had made its establishment possible.   The
individual's will became the expression of a transcendent will which
had its origin in God.   God made His will known through those
individuals who revered it by respecting its law.   Once the law was
respected the individual was subjected to it.   The officials of the
community, who were also those of the Church, were answerable

---

[149] Angélica Mendoza, *Fuentes del pensamiento de los Estados Unidos*
(Mexico City, 1950).

only to God, thus establishing a kind of theocracy of democratic origin. "The theory was democratic in the sense that it provided for the regular election of magistrates and church officers by all members," said Herbert W. Schneider, and in that sense it championed equality and representative government; but in another sense it was not democratic, since it denied that the elected officers are responsible to the will of the people and asserted that law and authority come from God."[150]

The intolerance which this statement produced would, therefore, have repercussions in the future and would lead to the full explanation of the liberal and democratic ideology of the so-called "enlightened" who were responsible for the movement of independence in the United States and the social and political organization consonant with that ideology.

In this way the contractual theory created by European Puritanism to undermine at least in part the privileges of the ministry and the authority of the ecclesiastical institutions, subjecting them to an election by their members, turned into a system which served as a basis for the democratic organization of the Anglo-Saxon colonies in America. "In New England," according to Schneider, "it was practical to organize by covenants or social contracts small independent communities, towns, or congregations, small kingdoms of Christ, or theocracies, in which popularly elected magistrates and ministers were jointly responsible for enforcing the law of God."[151] That new ideal of Modernity which we have analyzed in another part of the book, where man, without any obligation to a past for which he was not responsible, could create from the very beginning social organizations in accordance with the expressed desire of all its members became possible in America. The social contract, the voluntary acceptance of social obligations, actually existed on the new continent. Man no longer lived with obligations that he did not accept. Individuals, likewise, no longer had to contend with laws and social rules that were not imposed by them. It was the individual who freely established all laws and rules under which he lived with others in America. There were no obligations other than those the individual recognized as his own.

---

[150] Herbert W. Schneider, *A History of American Philosophy* (New York, 1946), p. 4.
[151] Ibid, p. 6.

The theocratic factor, however, became the predominant one in communities of religious origin, gradually undermining their democratic spirit. The Church endeavored to expand its power at the expense of its members. Secular reaction was not long in coming, claiming that the members of the community were being deprived of their rights in the name of a theocracy out of harmony with the democratic spirit that had created it. "Though the New England divines formed the habit of promulgating divine decrees from their pulpits and took on the airs and powers of a privileged order, the laymen were able in the long run to assert their covenant rights, and they gradually undermined the clerical theocracies in favor of democracies."[152] The clergy's outcry against this reaction was as useless as their condemnation of supposed impiety, because the new generations in the American communities were forging ahead and imposing the democratic order which was to be an example for other societies in the world. "In other words, what was in Europe primarily a revolt of the middle classes against ecclesiastical privilege became in America a positive basis for the founding of independent political communities in which the clergy gradually lost their power and kept their prestige only to the extent that they themselves adopted the 'lay' point of view." In the Calvinist New England communities modern man had tried to solve interests of a mixed character. His concern to rule the world without losing the possibility of salvation, if it existed, found an appropriate way out of the dilemma. The new Church would sanction economic freedom and material expansion, and would, at the same time guarantee the salvation of the soul of modern man. "The New England towns were neither mere investments for merchant adventurers nor holy commonwealths; they pretended to be both," according to Schneider, "but gradually there evolved a distinct type of independence which embodied a mixture of Platonic idealism and Yankee mercantile prosperity. The 'election' and the 'providence' of God became the sanction or ideology of independent commonwealths."[153]

---

[152] Ibid, p. 7.
[153] Ibid.

38. The Community of the Chosen

It was considered a special privilege to belong to one of the democratic theological communities, since these communities of the chosen were not open to everybody. To belong to them was a privilege of Divine origin, a kind of selection made by the Divinity. They were communal organizations that represented God's city on earth. The covenants which made these communities possible were guaranteed by, and found their highest sanction in, God. God was the guarantor of those privileged democratic and theological communities. Therefore, the New England Puritans governed the colony's communities in accordance with a series of agreements: "The covenant of grace," "the ecclesiastical pact," and "the civil contract."[154] The covenant of grace made possible a kind of alliance with God Himself and was entered into by just and pious men and the Divinity. It was therefore valid only for the "saints" or those that God recognized as such. The "ecclesiastic pact" explained the "covenant of grace," establishing its recognition and acceptance by members of the congregation; this pact linked the spiritual and Divine with the worldly. The "civil contract" on the other hand dealt with human relations, a sphere where the intervention of the state was permitted in order to organize the activities of individuals, regulate their personal lives, and assure the salvation of the group that constituted the community.

Nevertheless, the basis of the Puritan society was contained in the covenant of grace, which rested on the selection of the best, those most righteous and the most pious persons in the community. The Divinity made this possible and sanctioned it. We have seen that this covenant was the point of departure and the basis for other pacts. Puritan society was rendered possible by the existence of "saints," who enabled the union between God and the community, which would not have existed without them, to take place. Through just and pious men the manifestation of grace which Puritan society permitted became possible. God guaranteed the first covenant, which in turn guaranteed all the others. On a higher plane than the civil responsibilities were the moral ones between man and God. It was a relationship established by means of the "covenant of grace," which was a direct pact between the soul and God, and needed no

---

[154] See Ralph Barton Perry and Angélica Mendoza, op. cit.

mediators. A relationship of the soul available to the best or the chosen in the community. The individual who entered into this covenant promised to lead an honest and blameless life and God kept him in this state through grace. It was a life in which passions were repressed, which allowed the individual to achieve sainthood as a revelation of grace. The "ecclesiastic pact," the contract between the "pious," as well as the "civil contract" which governed the relations of men among themselves, depended for their success on "the covenant of grace." In other words, the community depended on the piety of its most esteemed members.

We have already mentioned the importance placed on work within this social organization. Work and its product were to be the touchstone of this order, because through them the hoped-for grace manifested itself. Puritanism made the work of the faithful an indication of the congregation's desire for the manifestation of grace. The honest and blameless life of the virtuous could best express itself in successful action. It was not sufficient to contemplate God in order to glorify Him, one had to act and work. The just man of whom the Bible speaks could be identified with the serious and patient man who made work and industriousness a duty for the sake of God. His success was therefore regarded as a proof of his good relationship with God. An ever increasing activity that was crowned by success was felt to be a sign of Divine election. The new Christians were expected to have new virtues, such as diligence, moderation and thrift, the same virtues that were to mark the modern businessman. These were the virtues of the men who were responsible for the expansion of the West over the rest of the world,[155] which in turn made possible the sanctification of the world, its subordination to the Divinity, whose tool was the chosen man of action. Predestination revealed itself and was proved by the result of a man's action. "The ideal to which the Puritan aspired in life had more of the honorable than the good life and had to be achieved in the arduous fulfillment of complete and visible uprightness as proof of Divine benediction."

By accepting these beliefs, the New England Puritan made of his society an institution that was Messianic in character. We repeat that his mission was to establish the kingdom of God on earth and to

---

[155] See Max Weber, *The Protestant Ethic and the Spirit of Capitalism*, op. cit.

banish evil. The Puritan knew that he was a member of a community of chosen men, that he was a man chosen by God whose mission it was to redeem the world by wresting it from the clutches of evil in its various expressions. It was a Messianic conception that in the future would justify the expansion of Puritan America over other countries, because in thus expanding it would see itself as a redeemer nation. First, the Puritans wanted to free the natives from the clutches of the Devil, or at least to save from their unproductive hands lands that ought to be used to yield crops; later they would bring civilization, progress, freedom, and democracy to countries that had continued to live in a life-style different from the American way of life. "Theocracy justified itself by firmly maintaining that it was a 'democracy' or the 'chosen' whose obvious goal was the restoration of God in America's virgin lands; the Calvinist doctrine of the state supported by its leaders, as well as the personal conviction of every Puritan that he was in a position of irresistible grace, with its corollaries on man's condition after original sin, gave it missionary substance and a comfortable assurance which made it possible to justify all kinds of enterprises the theocracy might undertake, and permitted the colonizers to develop a discipline and unusual energy when they realized that they were the tools of Divine decisions."[156]

In keeping with this outlook, the country which at present is the champion of democracy also feels that it is the nation predestined to establish it, just as the Puritans felt in the past that they were predestined to establish virtue throughout the world. God, in one way or another, is the guarantor that its goal are those of virtue and democracy. On the other hand, other nations are not called upon to fulfill such a lofty mission, because their admittance to virtue or democracy depends on the country chosen to establish these, and is therefore not incumbent upon them. This is the point of view America defends in her relations with nations that are under her political or economic influence. Consequently, the difficulties those countries have encountered or are encountering in establishing democratic institutions are not seen in relation to the diversity of their economic, political, and cultural reality, but rather in relation to their apparent incapacity for democracy, as happened to other nations in the past that did not adopt the virtuous life as it was understood by the Puritans. Democracy, like virtue, would be regarded as an

---

[156] Angélica Mendoza, op. cit.

institution within reach of certain countries only and these would be able to make democracy work in countries without that ability. Therefore, countries lacking in this capacity for democracy but desirous of achieving it would have to accept the democratic nations' "political pact" in order to belong. A pact sanctioned by grace, like those of Puritan communities.

From the very outset the United States began her history by seeking moral justification for each step she took. In her growth, her enormous expansion, she has always looked for the necessary moral justification vis-à-vis the strict conscience of her citizens and the world. Puritanism is always the basis of those justifications. The creators of the new empire arrived on the threshold of history conscious that they were guilty of the most irreparable of sins: that of human beings who are Adam's descendents and therefore heirs of his guilt and condemned without possibility of appeal. From this point of view the Puritan colonizer was like all other men regardless of color. Like the rest of humanity, he was a condemned man, predestined to nothingness. His salvation depended on love and on Divine mercy or grace. The Puritan knew that this grace was granted only to a few men, to whom it was revealed in the form of justice and love. How did one find out whether one was among the chosen? As we said earlier, by work and success. Success was a mark of predestination, because success was God-given since man could not succeed alone. God spoke through men's work. The Puritan in America began very soon to test his mission. His work would show whether or not he was an emissary of God on earth. Material success in relation to weaker countries indicated that he was predestined, and therefore whatever he did was necessarily good and just. His success, first against the Indians, later against his neighbors of Hispanic origin along his border, was a proof of his predestination, and his destiny was a "manifest destiny." Any action against countries on the fringe of America's interests was justified by the success achieved. It was an action undertaken against evil, backwardness or barbarism. No civilized or democratic Christian nation could refrain from praising action of that kind.

39. Relations Between the Americas

The relations of the Puritan colonizers with less fortunate
colonizers and the natives were therefore determined by the formers'
conception of the world and of life that arose out of their religious
ideas. As we have already seen, the mainspring of that concept was
action, work for its own sake. The Puritan did not conceive of an
activity without a practical end which in turn served another, thus
forming an endless chain.   Leisure had no meaning in those
communities, and if it existed it was of negative value and was
looked upon as a generator of vice. What was important was to
work, because it was only through the success of one's labor that
God separated the just from the unjust.

Charity in the Catholic sense had no meaning, either, and was
rejected by the new communities. Nobody could help anybody else.
Only the slogan "God helps those who help themselves" was valid.
Each individual was master of his own happiness in this world and
responsible for his salvation. Individualism has an absolute meaning
and the expression "every man for himself" was applicable here.
According to Tawney, for the sake of individualism Puritanism
sacrificed fraternity on the altar of freedom.[157] Beginning with his
self-sufficiency, the Puritan limited his sense of human solidarity.
All men were equal and if inequality existed it was due to the
weakness of the individual concerned. Some preferred to work and
others to be idle.   Circumstances had nothing to do with the
individual's wealth or poverty, because man must be able to rise
above them. The Puritan, therefore, did not see in the poverty of
those around him a circumstance worthy of compassion and
assistance, but rather as typical of a man's character, proof of his
moral failure which far from being pitied ought to be condemned,
because in that failure God has shown His condemnation of the
unjust who have forsaken their mission. There was no reason, on
the other hand, and regardless of the Catholic Church's
condemnation, to make wealth the object of suspicion; it should
rather be a cause of thankfulness, because it bore witness to the
Divine blessing on the just man who had fulfilled the mission
assigned to him. Wealth was an expression of what an energetic,
frugal character could achieve when he had made productive work the

---

[157] R. H. Tawney, op.cit.

center of his activity. Poverty and wealth were merely indicative of what individuals were. God rewarded or punished men in their work according to their moral inclination. The virtuous man could only reap success, whereas the bad man reaped failure. That was the reason for the Puritan's hostility toward the poor man and his refusal to see in him a representative of Christ on earth, as the old Christianity saw him. Poverty was therefore prohibited in Puritan communities and vagrancy persecuted, as expressions of an evil that must be stamped out.

However, the interpretation of work as the center of Puritan life was opposed by the countries which developed beyond America's southern border. Those countries had a different outlook. They did not make a moral institution of work for its own sake, they respected poverty and enjoyed leisure. They spent little time worrying about exploiting nature beyond their most urgent needs. They were countries whose society had its roots in a type of authoritarian community, nations that seemed to have developed in a different way from those that knew God had chosen them to establish goodness, civilization, progress, or democracy. When those countries had tried to organize along the lines of modern nations, they failed completely, as shown by the chaos they experienced when they became independent from Spain. They were on the fringe of the new world represented by America. They were countries with no role to play in the mission that had been entrusted to the new man. In spite of all their efforts and the help they had received from the modern nations, the Spanish American countries had not been able to assimilate progress. The Latin Americans continued to be unfit for industry and for liberal democratic institutions. Their countries were devoid of common sense, were rhetorical, conservative, and absolutist. Their governments continued to be ruled by the antiquated authoritarian forms of Spain and Portugal. In the land conquered by those nations nature was waiting for men who would wrest her secrets from her and put her to work for them. Man did not take more from nature than she graciously gave him. The forest preserved the wealth of its precious woods and the tropical jungle its exquisite fruit. The earth's interior was still hiding precious resources, metals even more valuable than the gold and silver that had inspired the greed of the Iberian conquerors, the metals that modern man would need to build new machines, and the oil indispensable for running them. Latin America was still enormously wealthy, but her wealth was beyond the means of her people to tap.[158]

America, on the other hand, with her steady growing success was responsible for a doctrine that, in accordance with Modernity, was to give an impetus to Western history and her own progress which we have already discussed. This doctrine would unite with the one of Puritan origin to turn America into the land of the chosen. The union of the two would become apparent in the theory of "manifest destiny." That theory made it possible once more to justify America's territorial expansion over Mexico in 1847, and her political and economic expansion over the rest of Latin America and over Western Europe at present. The theory would find its justification as it did during American expansion over the Indians of the Western plains, in the apparent inability of the Latin American countries to harness nature and establish the kingdom of God or democracy on earth. This theory of manifest destiny was in conflict with the admiration with which the Latin American countries had followed America's development. These nations had fought and were fighting to establish in their own countries institutions similar to those in America. They dreamed, as the Argentine Sarmiento said, of uniting to form the United States of South America. For the Latin American, relations between the two Americas would oscillate in the future between admiration and fear. The America of "manifest destiny" would be condemned as the personification of egotism and materialism, whereas the America that had given freedom and democracy to the world would be regarded as the model for the Latin American nations' loftiest ideals.[159]

Was the United States capable of understanding Latin America's two-sided attitude? Puritanism as an expression of the United States' first relationship with people different from her own failed in its purpose of attracting the natives to the new order mainly because of a lack of understanding of their situation and culture. The stubbornness of Puritanism and its conviction of the rightness of its outlook and methods caused it to disregard the native's point of view. It regarded that outlook as an obstacle and not as something it shared with people of a different culture. Therefore, when the

---

[158] Refer to my book *The Latin American Mind*, op. cit.
[159] Refer to my study "Norteamérica en la conciencia hispanoamericana." In *La filosofía como compromiso* (Mexico City, 1953).

natives resisted becoming part of an order they did not understand and in which they were not understood, it was decided to liquidate them. The Puritans did nothing to accustom themselves to, or to assimilate the new groups of human beings they encountered, an attitude that is repeated in present-day history, except that nowadays America's relations are no longer with Indians but for over a century have been with all Latin Americans and recently with people from the non-Western world, Africans, Asians, Arabs, and also with Europeans. It seems as if the words of Hegel were still being repeated today: "If the world does not understand us, that is too bad for the world. God, progress, and democracy know why they are not represented by other countries besides our own." That attitude in the past justified and gave rise to the great Westward movement, accompanied by enormous economic and material growth, that has turned America into one of the world's major super-powers. It would be difficult, however, for that same attitude to achieve the same success in the future. In order to guarantee the expansion so far achieved, it would be necessary above all to make the readjustment of which we spoke when we were discussing the West. The West, represented at present by America, has created new situations in the world to which it must adapt. If it were otherwise, expansion would have gone beyond the ability of Western man to adapt to the circumstances it has created.

Arnold Toynbee has shown in his magnificent book, *A Study of History*, that one of the reasons for the so-called "breakdowns of civilizations" may be found in the inability of civilizations to adapt to a set of circumstances their own action has produced. The ideological and material tools that were good for the development of a civilization are not necessarily the right ones for maintaining it within a set of circumstances for which it is responsible. Stubbornness has been the reason for the breakdowns of civilizations before that of the West. Civilizations fail when a given principle becomes an idol; when they idolize a given institution; when they stubbornly persist in adhering to a state of affairs not consonant with a new set of circumstances. It is then that institutions that were apparently universal turn into limited tools at the service of certain interest groups. The inability to create institutions consonant with a new set of circumstances was the reason why Athens, the teacher of Hellas, failed. Athens, with her great democracy, culture, and extraordinary institutions failed when confronted by a world that had adopted many of her ideals. She could not see in that world what she had seen in her own. Far from respecting and encouraging democratic institutions in those countries, she fought and destroyed them in order to maintain her political supremacy. The creator of Athenian democracy lacked th ability to make democracy among cities viable.

Toynbee has also said that some countries or civilizations, instead of examining the reasons for their failure, attribute it to outside forces, to adverse conditions, so that they do not feel responsible for a set of circumstances triggered by their own action. "The sense of drift," according to the English philosopher of history, "is the passive way of feeling the loss of the élan of growth, is one of the most painful of the tribulations that afflict the souls of men and women who are called upon to live their lives in an age of social disintegration; and this pain is perhaps a punishment for a commission of the sin of idolatry through a worship of the creature instead of the Creator; for in this sin we have found one of the causes of those breakdowns from which the disintegrations of civilizations follow."

Obstinacy in clinging to deterministic creeds is also an expression of this disintegration. In order to escape the crisis and the sense of drift,[160] nations try to steel themselves by accepting a determinism which isolates them from reality and reassures them concerning the outside world, which they see as the source of their misfortunes. The followers of determinist creeds whose faith has had a strengthening effect, continues Toynbee, seem to have had "the bold assumption that this human will is coincident with the Will of God or with the Law of Nature or with the decrees of Necessity, and is therefore bound, a priori, to prevail." These men and nations appear to be always sure of victory. However, "we have seen how Goliath incurs his doom by vegetating in the once invincible military technique of the individual hoplite champion without foreseeing or forestalling the new, and superior, technique which David is bringing into action against him." The defeat of determinism is in the long run the most irreparable of all. "The disillusioned determinist who has learned from experience that God is not on his side, acknowledges his own fault when he reaches the devastating

---

[160] See George N. Shuster, "The Culture of the United States of America." In *The Old and the New World. Their Cultural and Moral Relations*, op. cit.

conclusion that he and his fellow-men are merely helpless pawns in God's game." Determinism for victory can easily change, therefore, into determinism for defeat, except if one accepts what Toynbee calls" the sense of sin,"[161] or an awareness that the new situation is the direct result of one's own action and is not due to something external or remote; awareness that error and lack of adaptability have been the result of one's own acts or one's own free will; that the individual alone is responsible for his own failure and therefore the only one capable of repentance and the necessary readjustment. The individual or nation that accepts such an awareness would be able to readapt and thus face the new circumstances by adjusting to them. They could then create the tools and institutions which would enable them to remain in the new world their action has thus created.

---

[161] See Arnold J. Toynbee, *A Study of History*, op. cit., Vol. V, pp. 412, 617; Vol. IV, p. 465; Vol. V, pp. 618, 432. (Translator's note)

CHAPTER X

CATHOLICISM AND MODERNISM AS COMPONENTS OF THE LATIN AMERICAN MIND

40. Awareness of Latin America's Marginal Existence

Let us now return to the beginning of this book and the concern for Latin American originality as an expression of historical and cultural marginality. Latin America, as already stated, entered the modern world in a way different from that of her Anglo-Saxon counterpart because she was tormented by awareness that she had been established by nations which even then were on the fringe of history, because they were outside so-called Western culture. That culture was characterized by its opposition to Christianity, upon which, by contrast, Latin America was founded. Both Spain and Portugal were nations on the fringe of Western culture, as were the nations they colonized: Spanish America and Brazil. Something set those people apart and made it impossible for them to belong to the new world of modernity and Western culture, something that all the efforts to that end by liberals in the Iberian peninsula and in Latin America failed to change.

The Latin American countries' awareness of their marginal existence, which in the past took on a negative aspect, has become more positive in our time. Latin American philosophers no longer feel sorry for not being fully Western and see, on the contrary, that the non-Western elements in their countries form the basis for Latin America's participation in the establishment of a wide and more truly universal culture. The Brazilian Sergio Buarque de Holanda, among others, speaks of Latin America's marginal situation and cites the advantages this implies when he analyzes Brazil's relations with European or Western culture. Brazil, like the rest of the Latin American nations, is marginal but this marginality enables her to serve as a bridge between Western culture and other expressions of non-Western culture. It is a situation that has made it possible for Brazil and Spanish America to assimilate cultural patterns which often seemed in direct opposition to those of the West.

This ability to assimilate cultures apparently at opposite poles may be ascribed to the mixture of races. Latin America inherited this attitude from Spain and Portugal together with the Christian way of looking at the world and life which the West had discarded. Spain and Portugal are nations tempered by the contact with non-Western cultures and have always been disposed to cultural assimilation without discrimination of any kind. Spain and Portugal are countries of racially mixed origin, of a racial amalgam going back to periods prior to the discovery and colonization of the New World. According to Buarque de Holanda, "like Russia and the Balkans, Spain and Portugal are land bridges by means of which Europe communicates with other worlds. They constitute, therefore, a border zone of transition, less affected by the Europeanism which they preserve as patrimony nevertheless."[162] This explains the Iberian countries' peculiarity of letting the races mix freely, and this trait was not abandoned when they conquered and colonized America. It was a characteristic that already distinguished the Iberians from other Western European nations situated beyond the Pyrenees, namely, the Europe created by Charlemagne's empire. Américo Castro alluded to it when he compared Spain with the Europe on the other side of the Pyrenees. "Spain," he said, "was a part of Europe, with which she was in close contact, and with which she continually interacted. In one way or another Spain has never been apart from Europe; nevertheless her physiognomy has always been peculiar."

---

[162] Sergio Buarque de Holanda, *Raíces del Brasil* (Mexico City, 1955).

But it was a special kind of peculiarity that made her different from Western Europe. "Not with the peculiarity that characterizes England with respect to France," continues Américo Castro, "or France with respect to Germany or Holland."[163] It was a kind of peculiarity that Iberians and Latin Americans were able to assess only in a negative way, and in which they saw the reason for their failure in their desire to Westernize or Europeanize the Iberian peninsula and the Latin American continent. It was a peculiarity that those nineteenth century intellectuals tried to erase, when they began their struggle for the "intellectual emancipation" of Latin America.[164] The goal of that emancipation was to free their nations from habits and customs they had inherited from colonial times and which were hindering the creators of the modern world. In this respect, Brazil was the most practical, because without renouncing the best in her heritage, she consciously assimilated the values of the New World. Her practical and realistic outlook led her to achieve as much as Spanish America but without the accompanying violence, and was based on the peculiarity we have mentioned.[165]

41. Iberian Traits

What are actually those distinctive Iberian traits that have made the Latin American feel sometimes as if he were on the fringe of history and culture? When Sergio Buarque de Holanda compares the part of Europe that lies beyond the Pyrenees with the rest of the continent, he states that it "clearly shows a trait unique to the inhabitants of the Iberian peninsula, not shared to the same degree by any of the peninsula's neighbors on the continent. And this is because none of her neighbors know how to develop to such an extreme degree the respect for individuality which seems to be the most decisive trait in the development of the Spanish people since time immemorial." It is a trait based on "the special importance of the human being as such" and on "the individuality of each one of

---

[163] Américo Castro, *The Structure of Spanish History*, trans. Edmund L. King (Princeton, 1954), p. 5.

[164] Refer to my book *The Latin American Mind*, op. cit.

[165] See Cruz Costa, *O Desenvolvimento da filosofía no Brasil no século XIX e a evolução histórica nacional* (São Paulo, 1950).

her citizens in relation to his fellow-men in time and space." These are people who love their own community and who are at the same time its most important component and may even feel that they can do without the rest of mankind. The concept which best expresses this feeling is reflected in the Spanish word "arrogancia" ("pride"). This word is an indication of struggle and rivalry which encourages people to depend on themselves rather than on others, but which at the same time explains many Iberian weaknesses. "To this we may largely attribute," continues Buarque de Holanda, "the singular weakness in organizational patterns which require solidarity and order among those countries. In a land where everyone is a baron it is impossible to arrive collectively at an agreement unless this is brought about by a respected and feared outside force." Many of the strangest episodes "in the history of the Hispanic nations, including Portugal and Brazil," are the product of the weakness of the social structure and the nonexistence of an organized hierarchy. In those countries, concludes the Brazilian sociologist, the lawless elements developed easily, counting on "the complicity or indolence of the institutions and customs."[166]

That same pride, that same aristocratic attitude was responsible for the Iberian's dislike of any occupation that did not do something for him as an individual, regardless of his financial situation. Whatever was material was considered merely a tool at the service of higher goals and actions that transcended it. Attributing the greatness of an individual merely to wealth implied a lowering of individual status. According to Américo Castro, Fernando de la Torre mentioned these traits of the Iberian soul as early as the fifteenth century, when he addressed a confidential communication to Henry IV of Castile in 1455, stressing that these peculiarities might be exploited. According to de la Torre, Castile had fertile land and men of strong and magnificent courage for military enterprises. Men from those parts were not gifted mechanically, mainly because they were satisfied with the wealth of their soil. Materially they aspired to no more than the goods necessary to satisfy their immediate daily needs and once these were taken care of, they knew that they could concentrate on other endeavors. Fernando de la Torre was aware of the Iberian's technological incapacity and attributed this to the wealth of the soil, which gave him more than he needed to solve his limited material problems. He therefore did not have to look for material

---

[166] Sergio Buarque de Holanda, op. cit.

resources other than those the land offered him with the minimum of effort he devoted to it. The fertility of the land causes them, "to be proud and slothful and not so ingenious or industrious."[167] They were men who did not feel the need to accumulate wealth which was the reason why they did not make material wealth an end in itself. Consequently, de la Torre saw no shortcoming in the technological inability of the Spaniard, since it was an inherent trait inherited by all Iberians. This would be considered a definite drawback for other countries, particularly for those that have built their conception of life and the world around technology.

For the Hispanic observer, contempt for technology designed to achieve more than man needs is an indication of his superiority and shows that the Latin American is called upon to perform work of a higher caliber rather than to pursue purely material aims. According to Américo Castro, de la Torre is therefore not a critic who is pessimistic with respect to Hispanic peculiarities. "If greatness does not come to Spain from her industrial skill and her commercial wealth, it does come from her lofty spirit and her grandeur."[168]

Great men have gone forth from that country, "men who were emperors of Rome, and not one, but seven," said de la Torre, "and even in our own times we have seen in Italy and in France and in many other places very great and valiant captains." Those were men with a sense of empire whose desire was to achieve immortality through great deeds rather than gain wealth by accumulating material goods. They were men who wanted the kind of immortality of which Jorge Manrique spoke, eager for heroic exploits and glory, who regarded material wealth merely as a means of bringing their deeds to a successful conclusion. For the Iberian, the fertility of the soil was therefore more than sufficient and so he could devote himself to other tasks. Technology and commercial activities merely took hold of a man and channeled his activities into fields that were alien to his interest. "Commercial traffic," states Américo Castro, "uproots man from his own land, severs him from his vital context, draws him away from nature, and causes him to participate in frauds . . . As early as the Middle Ages, the Spanish Christian scorned mechanical, rational labor that was without mystery, without a background of

---

[167] Américo Castro, op. cit., p. 17.
[168] Ibid., p. 17.

eternity to transcend it."[169] To work on the land, on the other hand, prepared man for other activities, like those the Iberian would assign to himself in his quest for greatness. Juan Ginés de Sepúlveda referred to this when he said that agriculture is "an occupation that is very virtuous and near to nature, and that usually invigorates the body and the spirit and prepares them for work and for war; to such a degree that the ancients preferred labor in the fields to commerce, and the Romans drew many consuls and dictators from among the ploughmen."[170] The discovery and conquest of America would therefore not only provide Iberians with new and fertile land, but would also give them the opportunity they were waiting for, namely, to carry out an important mission, a mission which in the long run would fail when times changed and imposed values based on a different conception of life and the world.

Sergio Buarque de Holanda speaks of the Iberian's aversion to work that demanded the subjection of what he considered to be his goal as an individual. The Latin American countries, he said, had an insurmountable loathing for "any moral based on the cult of work." "Action over matter, the material universe, implied submission to an outside force, the acceptance of a law not in consonance with the individual. Such a law is not demanded by God, does not add to His glory in any way, and does not increase our own dignity. On the contrary, it may be said that it injures and debases it. Manual and mechanical labor looks for an end beyond man and tries to achieve perfection in work." It is understandable, therefore, that the modern religion of work and the appreciation of utilitarian activity has never taken hold among the Hispanic people. A dignified idleness was always better or more ennobling in the eyes of a good Portuguese or Spaniard than the arduous struggle for his daily bread. What both admired as the ideal was the life of a grand seigneur which excluded any kind of worry or effort." Thus, the solidarity so typical of Anglo-Saxon people, which called for a united effort in tasks they considered to be of common interest, was not practiced among the Iberian peoples. Iberian solidarity existed, however, on another level, that of a common mission and not merely working together. A mission and loyalty to goals that went beyond the individual or loyalty to social groups for a merely practical reason of work, as could be friendship or family ties. According to Buarque de

---

[169] Ibid., pp. 17-18, 21, 23-24.
[170] From *De appentenda gloria* as quoted by Américo Castro, ibid., p. 23.

Holanda, "solidarity exists only where there is a bond of affection rather than a relationship or interests at home or among friends. These groups of necessity tend to be restricted, more private, and oppose rather than favor associations established on a larger scale through trade unions or on the national level."[171]

Consequently, the modern world's conception of society was practically alien to the Iberians. The Iberian paid little attention to the so-called social conventions that were too abstract and were designed for entities that, except in a symbolic sense, were nonexistent. The Iberian also found the abstract symbolism of modern man repugnant. He preferred genuine relationships based on friendship or consanguinity. The anonymous societies created by modern man were meaningless to him. He preferred communities whose extension depended on the genuineness of the relationship of their members. Small communities, comprising a group of relatives or true friends, or large communities that are no less genuine such as those of an empire where all individuals know that they belong and form a real and essential part of it. Within these communities each individual knows he has personal and unique qualities that cannot be replaced. Nobody feels he is an extra man who can simply be added or subtracted, and everybody feels he is an important part of the whole. Within that type of community the Iberian can give of himself completely, with his life and wealth, without a second's doubt or hesitation, because he knows that such renunciation, far from destroying his personality, increases and asserts it. In return for this genuine and material renunciation he will gain recognition, lasting fame and posterity within the community of which he knows himself to be an essential part. He becomes a true component related to each and every one of the parts, related to the whole as a father is to his son or the son to the father or the friend to his friends. "The absolute rule of the individual," says Buarque de Holanda, "the extreme exaltation of individuality, fundamental passion which does not tolerate compromise, accepts only one alternative: the renunciation of that same personality for a greater good. Because it is rare and difficult, obedience appears sometimes to the Iberian people as the highest virtue of all. It is not strange, therefore, that blind obedience very different from medieval and feudal principles of loyalty has, until now, been their only really strong political

---

[171] Sergio Buarque de Holanda, op cit.

principle. The will to order and a disposition to follow orders are also typical traits."

The Iberian's ability for historical action depended on the generosity or narrow-mindedness of the community feeling. During the sixteenth century there was a moment in his history when this feeling grew until it encompassed all of the known world and gave him an awareness of his high calling. That world had grown with the discovery of America by Spain and the first circumnavigation of the globe, carried out by the Portuguese. For a time, the idea that the Iberians belonged to a group of men destined to unify that world within the Christian community inspired Spaniards and Portuguese alike. It was an idea already present in their minds when they went in search of new worlds to conquer. The discovery and easy conquest of new worlds made the Iberians feel called upon to organize the new "ecumene." In that mission every Iberian felt he was an essential part and prepared to fulfill his high calling. But failure overtook them, and along with it came a narrowing of the community. From Iberian imperialism they turned to Iberian regionalism, seeing to it that the interests that inspired them were reduced to those nearest to them. The Iberian community divided and subdivided into gradually smaller and smaller nuclei. Regional interests took the place of those that used to be associated with the larger Iberian community. As a result families, institutions, clans, and certain individuals became more important than the community.

In this way, the Spanish empire in America divided into many republics as an expression of regional and local interests. These republics in turn divided into factions that fought furiously to make their own interests prevail.[172] Consequently, what could have been a great Iberian family was transformed into a group of families in permanent struggle to ensure the supremacy of their own interests. Only the leaders ("caudillos") or strong men, dispensers of privileges, were successful in establishing an order that was, always however, threatened by anarchy. Since the ideal of a community larger than the family or regional one had been curtailed, the Iberian adjusted to obtaining privileges which enabled him nevertheless to live from day to day, without immediate problems, without thinking

---

[172] José María Luis Mora speaks of what he calls the interests of institutions ("cuerpo") as limiting the national outlook. Refer to my book *Positivism in Mexico*, op. cit.

of a future that no longer made sense when there was no longer a
mission to be undertaken.   The effort of nineteenth-century
reformers, who hoped that the Iberian countries could join a world
interested in other causes, was therefore of no avail.   Progress as a
means of accumulating material wealth had no meaning for the
Iberians.   For them it was enough to own a good piece of land and to
dominate the men working on it.   Confronted by the material world,
they kept their independence, but did not know what to do with it.
Independence without any particular goals easily turns into anarchy.
Obedience born of awareness of a definite goal becomes relaxed, and
therefore it is only obedience imposed by the strongest that has a
lasting effect.   For that reason "dictatorships and the Holy Office,"
says Buarque de Holanda "seem to be as typical of their character as
is their inclination to anarchy and disorder."   The order that they
created ran the risk of disorder; their unity was obligatory and for
this reason always bordered on anarchy.

That was why nineteenth-century Latin American philosophers
and ideologists saw only failure in the Iberian world: strong men,
dictatorships, anarchy, and the Iberian's incapacity for the
technology that would have made him eligible for progress.   Thus,
we may say that the Iberian belonged to a world outside history and
culture, outside the Western world and culture which coincided with
the point of view expressed by Westerners about the Iberian world.
The Iberians tried to make up for lost time when confronted by their
inevitable contact with the modern world which, as it expanded,
swept over the Iberian countries.   That expansion was difficult to
stop and the ideologists were powerless in the face of it.   The only
thing that could be done was to re-educate the Iberian by giving him
the habits and customs of the men who were creating the new world.
During that re-education, Spain's past, the Iberian world, and its
particular traits were seen as obstacles.   It was even thought that the
Iberian heritage ought to be rejected.   The name of Spain, said
Bolívar, would be "detested" within a hundred years by all
Americans.   That past must be forsworn because of the urgent need
to turn the Latin American countries into pragmatic nations, that is,
into countries capable of resisting the expansion of the West by
becoming Westernized.   And in accordance with that urgency the
Iberian past became something detestable.   "If we take as a criterion
of historical judgment the instrumental pragmatism of the last
century," said Américo Castro, "the Iberian past consists of a series
of political and economic errors, the results of which were failure

and decadence, which the other European peoples avoided because they were free from bellico-religious passion and static and seignorial personalism." The positive aspect of that rejected world was hardly noticed, because "the way has been blocked by the Anglo-American's attitude of superiority, and by the resentment of the majority of Spanish Americans, who find in the colonial past an easy excuse for their present political and industrial weakness. A further obstacle was the state of unawareness in which Spain lived with respect to herself and her past during the nineteenth century, an unawareness for which the rhetorical gestures of today's self-justifying politics are no compensation."[173]

It was and is that outlook which has made Latin Americans and even Iberians feel that they are on the fringe of history. Iberian traits are therefore looked upon as a negative influence, as the reason for that marginal position. However, as we pointed out at the beginning of this study, in the same century in which this feeling of frustration originated there were voices drawing attention to the other side of the Iberian coin. One of these was Andrés Bello, whom we have already mentioned. The evils of which we accuse this world, said Bello, are those inherent in all countries. "We must not accuse any nation of these evils, but rather ascribe them to the nature of man." With respect to the inherited character traits, Latin America owes a great deal to them, including her desire for freedom. "No country that is completely degraded, annihilated, lacking in virtue would have been able to perform the great deeds that illuminate the patriots' campaigns, the heroic acts of self-denial, the many sacrifices with which Chile and other parts of America won their political emancipation." The spirit which inspired those acts was Iberian. "Whoever observes philosophically the history of our struggle against the mother country will see immediately that what made us victorious was above all the Iberian element. The native Spanish perseverance has been defeated by the innate perseverance of Spain's descendents." Latin American bravery was marked and sprang from the same spirit that had inspired the Spaniards' valor in Numancia and Saragossa. In her struggle against Latin America, Spain was fighting against herself, since in America the ideal of freedom and independence prevailed over blind obedience. "The captains and veteran Iberian legions were defeated and humiliated by the leaders of a younger Iberia's improvised armies which,

---

[173] Américo Castro, op. cit., pp. 5, 5-6.

forswearing the name of the motherland, preserved her indomitable spirit in the tradition of the ancient defense of their homes." This was what the Iberian world was like, and her problem to try and establish another and alien way of life by rejecting the one she had been accustomed to. The Iberians wanted to renounce what they were, in order to become something else. For Bello, the modern world, or the ways of the West, was something alien to the Iberian spirit and would have to be adapted to it beforehand. There was something the Latin American had inherited, something which he had no reason to reject, namely magnanimity, heroism, pride, "and unselfish independence."[174] That same spirit inspired the political and intellectual emancipators of Latin America to free her from the negative features of the Iberian world, those which in a way had hindered the realization of what seemed to be the mission of the Iberian world at a time when an antagonistic world was making its appearance, the modern world of the West which soon made the Iberians feel left behind.

42. The Awareness of a Mission

"The Spanish Empire, founded by Ferdinand and Isabella," said Américo Castro, "was not a happy accident but the same form of Spanish living, enlarged at the moment when Spain was becoming aware of herself vis-à-vis the other peoples of Europe." Her citizens, whose valor the European countries began to admire in the fifteenth century, merely needed the incentive to engage in great adventures. "Impetuous valor, like boundless faith, is not satisfied with limits and national boundaries, for it seeks the infinite in time and space, precisely the opposite of what the reasoning mind pursues with its measurements, limitations, and conclusions. Castile, in the middle of the fifteenth century, felt sure of her valor and her will, and she aspired to nothing less than an infinite dominion, 'Cismaritime lands and Outremer.' Catalonian-Aragonese imperialism in the Mediterranean, in the fourteenth and fifteenth centuries, and the Castilian and Portuguese in the fifteenth and

---

[174] Andrés Bello, *Investigaciones sobre la influencia de la conquista y del sistema colonial de los españoles en Chile* (Santiago, 1842).

sixteenth, provided tasks that gave satisfaction to certain wills that were untamable, and incapable of rationally modifying the natural world in which they found themselves."[175]   During the fifteenth century Spain merely waited for the leader who would coordinate his designs with the supernatural signal of his destiny.   That leader was Charles V, King of Spain and heir to the empire created by Charlemagne in Europe.   The signal was the discovery of America. Spain and Portugal embarked on the great adventure which providence had provided for them.   There were many leaders determined to enlarge the Iberian world.   Discoverers and conquistadores sailed the oceans carrying the flags of their king or emperor, and their religion, with but one purpose: to add land and vessels to the crown.   They sallied forth to open the way for Western expansion which was to follow, and which in turn would sweep those leaders away by wresting their conquests from them and strangling their lines of communication until they were driven away and silenced.

Shortly before this happened there was a moment when the Iberian world seemed to be the one called upon to impose its way of life on the rest of the world through Christianity or Catholicism as its main form of universality.   However, this was also the moment when the modern world with its ideals of freedom of thought and criticism of authority appeared.   These ideals also showed a desire for religious renewal and reform.   It was an ideal that prevailed during the reign of Spain's Catholic Queen Isabella and could be found in men like Cardinal Cisneros and the Spanish Illuminati, forerunners of the Erasmians who were to advise young Emperor Charles.   The ideal of religious renewal divided Europe into two factions, the Papists and the Lutherans.   Confronted with that division the Spaniards, conscious of their mission to unify the world, refused to take sides in the struggle and would only accept the role of unifying a threatened Christendom even though it might be necessary to subject the Pope as well as Luther.   This was the role they assigned to their emperor.   His mission was to serve Christendom above and beyond any other interest, even if it were political or economic.   The modern spirit of compromise which already made itself felt in Machiavelli did not enter into his plans. We are referring here to Machiavellianism as practiced by Rome and the German princes who supported Luther.   Neither did the Iberians

---

[175] Américo Castro, op. cit., p. 18.

understand the game of competing in the political balance of power which Francis I of France and Henry VIII of England had played. The only thing that mattered to them was the unity of Christendom above and beyond the national interests and those of the Vatican, which was acting already like another state. In order to achieve this unification, Spain had asked for assistance in a crusade to drive the Turks from the Holy places. The goal of that crusade was to create a new feeling for Christian unity in a Europe which was beginning to become divided by nationalism. The man who had driven the Moors from the Peninsula could easily direct the battle of a united Christian Europe against the infidels, a battle which in turn would put an end to the existing division among Christians.

But they were to go still further: the idea of Christian unity would transcend that of Europe. Europe had one mission in the world: to bring the Christian faith to all the peoples of the world, including the Turks. The Christian world must extend to every country on earth, since that was the mission of Europe and, with that continent, of the Iberian people. Marcel Bataillon speaks of the spirit of Christian unity, which was an awareness felt by many Europeans and which in the Iberian world, turned into an awareness of a mission. The messianic restlessness, he says, "stems from an acute feeling of a gigantic development crisis which was translated into a dream of Christian unity that included a converted Islam, into an intellectual crisis that expressed itself in violent aspirations for reform. Those two aspects of that period cannot be dissociated. Even Savanarola in his predictions had foreseen a Christianity renewed from within which could not fail to convert Turks and pagans without the help of the sword. In Spain we would very soon find that same inspired prophesy."[176] In Spain this prophesy was first made by Cardinal Cisneros, who had already had the experience of converting the infidels after the conquest of Granada. The system of evangelization used in the case of the conquered Moors was the one later applied to the natives of America.

The first Archbishop of Granada, Hernando de Talavera, learned the rudiments of Arabic and insisted that his clergy learn them too, so as to be able to communicate with the converts. In order to be understood by the conquered, states Bataillon, the Archbishop was "not afraid of seeming revolutionary. His sermons

---

[176] Marcel Bataillon, *Erasmo y España* (Mexico City, 1950).

avoided dogmatic subtleties and were based on the straightforward topic of moral action. This could be understood by an ignorant old woman as well as by the most educated man. What he tried to do was to attract the common people to the Church, giving them a greater opportunity for participation in the liturgy, and he therefore replaced the responses by devotional hymns appropriate to the lessons and in this way was able to induce the faithful to attend both matins and mass. He also used the religious theater to appeal to their emotions. Many protested against this innovation considering it an insult to the church, but he paid no attention."[177]   The Spanish Reformation, as Bataillon calls it so succinctly, would thus be propelled by that missionary zeal which Spain considered to be her task on behalf of the world. There was the desire to reform the church so that it would be more easily accessible to other countries. Since Spain was in permanent contact with non-Christian countries and those of other religions and customs, she understood the need for resiliency in order to understand and in turn be understood by other nations. Moved by true Christian zeal she wanted the whole world to be Christian. From the Arabs she learned the difficult art of living with other religions, but not the respect the Arabs had for them.   In this sense Spain was not ready to permit religious coexistence, but was willing to make the necessary effort to attract to Christianity believers from other religions.   She easily passed therefore, from the utmost understanding as a method of assimilation to the most absolute fanaticism if that understanding was not sufficient.   The goal was the Christianization of the world, regardless of the methods used to insure its achievements.   Spain was, therefore, agreeable to modifying within certain limits the organization of her church and liturgy, thus putting Christian religion within easy reach of other countries so that they would not remain on the outside.

That was the reason for the great Spanish reform movement which began with Cardinal Cisneros and which was prolonged by the followers of the so-called Philosophia Christi and Jesuitism in its first stage. The ultimate goal of that reform was the expansion of Christendom so as to include all the nations of the world without racial or economic discrimination. As a reform it was very different from the Western European one, which strengthened individuality in

---

[177] Refer to chapter IX on Puritanism and also see A. Ortega Medina, op. cit.

the most absolute sense. It was an individuality without limitations except for those strictly necessary for living together, but one not made for communal living. Thus one might almost say, that if the Spanish Reformation had been successful, the different denominations or nationalities supported by Western Europe's Protestant Reformation, into which Europe was ultimately divided, would not have appeared. That Reformation did not have as its goal the expansion of the Christian community, but rather the strengthening of the personal, independent, and critical spirit on which the world we have called the West, with all its qualities and defects, was based. We have seen earlier in this study how, within that world, the individual can do nothing to persuade others to join his "ecumene." This desire to join is so personal, individual, and unique that each person must decide for and by himself. If the individual cannot do for others what they cannot do for themselves, then others cannot do anything for him that he cannot do for himself. In the religious sphere only God can do something for others; therefore, one can belong only to Puritanism, to the order established by God because it is preordained, and the same is true of the civilization or progress of which one is part, because it is so ordained. That is not what happens to the Iberian. The Iberian not only believes that he can induce other men to join the Christian order to which he belongs, but is firmly convinced that God has chosen him for this mission. How it is to be accomplished does not matter: be it through understanding and necessary reforms or by force, the sword, or the Inquisition. "The means are unimportant: what matters is the goal." All men and nations can and must be saved even if their salvation depends on war. Side by side with means of persuasion used by the archbishop of Granada to attract the infidels, there appear, therefore, violent methods such as the Inquisition, which was established by Cardinal Cisneros.

When the persuasive method seemed too long and insufficient for the Iberians' pretense to universal evangelization, they had recourse to other methods. "All want more decisive results," says Bataillon, "and Cisneros, called on to collaborate with Talavera, put into practice other ways and means. He tried to win over the Moorish aristocracy, exerted pressure on the 'alfaquíes' or lawyers, promoted mass conversions which produced violent reactions, and burned Moorish books. One rebellion gave him the right to revoke the concessions made during the days of the reconquest. Any Moor was very soon considered a rebel and as had happened a century before with the Jews, the new converts constituted an unassimilated mass of 'new Christians' whose Christianity was looked upon with suspicion.   Then, more than ever, the Inquisition established to supervise the new Jewish converts to Christianity became an essential institution of the nation's life."   That was the other side of the Iberians evangelizing zeal, which would end by rendering void its self-imposed work and mission.   Violence as a means of enforcing entry into the Christian community would end by becoming an instrument of isolation, and this process was to culminate a few years later in the intransigent empire of Phillip II, an empire that would retreat before Western Europe, which intimidated it.   It was a fact that the Iberians longed to establish an empire of Christian culture throughout the world, an empire which, like everything human, was to be an image of the qualities and defects of the men who tried to establish it.   It was an empire very different from the one finally established by Western Europe or the West.

43. Two Kinds of Imperialism

While the various nationalities into which Western Europe was to divide were developing, Spain presented herself to the world as the champion of European unity and the symbol of Christian unity. The Europeans were aware of this fact, felt the division that corroded them, and understood the role Spain could play.   "The responsible intellectuals of the period," says Bataillon, "hopefully turned their eyes toward Spain.   Actually, the inevitable decline of the Papacy and the Empire left intact the ideal requirement for unity in a Christendom that was being destroyed.   And Spain was one of the frontiers where Christendom fought against Islam.   The idea of a crusade became intellectualized in an aspiration for the universal kingdom of Christ.   The idea of a crusade no longer entered into policies of royalty.   Only the Spanish monarchy, still elated by the final thrust which enabled them to reconquer Granada, gave that idea some thought."   Spain felt called upon to undertake that crusade and to impose the Christian order.   This task, which began with the conquest of Granada, "had to continue with the annihilation of Islam, the rebuilding of early Christianity and the reconquest of Jerusalem." That was what the archbishop of Toledo had planned and was envisioning as the task of the Catholic Kings. In 1506, therefore, Ferdinand decided to ask for the help of the Portuguese and English kings. The former, since he was an Iberian, accepted the project and indicated that he was already engaged in this crusade because "in the Indies we are looking for precious spices and God's glory."[178] The Spaniards were engaged in the same enterprise in the West Indies discovered by Columbus, where they were seeking gold but also the higher glory of God.

Spaniards and Portuguese in their discovery and conquest of new lands were fired on the one hand by an ambition which led to their finding valuable spices and gold, and on the other hand by a desire to bring Christianity to those lands. Behind the ambitious warrior there always followed the modest missionary. Ambition and desire were often at odds, as was shown by the discussions which raged in Spain about the nature of the indigenous element. It was an unbridled ambition that clashed with the attitude of the evangelizers, who hoped for something more than bartering for spices and gold. Hegel has shown already how the mind uses man's passions in order to achieve his ends. In this case, Iberian ambition served as a springboard for the evangelical mission that the Iberian world had set itself. The difficulty resided in the need to keep a just balance between the means and the desired goals. Unlimited ambition always led to barbarism and was denounced by missionaries as well known as Las Casas. An important fact was that there were always men like Bartolomé de las Casas ready to fight and denounce the abuses of ambition, or men like Francisco de Vitoria granting all men the right to become a part of the great Christian community on a level of complete equality and without any racial or cultural discrimination.

Keeping this point of view in mind the great preoccupation of the Iberians, or rather of the Spanish and Portuguese, in their far flung expansion all over the globe was inspired above all by the desire to incorporate that world into the great Christian community of which they were the champions. It was an expansionist preoccupation entirely different from the one that was to manifest itself during the seventeenth or eighteenth century in Western Europe. The diversity of problems and goals to be pursued in either expansion would ultimately be revealed in the results achieved. Arnold Toynbee points out the consequences of the different

---

[178] Marcel Bataillon, op. cit.

expansions over the world and the consequences of various imperialisms. The attempt of the Spaniards and Portuguese in the sixteenth century, he says, "was more or less successful in the New World - the modern Latin American communities owe their existence to it - but, elsewhere, Western civilization as propagated by the Spaniards and Portuguese was rejected after about a century's trial. The expulsion of the Spaniards and Portuguese from Japan, and of the Portuguese from Abyssinia, in the second quarter of the seventeenth century, marked the failure of this attempt." Another attempt "was begun in the seventeenth century by the Dutch, French and English, and these three West European nations were the principal authors of the world-wide ascendency that our Western civilization was enjoying in 1914. The English, French and Dutch peopled North America, South Africa, and Australia with new nations of European stock which started life with the Western social heritage, and they brought the rest of the world within the European orbit."[179] Therefore, the varied success of this European expansion over the world was due to the different goals which inspired the Iberians and the Westerners who carried it out.

The Iberian expansion has in addition to a political and economic goal a cultural end in view: namely to incorporate the conquered people into the Christian community. The expansion of the West, on the contrary, merely hoped to maintain its economic and political dominance and the cultural aspect was only of secondary importance, as much to their regret was often the case.[180] It was a different kind of expansion that expressed a different kind of outlook and therefore envisaged different goals. The Spanish and Portuguese justification for their expansion was what they called "the greater glory of God," meaning that they were widening the sphere for world-wide recognition of Christianity. What was important in that expansion was not so much the land and the resources that had to be conquered but rather the human beings who had to be incorporated into Christendom. Of course, we know that many Iberians who embarked upon the conquest of new lands did so inspired by the wealth and well-being it might bring them; but it was a conquest without moral justification and, therefore, what was important in that expansion was the conversion of the infidels. The expansion of the West, begun during the seventeenth century, had another

---

[179] Arnold J. Toynbee, *Civilization on Trial*, op. cit., p. 101.
[180] Refer to chapter IV of this study.

significance. It was an expansion that set out to conquer the land and its resources as a new expression of "God's glory," namely, as that term was understood by Puritanism. For the "greater glory of God" here means the maximum advantage to be derived from the land, fauna, and flora, which was there for man to bend to his will. Here man sees it as his mission to exploit the available resources by making the utmost use of them. For this reason there is disdain for the original inhabitants, who did not know how to harness the natural world. Interest in having these men belong to Western communities did not exist. Consequently, while the Iberians were basically interested in having men and communities join the great Christian community, the Westerners were more interested in making the lands they had discovered a source of new wealth from which only those who knew how to exploit them and their peoples would benefit. The Iberian expansion was primarily interested in assimilating countries or peoples, whereas Western expansion was interested only in the raw materials that the lands of those countries and peoples could offer, raw materials which were going to be a source of wealth and whose accumulation was responsible for the great modern system of capitalism.

Iberian expansion in general would be directed toward the most populous centers of the world, where in a totalitarian sense they tried to dominate and subject nations to the community and culture of which they were the leaders. Europe in its expansion was not looking for that kind of subjection: rather, what interested her was the domination of the land and its resources, but not of its people. Whereas the Iberians created countries that were mixed as to their cultural and racial composition, the Westerner did not follow that pattern and was careful not to mix either racially or culturally with the natives, respecting their habits and customs which they had no desire to change and even going so far as to join the local forces preventing contagion of the nation by the West. In this way they maintained the same social, cultural, and political conditions that they had found when they came. Given those two divergent attitudes, the Iberian conquerors were successful in places where the cultural resistance was weakest, as in America, which lent itself to rapid assimilation of the conqueror's culture by means of changes of attitudes brought about by the missionaries who were working with the American natives. On the other hand those same conquerors failed in the Asiatic countries, whose culture was so deeply rooted that it was impossible to assimilate it or replace it with Christianity, as happened in America. That was the reason for ' Japan's unrestrained persecution of Christian evangelization during the seventeenth century, although it would later accept Western technology. And the same can be said of other Oriental countries which rejected Iberian colonization but could not avoid being engulfed by the expansion of the West. In Asia, therefore, where the Iberians had failed in their attempt at cultural assimilation, except in the Philippines, they were obliged to turn back or to resign themselves, as did the Portuguese, to maintaining a kind of colonization similar to the Western, based on economic domination, and dispensing with cultural assimilation. Political and economic colonization was thus achieved, but cultural assimilation was arrested. The expansion of the West, on the contrary, was successful all over the world, because it was limited to the economic and political spheres and used them to strengthen Western business interests. There are of course places where the West's expansion has also been cultural, as in North America, Australia, and South Africa, but there the natives were either exterminated, banished, or intimidated in such a way that they no longer represented any threat to total expansion by and for Westerners. In the rest of the world, where such extermination or banishment was impossible, the natives were culturally ignored. They did not represent a cultural problem that needed to be solved because they were regarded merely as things, objects to be used like the country's flora and fauna, and exploitable like the land on which they lived.

44. The Dream of a Christian Empire

The Christian Empire's highest ideal, to which the Iberian people aspired as a consequence of their evangelical vocation, found expression in Spain during the sixteenth century at a time when the group of the so-called "Spanish Erasmians" were influencing the affairs of the Spanish crown. And I say "so-called" because they were something more than Erasmians. Actually, Erasmianism served them merely as an ideological tool in the Iberian world's self-assigned mission. The spirit of the Spanish Erasmians was in fact different from the spirit that inspired Erasmus and his followers in the rest of Western Europe. Erasmus and the Erasmians of Western

Europe were merely the highest expression of the individualism that appeared with Modernity, an individualism which was responsible for those modern institutions based on individual freedom and on the condition of freedom for all. It was the ideal of the modern liberal democracies. It was also that other side of modern individualism, and therefore synonymous with the egotism to which we referred earlier. Modern individualism, like the spirit of the Iberian community, had two sides to it: one positive and the other negative. European Erasmianism represented the positive side of modern individualism in the same way that Spanish Erasmianism represented the positive side of the Iberian community spirit.

Of course, Erasmus and the European Erasmians also hoped for European unity within Christendom based on mutual understanding and respect. They regarded Christianity as the highest expression of Humanism. Christianity united all people by recognizing their human qualities. All people, as sons of Christ, were equal, alike in spite of individual differences. Any human difference was, therefore, treated with respect because it was common to all people. Beyond any difference there was always man's essential quality: reason. Reason was to be the center of modern humanism by granting equality to all people, bringing with it a sense of collaboration and assistance for the individual on whom it was centered. For an Erasmian like Sir Thomas More this ideal of a human community would be manifestly based on individual awareness and consent, which could only be given to what was "clear and distinct" and understood beforehand. In *Utopia* the ideal community of European Erasmians is pictured with a minimum of social intercourse, the bare essentials necessary to insure that the individual could remain within it. This type of community had few laws, but those that existed were effective. In *Utopia* everyone participated in the community's work but only in what was strictly necessary, thus making it possible to devote the rest the time to personal business. "For the magistrates," said More, "do not exercise their citizens against their wills in unneedful labors. For why? In the institutions of that weal public this end is only and chiefly pretended and minded, that what time may possibly be spared from the necessary occupations and affairs of the commonwealth, all that the citizens should withdraw from the bodily service to the free liberty of the mind and garnishing of the same. For herein they suppose the felicity of this life to consist."[181] In other words the community was serving individualism. That same ideal of an individualistic community, in the way that Tönnies would see it, would also inspire the social ideas of Locke or Rousseau. These would be societies based on the will of all and each of their members and would be established to serve them. Another facet of this same individualism is shown in Machiavelli's or Hobbes' thesis. According to the former, the will of the individual can be transformed into that of the state, which, as the sum of various opinions, becomes the will that transcends them all embodied in the will of a single individual who justifies his actions on the grounds that he has been given a mandate. In the case of the English philosopher, society is merely a necessary evil, a protective tool that the individual has invented in order to live, a mutually protective tool against the voracity of the wolf that dwells in all human beings. That protection would be denied to all individuals on the fringe of society, because that was precisely why it was created. Individualism in the Machiavellian and Hobbesian sense was to be responsible for aggressive nationalism when it changed to an imperialism serving certain interests only, an imperialism that was merely an extended individualism devouring everything in order to make it its own. Modern individualism is also responsible for modern imperialism, the other facet of freedom and sovereignty.

The Spanish Erasmians had other ideas: their main desire was for the Christian unity of Europe and the world. They greatly valued the individual and individualism but did not make them the ultimate goal, seeing them rather as serving the Christian community which transcended them. That kind of individualism was broadened within the community to which it belonged, and the individual could be considered as belonging to a community without thereby feeling in any way humbled or altered. This was the feeling revealed in the Hispanic Erasmians. They were a group of men able to exert their influence at the beginning of Charles V's empire, because of the personal contact some of them had with the monarch. On several occasions this familiarity made it possible for them to influence the policies of the empire in a way considered appropriate for the successful attainment of Christian unity. Beyond incipient nationalism and religious strife there was always Christendom. Spain's mission was to restore Christian unity in Europe in order to

---

[181] Sir Thomas More, *Utopia* (New York, 1928), p. 108.

bring Christianity to the worlds that providence was helping them discover. That was the mission of Spain as well as that of each Spaniard who fought for the emperor. Erasmus' conciliatory spirit, which envisioned an end of the discord dividing the Christian world, was therefore adopted. But they were attempting something more than the Dutch humanist had in mind. Nowhere in Europe was Erasmianism supported with greater enthusiasm than in Spain, an indication of the different interpretations it would be given. These interpretations and goals could not have been further from Erasmus' own thinking. It was significant, therefore, that in spite of the enthusiasm of his Hispanic readers, Erasmus never made any effort to visit the Peninsula and even rejected an invitation. For this Westerner Spain was a strange world with an idea of Christianity to which he no longer subscribed.[182]

The defeat of the Pope and the sack of Rome by the Emperor's troops was seen by the Spanish Erasmians as a sign of the divine mission of Spain and her monarch: to achieve European unity under Christ's empire. It was an indication that God had put the fate of the Church into the hands of Spain. A church divided by strife which neither the Pope nor Luther had been able to reconcile. The lightning victory of the Emperor's troops, "against the Pope" says Bataillon, "would have carried to paroxism the faith of Spain's select minority in a religious reform imposed by the Emperor."[183] Like Erasmus, the Hispanic Erasmians believed in reconcilement, but they also believed in something more than did the Rotterdam humanist, because they felt that violence was sometimes necessary to achieve that end. This hovering between war and peace so typical of Spain manifested itself also in the Erasmian conciliators. Luis Vives wrote to his friend Fevyn: "It is reported that a large number of enemies have conspired against Charles. But that was Charles' fate: to defeat large numbers of enemies so that his victory would be celebrated all the more. Actually, these were God's decrees to show men how weak our forces were against His power."[184] Charles and Spain were destined to bring the Christian community to all the countries of the world, but in order to do so European unity had first to be established. God had already given several indications of that Spanish destiny, one which would raise the Emperor above all obstacles and justify all the

---

[182] Marcel Bataillon, op. cit.
[183] Ibid.
[184] Ibid.

measures taken to insure its fulfillment. "By virtue of that mystique in which war and peace intermingle in such a strange way," states Bataillon, "the Emperor appears to his faithful as the tool of Divine will, stronger than all obstacles including the Pope. The imperial policy, as it becomes decidedly anti-Roman, adopts the idea of the council and attempts to remake Christian unity by means of a strictly just decision which the victorious Emperor would impose on the Pope and the Lutherans."[185]

With respect to this point, the Hispanic Erasmians considered themselves the disciples of an Erasmus, who strove for a reconciliation of the churches within Christendom. However, Erasmus did not want that reconciliation to take place under the leadership of a given country or emperor although this was exactly what the Hispanic people wanted. Erasmus, continues Bataillon, "does not follow Charles V in his dream of universal hegemony, because he believes that peace among the Christian princes is to be more highly prized than imperial victory." As a modern man, Erasmus preferred a balance of power between princes and nations, which was to be the principle Western Europe would adopt as her policy for the future. Erasmus would be more in agreement with Francis I's idea regarding national sovereignty than with Charles V's idea of Christian unity. The only acceptable unity among nations and princes should be based, as among individuals, on a code mutually agreed upon, that would do justice to all the interests involved. It was on this point that the Spaniards differed from their Dutch teacher: in spite of the diversity of particular national interests there would always be the one interest in Christianity. God was on their side and, therefore, they were able to defeat their enemies. God's will was shown in the victories achieved over Christ's vicar on earth. Alfonso de Valdés justifies thus the sack of Rome in his *Diálogos de las cosas ocurridas en Roma* (Dialogue describing what took place in Rome). In this dialogue Rome is indicted because she had separated from Christendom. This is given as the reason for her defeat, which was necessary in order to establish peace and the unity she had lost through wars which had unchained ambitious and narrow-minded interests. God himself permitted the violence perpetrated in Rome by the Emperor's Christian soldiers. Out of this defeat must come the desired unity and the only true Christian

---

[185] Ibid.

peace.[186] "Thanks to Valdés," says Bataillon, "the sack of Rome was for the Spaniards of that period something more than a dreadful scandal from which all of them turned away in horror. This event, known in all its details, was accepted by the more enlightened Spaniards as a clear sign of Divine will, as the announcement of a Christian renewal which would end Rome's mistakes and bring about a return to the spirit of the Gospel."

The Iberian world led by Spain considered itself the champion of a cause doomed to end in failure. History was taking another direction and its leader was to be the West. More important than community interests were to be those of the individuals who made the new history possible. More important than the community of Christian nations was to be the interest of each country independent of its Christianity. Francis I with his idea of national sovereignty was following a more realistic policy than did Charles V with his policy of a Christian empire. Thus, while the latter tried to unify Europe and evangelize the newly discovered worlds, Francis I for his part tried to enlarge France, growing in power with her. While Charles V preached a new crusade against the Turks, old enemies of Christianity, the French king taking care of so-called matters of state or the needs of what was to be the French nation, became an ally of Suleiman and the Turks in order to stop Charles. Even Rome was more preoccupied with material than with spiritual power in view of the growing strength of national power. "The Pope," according to Valdés, "was Christ's extension on earth and represented the evangelical spirit, but was not a head of state who had to defend his possessions arms in hand. The dominion and authority of the Church were more concerned with human beings than with governing cities. It was necessary and beneficial, adds Valdés, that the Holy Fathers should have temporal power or they would not respect it. It was true, however, that they could understand spiritual matters better if they were not concerned with secular ones."[187] Well said, but this did not fit the new course the world was taking. History moved in another direction than that chosen by the Iberian world: "The emancipation of Rome, the hoarding of treasures, nationalism;

---

[186] Compare the *Diálogos* by Valdés with Thomas More's *Utopia* to see the differing conceptions of social relations between the two, the Christian and the modern.

[187] As quoted by Marcel Bataillon, op. cit.

Reformation, capitalism and the great powers," says Eugenio Imaz.[188]

Instead of an empire there appeared in Europe great and small nations, kingdoms and weak nations; powers that exercised their might over weaker nations, thus giving rise to a new kind of imperialism; powers that respected only each other and were kept alive by the fear of defeat. This was the origin of the modern problem: Europe's balance of power based on pacts and alliances or against pacts and alliances, pacts and alliances that would be broken easily when one of the members felt sure of being able to succeed in subjecting any of the other parties. This meant the subjection of the weak and provided a balance of power vis-à-vis the strong nations. As an expression of interests it reflected a nationalism which was to give rise to that other form of imperialism of which we have spoken already. An imperialism which is merely an enlargement of the sovereignty of one nation over weaker ones. An imperialism which would refuse to grant weaker nations the same rights it expected them to recognize with regard to its own citizens. Finally a new form of imperialism based on material power over other countries, but not on awareness that those countries might become part of a great mission in which all nations could share equally without discrimination. [189]

But let us return to that dream of a Christian empire under Iberian hegemony. What sort of empire did the most capable men of the Iberian world want to establish during the sixteenth century? What was the essence of the so-called Philosophia Christi that inspired them? They wanted to unite and integrate a world which was threatening to destroy itself by a division that arose out of a new discovery. That discovery was freedom: freedom of the individual as the source of all culture. Freedom and individualism were undermining the values that up to then had given meaning to the Christian community, which comprised all of the known world in spite of the policies of kings, popes, princes, or nations. The group of men who decided to reshape that community thus thrown into a crisis was quite aware of the danger threatening it. "The

---

[188] "Topía y Utopía." Introduction to *Utopías del Renacimiento* (Mexico City, 1941).
[189] Several studies have been published recently in the review *Comprendre*, Nos. 13 and 14, discussing the positive and negative aspects of Western imperialism as a vehicle of culture.

representatives of the philosophy of Christ," adds Joaquín Xirau, "were clearly aware of the abyss that would open for Christian civilization in the future."[190] Above all, reform would be necessary to save it from the inevitable abyss, but it must be a reform opposite to the one Western Europe had undertaken. The triumph of the Protestant Reformation had meant the division of the Church, which until then had served as a common bond, into different churches. It might be said that every individual became a church unto himself if one started from the possibility of direct relationship between God and each of His faithful.

The Spanish Reformation was looking for something else. Had it succeeded, it would have been an internal matter and would have taken place within the Church itself. It would have tried to reconcile the new interests with those of Christendom, and in that reconciliation the already existing individualism would have played one of the most important roles. From this point of view it might be said, therefore, that the Spanish Reformation was a Catholic Reformation because it insisted on maintaining the idea of the Church as a community. This could be achieved, however, only within a changed and flexible Church ready to assimilate the new values of modernity in the same way the Christian missionaries had assimilated cultures in the newly discovered lands that seemed alien to Christianity.[191] The Iberian reformers, therefore, tried to find a formula that would reconcile the values of Christianity with those of Modernity. Confronted by this situation," says Xirau, " it was necessary to find a formula which, while it integrated freedom's conquests would remain within the limits of the oldest traditions and would grant Christian civilization a greatness where nothing would be impossible, thus insuring the continuation of its destiny." It was necessary to coordinate the ancient world with the one being born, tradition with progress, and the community with the freedom of the individual. There was no reason why the Christian spirit should be at variance with the practical modern spirit. One could hope for

---

[190] Joaquín Xirau, "Humanismo español." In *Cuadernos americanos*, Mexico City (January/February 1952).

[191] Bataillon calls this movement Reformist. The greatest mistake, he says, consists of using this word as synonymous with Reformation, "a synonym that is anachronous with respect to Protestantism when it ascribes to the Counter-Reformation whatever was vigorous and new about Catholicism after 1517, when actually what merits the name of Counter-Reformation between 1517 and 1560 is a negative attitude, hostile to any kind of reform be it Catholic or Protestant." op. cit.

happiness in the hereafter without renouncing it on earth. Vis-à-vis the difficulty of choice as stated by Christians and partisans of Modernity, the new Christians or Iberian reformers would try to reconcile the two worlds by choosing the best values of both, thereby creating a synthesis in which no one would lose. They would be against a narrow-minded and restrictive Christianity which stifled man's potential, but they would also be against a humanism whose individualism might culminate in an unlimited anti-social egotism. Neither earthly happiness nor Humanism was at variance with Christ or Christianity.

However, the idea these reformers had regarding the role of princes and heads of state was weighted in favor of the community as against the individual. The prince or head of state was charged with watching over the individual's happiness, but in relation to the interests of the community for which he was also responsible. He had to watch over the happiness of all individuals, not of a particular one or a particular group. On his ability to fulfill this role depended the unity of the community. Therefore, the Prince who forgot that role became a bad ruler or a tyrant, thus losing his quality of leadership. "Does not to rule and govern nations also mean to defend them, watch over them and protect them as is done with children?" asks Luis Vives, "And is there anything more irrational than to attempt to protect those who do not wish such tutelage? Or to try to attract those who say they wish to benefit even if it means hurting them? Or is killing, destroying and setting of fire also trying to protect? Be careful not to show that what you are trying to do is not to govern but to dominate, and that it is not a kingdom you long for but a tyranny. What you want are more subjects, not so that they may live more happily but that they may fear you and unquestioningly obey."[192]

The ruler is the defender and protector of the nations God has entrusted to him. On him depends their happiness, and therefore the permanency of the community. "Do you know that you are the pastor and not the master, and that you must account for those sheep to the shepherd who is God?" asks Alfonso de Valdés. "It is a bad sign when the shepherd wants more sheep than the Master wishes to entrust to his care, because this shows that he wants to take advantage of them and that he does not want to govern them but milk

---

[192] As quoted by Joaquín Xirau, op. cit.

them . . . the good prince is the image of God, as Plutarch says, and the bad prince a minister of the Devil. If you want to be taken for a good prince try to emulate God and do not do anything He would not do."[193]

The good Christian prince not only tries to maintain the Christian community intact but easily extends it, as is done by Polidoro in Valdés' *Diálogo*, whose good government has Turks and Moors asking him to become a part of it, accepting baptism and paying the tribute that is theirs without being forced to do so. Such a prince could bring Christianity to the whole world without provoking death and without spilling Christian blood. What is important, however, is the relationship the ruler has with God, since he must answer to Him for the good or evil he has done to his subjects. A good ruler is one who behaves to his subjects as he would to God. From God he receives the enlightenment which permits him to act for Him. In this relationship, therefore, one cannot properly speak of a "pact" in the sense that it is understood in modern society. The authority of the Christian prince is not actually derived from his relationship with those he governs, but rather stems from his legitimate relationship with God. A bad ruler is one who has lost that divine relationship which made it possible for him to serve those he governs. This is reason enough for the governed to change him without going against God's will. Consequently, the loss of his alleged enlightenment must entail the downfall of the ruler. According to Bataillon there is nothing in this idea that resembles the affirmation of popular rule. It is rather a kind of government that can be authoritarian if this is necessary for the well-being of the members of the community. Such a government must therefore want peace, be peaceful, and in a wider sense seek peace with all the means at its disposal, as an extension of Christianity, although this does not mean the total condemnation of war, which is permissible if there is evidence that it is necessary. Valdés therefore justified the Emperor's war against the Pope. He saw it as a necessary war in order to maintain the Christian community's unity, which had been endangered by Rome's ambitions. In any case, Christian government ought to be tempered by virtue and led by Divine grace. According to Bataillon, we are dealing not so much

---

[193] Alfonso de Valdés, *Diálogo de Mercurio y Caronte* (Madrid, 1925). Also see Marcel Bataillon, op. cit., and J. A. Ortega y Medina, "La 'Universitas Christiana' y la disyuntiva imperial de la España del siglo XVI." In *Filosofía y Letras*, Universidad de México, Nos. 51-52 (1953).

with an enlightened despotism, but rather with an "enlightened royalty." The ruler's authority is not based on the pact uniting him to his subjects; that pact merely expresses the necessary reciprocity of good and bad procedures between the ruler and the nation.

Enlightened despotism, which was to appear later in Spain and the Latin American countries, would have a great deal of the "enlightened royalty" of which Bataillon speaks. The Latin American liberators would act as enlightened men toward their countries, although by other, transcendent forces only nominally different from Divine ones, always having in mind the well-being of their countries, even against their subjects' will; ruling and protecting them as if they were sons; protecting and watching over them so that they might become free in spite of themselves, and using force if necessary. This spirit manifested itself in the liberal dictatorships that appeared in Latin America once the latter had achieved her political freedom during the nineteenth century. To insure the freedom and and material well-being of these countries, the most progressive groups imposed the political and educational institutions they considered best suited to this high purpose.[194] Finally, instead of creating, as we might say, "a government of the people, for the people," says Daniel Cosío Villegas, "they simply attempted to create a government for the people, that is to say, in their name and for their benefit. To that need responded . . . in a large number of Latin American countries true oligarchical governments that were enlightened and beneficent, and due to their efforts initial political progress was made, even if today's demagogy has succeeded in disgracing the idea and the word 'oligarchy'."[195]

45. The Failure of an Idea

Internal and external pressures contributed to make the Iberian Catholic reform movement end in failure. The other face of the Iberian world took charge in the long run and in spite of everything

---

[194] Refer to my book *Del liberalismo a la revolución en la educación mexicana* (Mexico City, 1956).
[195] Daniel Cosío Villegas, "La república restaurada." In *Historia moderna de Mexico* (Mexico City-Buenos Aires, 1955).

aligned with the external forces which had taken hold of Western Europe. In Europe, modern individualism had triumphed over the Christian community's limited efforts. From Western Europe the Hispanic peoples who were the last defenders of that spirit were expelled. The desired reconciliation became impossible in Spain, and in its place arose a fanaticism which denied without trying to understand. Soon Erasmianism fell victim to that new activity. The chance that the Iberian world might assimilate Modernity without renouncing its ideal of a Christian community was therefore lost. In Spain men would come to the fore who opposed that reconcilement. "Every time Spain, anxious for spiritual renewal, tries to admit a foreign influence," says Bataillon, "that unconquerable land appoints one or several of her sons to say 'no' to the invader." At that time, the foreign influence was represented by "Erasmianism," which Hispanic reformers had used in trying to extend and strengthen Christian unity. The spirit of reconciliation of the Erasmian reformers was confronted by a narrow, provincial, and scholastic spirit proud of what Spain represented as the orthodox defender of Christianity. That spirit was no longer concerned with the reconcilement and extension it implied, rather, it felt it was sufficient to be orthodox and try to maintain this by all available means, including even force. It was hardly in favor of conciliatory arrangements, pacts, and agreements; it much preferred to dissuade those who opposed it rather than to convince them. It was the same Spanish spirit which had turned the Inquisition into a tool to save men's souls, even if that meant destroying their bodies. This narrow-minded approach was first noticed in Diego López de Zúñiga's pedantic and arrogant criticism of Erasmus, whereby he tried to prove that the Dutch master was prone to heresy. The same spirit was responsible toward the end of Charles V's and at the beginning of his son Phillip II's reign for the persecution, torment, prison, and death of many of the most outstanding Hispanic Erasmians.

The uncompromising Spanish attitude was in turn stimulated by Charles V's failure in his efforts to impose unity on an increasingly divided Europe, and also to unite Europe under the banner of Christian crusade against the Turks. While Spain was persisting in that unity, modern nationalist movements appeared in Europe. England and France, the German principalities, and the Italian cities were more interested in defending their own interests than in the unity sought by Spain. Alliances, pacts, and preventive wars interested them more than a crusade in which they saw no advantage.   Very   soon,   the   most   daring   representatives   of nationalism would lead the rest of the world in a new type of crusade in which neither religion nor the intellect was of any importance. The nationalist movement began by expelling from the national territories those annoying Iberians who persisted in subjugating them, whom they did not consider Europeans at all, and who for that reason were aloof from European problems.

On the other hand, the uncompromising attitude of Rome and the individualistic arrogance of the Reformation born in Wittenberg made any scheme to reunite Christianity, as Spain had hoped, impossible.   Emperor Charles did not dare to follow the Erasmians' advice at court that the Pope's material power should be changed to that of the spiritual leader of Christianity, and that the Papacy and Luther should be asked to reach an agreement that would end the existing division.   "The providential mission of Charles V was an illusion.   The sack of Rome," says Bataillon, "did not mark the beginning of a new era." Luther put an end to the Emperor's dreams when he rebelled, abetted by the German princes.   From that moment on, Spain abandoned her spirit of reconciliation and along with it the dreams of her reformers; henceforth she would try to achieve by force what she could not obtain by agreement.   Spain thought that she was being faithful to her mission by pursuing the heretic wherever she might find him.   But that attitude, far from realizing her dreams, ended them.   Spain was to appear to Western Europe exactly as it had pictured her, as something "other" or different, alien to Europe and to the new world that was to be established. Charles' testament, in which he asked his son Phillip II to "put an end to the heretics," was the document that ended the dream of a Christian empire.   After the effort to reconcile all points of view, there followed a useless struggle to impose one spiritual outlook, one single truth.   Thus, one could sweep aside, with a clear conscience, any attitude that might be in error or indicate a simple difference that might lead to discord.   Spain wished to impose agreement, but without feeling and with the blind will of fanaticism. "In Spain's soul," says Xirau, "all ideological differences would gradually disappear and with them the individual features of all nations.   The whole world had been reduced to the unity of a true and irrefutable Catholic thought."[196]   The Spanish mind turned to

---

[196] Joaquín Xirau, op. cit.

fanaticism and persecution that tended to favor a violent solution; this was revealed already in Cisneros, culminated during the reigns of Phillip and his successors, and turned the country into a nation outside of history, removed from the reality that was shaping the world. With Phillip and his successors, says Juan Ortega y Medina, "the Spanish mind stiffened and responded only with violence to any stimulation . . . for the Spaniards there remained only one solution: to refuse admittance to dissidents and infidels neither granting nor asking for clemency; it was total war to the death."[197]

Spain and the Iberian world, far from being a tool in the unification of the new Europe, ended up by representing all that was anti-European and anti-Western. The universal Catholic concept for which Spain believed she was fighting narrowed and ceased to be universal, changing instead into simple Romanism or Papism. Spain became, that is to say, a nation favoring merely another religion among the many different faiths competing with one another in Europe, and her church became no more than a church among other churches. For the Lutherans, Calvinists, and Anglicans the Spaniards were merely Papists. But, what was more serious still, within that denomination they appeared "more Papist than the Pope." Even Rome, contemplating the new situation in the world, was not ready to be led in the direction that Spain wanted to dictate. The Pope acted more like the representative of a secular than of a spiritual power, and therefore showed no embarrassment in condemning the Spanish policy and in excommunicating the son of Phillip II, the defender of Christianity and the Church, and the champion of Catholicism.

46. The Church Led by Calvin

Spain was no longer the nation chosen to establish Christendom throughout the world, but just a country among other countries, one more country in which nationalism was imposed. Her persistence in establishing her catholicity was simply regarded as one of her peculiarities, as a national symbol contrasting with those of

---

[197] J. A. Ortega y Medina, op. cit.

other nations. The universal empire was changing in one more country, in spite of herself, but in one that was minor, marginal, and subordinated to the interests of nations that regarded themselves as major powers. Spain was one of the nations that served as pawns for the major powers in their struggle to achieve world domination. The new nations, the creators of the so-called West, had intimidated the Iberian world until it had been converted into a tool for their interests. As regards the empire that the West had established overseas, this would also be fought for in the name of freedom, in the same way that England had striven for supremacy on the high seas in the name of "freedom of the seas." It is true that neither Spain nor Portugal was a nation in the way the modern world understands that term. The spirit which had made England, France, Holland, and other countries into nations in Western Europe was alien to Spain and the Iberian world, which did not share the high sense of individualism, the commercial and industrial ability that characterized the new nations. Although it was of secondary importance to her, Portugal showed greater ability in adapting the spirit of Modernity, in as much as she was able to hold her own in the commercial competition with the West in Asia.

But Spain did not adapt to the new ways because she preferred to cleave to her own ways. As we have already seen, she was not able to establish a middle class similar to that of Western Europe. On the contrary, carried along by what she considered her "religious faith," she had expelled and continued to expel those elements that might have helped her to become a part of Modernity, like the "marranos" who emigrated to Holland, succeeding there in work that was lost to the Peninsula. Instead of depending on the achievements of an active middle class, Spain relied on what remained of an impoverished nobility, trained for war and conquest during their country's heroic era, but who from then on merely spent their lives in yearning for the return of the Spanish Golden Age, recalling the feats of their forebears in the hope that the aristocrats and noblemen would feel that the practical effort which had produced the greatness of Western Europe's nations was a disgrace. These were men satisfied with a good piece of land that would yield them enough for their daily living requirements. Neither more nor less, with no thought of the morrow, living for the day only, following "the will of God."

The Church and the Catholic clergy contributed to the marginal existence of Spain and the Iberian world. In her desire to defend orthodoxy the Church became an ally of the very heterodoxy she had opposed. In trying to fight the modern world and its ideas she became its best ally, making its expansion over a divided world easy. One could speak here of "the Church led by Luther," but even more so of "the Church led by Calvin." The Calvinists, whose outlook justified from a religious point of view the expansion of the West over other countries, knew how to use to best advantage the attitude of the Catholic church and thus, although the Iberian world could have remained Christian and Catholic, its opportunity to enter modern times was lost, and the efforts made by Iberian reformers, Spaniards at first and Latin Americans later, were in vain. The Church, by resisting and fighting the efforts that Spain and the Latin American countries made to reach the level of Modernity without in any way renouncing their Christianity, paradoxically became an unwitting ally to the world expansion she had persisted in fighting blindly. The Iberian countries engaged in long and bloody combat regarding their future, a struggle in which the Church opposed any kind of reform that would alter already limited interests, and were thus weakened and became an easy prey for the nations that had created the modern world. Within that world, the Latin American countries were merely subordinated colonial countries in a new form of colonialism, the same kind of colonialism to which other countries in Africa and Asia had been subjected. In the Iberian countries the Church took on the same role that had been played by the feudal forces of which Fritz Sternberg spoke: with her intolerance she stopped material development in those countries, and fought, as if it were a heresy, any insistence to have them adapt, in a struggle they could not avoid. The West, as we have stated in another part of this study,[198] could accelerate its development and expansion, as well as eliminate any eventual competitors. With all the means at its disposal it reduced other countries to the status of mere providers of raw materials and obligatory consumers, but not producers. Industrial development in those countries was prevented or slowed down.

In the Iberian world (Spain, Portugal, Latin America) the Church, and along with her the heirs of privileged position in a world that had failed, became allies of the world of men who saw in

---

[198] Refer to chapter III, section 13 of this book.

their success a sign of predestination. Calvinism, in its material expression, expanded and was helped unwittingly by a Catholicism that had lost its universal meaning. Consequently the new imperialism found in the old and backward Iberian feudal class the best allies for its expansion and maintenance. The Church continued to be led by Calvin, and in return for preserving local orthodoxy became a tool of heterodoxy, which triumphed all over the world. That heterodoxy placed on the fringe, outside of history, away from the world of freedom and personal well-being which it had established, a world that had decided to remain in the past and refused any kind of reconciliation with the future. That heterodoxy used Iberian orthodoxy as it had used all forms of religious, social, and political orthodoxy it had encountered in its expansion to other countries. By respecting, even encouraging, that orthodoxy it maintained peace, the condition best suited to its expansion. The West continued its march toward the future in that seemingly unending line of permanent progress. It met no obstacles or competitors in an order where the most privileged were also the best and most able. In the past remained those countries which for a moment had seemed to be the West's strongest competitors, reconciling the best in their past with a future for which they felt they were predestined.

The Iberian reformers were aware of all this; and they included not only the Erasmians but also those who took their place in a mood of conciliatory and humanistic eagerness: eclectics, liberals, and followers of Krause. They never attacked the Church for her Catholicism or religion; they fought her only as a political tool in the conscious or unconscious service of interests that were contrary to the development of her people in a world already ruled by other values. Our reformers were anti-clerical but never anti-Christian, anti-religious, or anti-Catholic; that is to say, they were enemies of the group or class that persisted in maintaining, in the name of orthodoxy, situations that hindered the development of the incipient Iberian nations. They were for ecclesiastical power as such, but not for using it as a political power. "The ecclesiastical power," said the Mexican José María Luis Mora, "reduced to the purpose for which its institutions were established, working in the purely spiritual sphere and through the spiritual order, would be a beneficial element, necessary to humankind and without which society could not flourish." Those reformers had nothing against Christianity. Being Catholic themselves, they distinguished between faith and the material pretensions of the Church. They felt that their desire to turn their countries into nations in so far as circumstances permitted did not interfere with their beliefs.

47. The Extension of an Idea

The ideal of the Iberian reformers, which found one of its highest expressions in the Erasmians, was to manifest itself in spite of many obstacles in the Peninsula and in Latin America. To America the Iberians went in their eagerness to extend the frontiers of Christianity. On that continent they found other nations and people, a world where there were not only people to convert, but also people and some lands to be exploited. In that world the two Spains and their opposing philosophies would be in evidence: the outlook of the reformers, and that of the orthodox, who were happy with a world unchanged by any new ideas which provided them with land and the necessary laborers to cultivate it. Parallel to that limited outlook, which hoped for an order that would not change anything, there appeared the philosophy of another Spain, which had decided on an evangelizing mission by extending the frontiers of Christianity through understanding. Therefore, side by side with the greedy and egotistical adventurer, was also found the missionary, who came for something more than gold, land to live on, and slaves to cultivate it. He came because of the people who had inhabited those lands before the Iberians arrived, and in order to have him belong to an empire envisioned for all people without distinction. Confronted by people who were so different in their habits and customs from the Christians and Europeans, the mission of the Iberians was more obvious than it had ever been: Providence had placed these peoples in their path so that they could be assimilated. Until then, a whole continent, thousands of villages and millions of people, had remained outside of Christianity. Why had they been discovered at this time? Why were they now within the reach of the Iberian world and not of another country? Spain's destiny was clear: to serve Providence by reincorporating into the community she had established those sons who had been led astray. But it was to be a community where all people were equal. God had given pupils and not slaves to the Iberian world.

Thus a conflict arose between those who regarded the discovered people as slaves and those who thought of them as pupils. This conflict formed the basis for a discussion on the nature of those people, a discussion of which we have already spoken in another part of this book. What were the natives, persons or beasts? The discussion ended in favor of those who saw them as persons like themselves who ought to be made a part of the new empire, a moral triumph that was not always translated into action and not always accepted by those who persisted in seeing them as beasts to be exploited. But this triumph made it possible for these large masses of natives to be legally incorporated into the Christian community with all its rights, although they would have to fight for these later.[199] The rights of the natives were established: what was needed was to see them become a reality. In this way Sahagún, Las Casas, Gamarra, Vasco de Quiroga, and many others in Latin America were fulfilling the ideal of the Iberian reformers which had failed in the Peninsula. Like their teachers in Spain, they were trying to discover and understand what was human in the people's habits and customs. This discovery would enable them to be incorporated without difficulty into the Christian community, of which the Iberians were the agents. They did not impose their truth or their faith, but they tried to make it understood through the native's habits and customs. Sahagún, instead of seeking differences between the native's habits and customs and the Christian's, looked for similarities, which he found, and this provided an easy way of introducing and spreading Christianity among the indigenous population. In contrast to the Puritan evangelizers in North America, the Iberian missionaries accepted the native's capacity for Christianity, and thus assimilated them without difficulty.[200] If the natives for some reason strayed, the evangelists did not interpret this as a sign that God had turned away from them, but merely as an inability on the missionaries' part to make themselves understood, even though they thought this had previously been achieved. That was why the missionaries were interested in understanding indigenous culture. They wanted to understand in order to be understood and of course succeeded although, like Granada's and Toledo's evangelizers among the Moors, they had to change and reform the religious framework of Catholicism. This meant they had to make its ways and profession

---

[199] See Lewis Hanke, op. cit.
[200] See chapter IX of this study and the previously mentioned book by J. A. Ortega y Medina, *Evangelización anglosajona en Norteamérica.*

of faith more attainable. Beyond the literal meaning of a phrase, a close orthodoxy, there was always the end they pursued: the assimilation of the natives and the widening of the frontiers of Christendom. The Catholic reform dreamed of by the Hispanic Erasmians became a fact in America.

As I have already mentioned, the discussion about the nature of the natives was also a triumph for the spirit of reconciliation which had failed in Europe. "For those who live in the New World," says Lewis Hanke, "it will always remain a source of deep satisfaction that the first blow struck for human freedom took place in America."[201] That same spirit that envisaged a Christian empire, situated beyond all individual and national boundaries, was shown in Francisco de Vitoria's *Relectiones de Indias* which, as Antonio Gómez Robledo pointed out, was "our first continental constitution of independence." The conquest, according to Vitoria, did not give Spain any right over that continent. Vitoria "could not accept that the Empire had any rightful claim to the New World that had been discovered, nor did he feel that it rightfully belonged to the sovereign. Against the latter and in favor of the Americans he wrote: "Imperator no est dominus totius orbis."[202] Above the will and the interests of his master, the Emperor, were the interests of justice, the only basis for a true Christian empire, which went beyond the nationalist empires supported by individual and group interests and that were the source of all injustice.

This spirit would also make itself felt among the intellectual precursors and the achievers of the Latin American nations' independence. In the former this was seen in the eclecticism of their philosophy. They were men who knew that the idea of freedom could be satisfied by belonging to a community or an empire that represented something more than the imposition of certain interests over others. God and religion were not incompatible with the idea of freedom. Men like Gamarra, Varela, and many others in America knew how to reconcile their ideas of freedom with their faith, and Modernity with Christianity. They hoped to liberate their countries, but this freedom did not imply necessarily a renunciation of what

[201] Lewis Hanke, op. cit., p. 22.
[202] See Antonio Gómez Robledo, *Política de Vitoria* (Mexico City, 1940). On Erasmianism in America see the appendix of the work by Bataillon already mentioned and the book by J. Almoina, *Rumbos heterodoxos de México* (Ciudad Trujillo, 1947).

was best in their history, their religion or their Iberian past. With respect to those who achieved political independence in Latin America, their efforts toward reconciliation were apparent in their eagerness neither to separate from nor to break with a world to which they knew they belonged. They wanted their nations to be free, but within the Iberian empire, an empire that was viewed as the common goal of action for all the Iberian peoples. Therefore, in every one of the Spanish American countries the cry for independence began in the name of the king of Spain, Ferdinand VII, who was a prisoner. What those countries asked for was simply autonomy, not independence. Almost all of them offered the throne to the Hispanic king, a prisoner of the French. This attitude contrasted with the blindness of Spain, which answered with violence, refused reconciliation, and would not accept as equals the people born in her colonies. The Portuguese empire in America was to be more fortunate. John VI, likewise fleeing from the French, sought refuge in Brazil and granted his new homeland the rights that Spanish America had demanded of her king in vain. John VI enacted the constitution of the United Kingdom of Portugal, Brazil, and the Algarve; he encouraged culture and upon his return to Portugal named his son Pedro regent, thus preparing the way for the peaceful achievement of independence by Brazil, which was to become a new empire under her regent Pedro who, as Pedro I, became her first emperor.

    In Spanish America the struggle against Hispanic orthodoxy was to be very hard, and several generations of Spaniards intervened in every one of the nations that had been established after emancipation from the Spanish mother country. In that struggle those countries endeavored to strip themselves of habits and customs they regarded as belonging to a narrow orthodoxy that was hostile to any kind of reform; they attempted to abandon the past as imposed by Spain, going so far as to renounce the mother country.[203] But in this conflict the Spanish Americans were not alone, because in the mother country, which was the seat of the empire, the same struggle was taking place. The Spaniards, like the Spanish Americans, were also fighting in order to free themselves from the negative aspect of the Spanish mentality and thus assert the spirit of reconciliation that had failed. There, too, a great struggle began to bring about reform, but a reform that did not imply renunciation of the Iberian world's highest values. "The movement that began during the eighteenth

---

[203] Refer to my book *The Latin American Mind*, op. cit.

century in Spain and Spanish America," says José Gaos, "presents
itself as a unique movement for intellectual and political freedom."
Spanish America was first in achieving intellectual emancipation and
she was followed by the Antilles. "Spain was her own last colony,
the only Iberian nation which was left over from a common imperial
past and still had to become spiritually and politically
independent."[204] The joint interest of Spain and Spanish America
was in evidence sometimes, but at other times it was not. Many of
the Spanish liberals fought in the independence movement, and
joined it. But, in general, Spanish liberalism was hostile to the
demands for Spanish American freedom, as in the case of Cuba,
which tried unsuccessfully several times before she gained full
freedom from the mother country. Sometimes the Spanish liberals
saw the colonial war against the mother country merely as a civil
war, the same that they were waging against an orthodox Spain.
Others, however, did not see it this way but felt rather that it was a
struggle of inferior countries against a superior one, namely, Spain.
"Many of the Spaniards residing in Spanish America and even some
of those residing in Spain," adds Gaos, "simply understood, with
greater or lesser historical sagacity, the solidarity of a new Spain
arising after the conversion of the colonies into nations. By contrast
the first Spanish Republic did not understand her own role when
confronted by that change in status. More discerning and generous
than the mother country, the new Spanish American representatives
and Mexico in particular understood their own role vis-à-vis the
second Spanish Republic by helping her in her battles and receiving
her citizens when they were defeated and exiled, thus replacing the
anti-Hispanic feeling which had persisted against the old Spain by
one that seemed to be a definitive perception of the new, and by the
adoption of an attitude toward Spain similar to that taken by the
Spanish American nations which had already achieved independence.

Solidarity and relationship grew up among the Spanish
American or, in a wider sense, Latin American nations that were in a
position to realize the old and cherished ideal of all Iberian reformers
to create a new kind of universal empire. It was an outlook different
from that established by the West in countries that did not belong to
her world and interests, and it stemmed from something already to
some extent inherent in the heritage of the Latin American countries.
There was already an awareness of that ideal during the nineteenth

---

[204] José Gaos, *Pensamiento en lengua española* (Mexico City, 1945).

century in the minds of Latin America's intellectual leaders. Not everything had to be renounced for emancipation; there was indeed very much in the Iberian heritage that should be kept and encouraged. Many of the inherited traits had given rise to historical attitudes in the Iberian countries that were more valuable than those originating in the modern world. The Chilean, Francisco Bilbao, referred to many of these inherited attitudes typical of the Iberian world when he compared Latin America with the world developed by modern man in the United States. There is much that we can learn and admire in big and powerful countries like the United States, Bilbao thought; however, in spite of all our feelings, we have shown a strength of mind that is no less admirable.

To equip them to play an active role in the new world originated by the West, the Latin Americans did not inherit anything comparable to the inheritance of the United States. It was to be regretted that our heritage was the negation of that world: "There was light in the grief stricken heart and we broke the tombstone." Afterwards, "we had to organize it all according to the dictum of theocratic education." But in spite of all the difficulties, "we caused slavery to disappear from all the republics, and that was not due to you who are happy and rich. We have assimilated and continue to assimilate the primitive races . . . because we believe that they are men of flesh and blood like ourselves, but you have exterminated them in Jesuit fashion. We do not see man's ultimate end in earthly pleasures; the black man, the Indian, the disinherited, the unhappy, the weak find in us the respect due to the dignity of the human being . . . This is precisely," concludes Bilbao, "what the South American republics dare to weigh in the balance against North America's pride, wealth and power."[205] That heritage as shown by our difference, we might add, is what we could contribute to many of the New World's unquestionable values, within a larger community than the one created by outdated provincialism and narrow modern nationalism.

---

[205] Francisco Bilbao, *El evangelio americano* (Buenos Aires, 1864).

48. The Bolivarian Ideal

Another American who belonged to that group of Iberian reformers also envisioned a great community which would begin by being Hispanic and later would become truly human. That man was the Liberator Simón Bolívar. In his famous Jamaica letter he described the dream that gave expression to the Iberian community's feeling for humanity. "More than anyone, I desire to see America fashioned into the greatest nation in the world, greatest not so much by virtue of her area and wealth as by her freedom and glory." That is to say, he was dreaming of a great nation constituted by a community of nations bound to one another by something more than greed for expansion and wealth, which always ends by dividing what seems united. Bolívar dreamed of a great community, not a modern society, that could only subsist if certain interests prevailed, a community of nations united for something more than the egoism of modern societies, which aspire at best to achieve a relative equilibrium induced by fear, only to upset the balance when chance offers an opportunity for easy domination. The objectives, like all true goals that appear in dreams about the Iberian communities, would be "freedom" and "glory" and "dominion" and "enrichment." Such an ideal community, that the whole world dreamed of, would be initiated in America among the Hispanic countries, since they share the same origin, blood, language, and religion. "It is a grandiose idea to think of consolidating the New World into a single nation, united by pacts into a single bond. It is reasoned that, as these parts have a common origin, language and customs, and religion, they ought have a single government to permit the newly formed states to unite in a confederation." That is what Bolívar felt might be initiated some day at a great gathering of the Spanish American nations in Panama. "How beautiful it would be if the Isthmus of Panama could be for us what the Isthmus of Corinth was for the Greeks! Would to God that some day we may have the good fortune to convene there an august assembly of representatives of republics, kingdoms, and empires to deliberate upon the high interests of peace and war with the nations of the other three-quarters of the globe."

One ought to insist that this unity be initiated in countries of the same religion, customs, language, and origin. Bolívar admired the modern countries, the great Western nations, but he knew at the same time that in order to deal with them it was necessary first of all to become strong, to appear as equals and not as nations ready to be subjected. Bolívar hoped that one day all Spanish American nations would reach the same stage of development as the great modern nations, but in accordance with their own ways and peculiarities and by assimilating the Iberian heritage. Bolívar paid special attention to England and the United States because they embodied many of the values that should be acquired by Spanish America with due regard to her difference from the West. Spanish America, like those great nations, longed for freedom, but she also aspired to that other Iberian goal: glory, which could be attained only if freedom was made universal. The Iberian countries had no need to expand by destroying others, nor to enrich themselves at the expense of other people's poverty. Their sole desire was for the largest possible community, where freedom could be extended to other nations and be recognized. Bolívar hoped, therefore, that his ideas would be supported by the West's great champions of liberty, and that support would be forthcoming for the Iberian countries' efforts on behalf of freedom.

But things were not fated to turn out that way, because the champions of liberty in the West and in North America were in no hurry to see freedom extended to the Latin American countries, because they were interested only in their own political and economical domination. In that same letter the Liberator complained with bitterness: "How vain has been this hope! Not only the Europeans but even our brothers of the North have been apathetic bystanders in this struggle which, by its very essence, is the most just, and in its consequences the most noble and vital of any which have been raised in ancient or in modern times. Indeed, can the far-reaching effects of freedom for the hemisphere which Columbus discovered ever be calculated?"[206] Bolívar knew that freedom within a community established for the sake of freedom could only be achieved through the efforts made in that direction by the Latin American countries themselves. It was their union that would make possible their active participation in the modern world. They could bring to that world values not to be underrated. Anglo-Saxons and Iberians were different peoples, but in spite of this, and on a basis of mutual respect, they could collaborate. The Iberian countries

---

[206] "Reply of a South American to a Gentleman of this island, Kingston, Jamaica, September 6, 1815." In *Selected Writings of Bolívar*, op. cit., Vol. I, pp. 115, 118, 108.

would not secure that respect unless they united and became strong. Bolívar did not desire, as did some Hispanic intellectuals later, to make Latin America a copy of Anglo-Saxon America. Consequently, in a letter written to Colonel Hinton Wilson, he refuted United States' criticism that his policies did not follow Anglo-Saxon lines. "I am well aware," he said, "of the current opinion in the United States respecting my political conduct. It is unfortunate that we cannot achieve the happiness of Colombia with the laws and customs of the North Americans. You know that this cannot be; it is even less probable than for Spain to be like England."[207] They were different countries, but with freedom as the common goal which however, they must attain, each in its own way. "I think," Bolívar said in another place, "it would be better for South America to adopt the Koran rather than the United States' form of government, although the latter is the best on earth. Nothing more can be added; simply witness the unhappy countries of Buenos Aires, Chile, Mexico and Guatemala. We, too, may recall our own earliest years. These examples alone tell us more than entire libraries."[208]

Latin America must follow its own course just as the modern nations did, and grow with them. The Anglo-Saxon countries had done just that and had grown while heeding their own free and individualistic spirit. The Iberians could also do this by following their old community spirit, which was not incompatible with freedom. Latin America could not function by following even the best Anglo Saxon ideas. Above all, she must be attentive to her own reality and way of being. "People want to imitate the United States," the Liberator said, "without considering the differences in climate, men and things. Believe me, General, we are made of different stuff from that nation whose existence can be counted among the marvels that politics produces from one century to the next."[209] Bolívar knew all about the different make-up of the Anglo-Saxon people, of the modern nations as compared with those of Iberian origin. The former have made the individual the center of their social relations, whereas the latter can depend only on an implicit sense of community. Therefore, the former have created societies whose goal

---

[207] "To Colonel Belford Hinton Wilson, Guayaquil, August 3, 1829." In *Selected Writings of Bolívar*, op. cit., Vol. II, p. 729.

[208] "To General Daniel F. O'Leary. Guayaquil, September 13, 1829." In *Selected Writings of Bolívar*, op. cit., Vol. II, p. 738.

[209] "To General Antonio Gutiérrez de la Fuente. Caracas, January 16, 1827." In Simón Bolívar, *Obras completas*, op. cit.

is the aggrandizement of the individual, while the latter can only generate relationships that have as their goal the greatness of the community. In modern society, social life is the result of the spontaneous will for union by the people who belong to it; in communities, people live together by instinct and living together is the result of natural inclination, custom, a common desire with which all people can identify. This has been the kind of living together that the Iberian reformers dreamed of in the past, with the Christian empire in mind. At one stage in history the ideal for this kind of living together had made Spain great. According to the Liberator, that same ideal could contribute to the greatness of Spain's descendents in America.

It would also be the Spanish American, or in a wider sense, the Latin American community which would enable the Iberian countries to participate in modern society, as established by Western nations. without diminishing their freedom, sovereignty, or interests. Bolívar knew that this type of international coexistence was imposed on the world by nations like England and the United States. It was a kind of coexistence within which the weak nations remained always subordinate; hence, the need to unite Latin America by a series of common bonds, thus making it possible to enter the international arena on a plane different from that of mere subordinates. The Latin American countries had a common origin and interests.[210] Only if they were united could they make known the legitimacy of their objectives, as well as their right to freedom and sovereignty. The society established by the West was inevitable and must be accepted, but in such a way that the Latin American countries could participate in it as equals. For that reason Bolívar advocated a community of nations of Iberian origin, the Spanish American countries as he called them, and at the same time favored an association with the West, but one based on equality and mutual respect. The Spanish American countries could not follow in the footsteps of the West because they were latecomers to that world, but they could act like a great Iberian community whose interests were respected and which in turn respected those of others. Bolívar knew that if the Latin American countries did not unite they would merely

---

210 Bolívar did not consider the empire of Brazil which he felt was outside that community; he did the same with Argentina, whose interests he believed were contrary to those of the rest of Spanish America. However, in our time, we have seen the injustice of that discrimination within the unity of a world with the same origin, as is the Iberian world.

be a field for exploitation by countries which had made material growth and the wealth of their individual citizens the principal goals of their expansion.

What can be deduced from that ideal? The Pan Americanism of which some journalists speak today? It can be workable in some ways, but in order to achieve it the Latin American nations must have equality with the United States. Or, in a larger sense, the Iberian world must participate in the empire established by the West, but by giving it a different meaning from that intended by its founders. Yes, an empire, but if an empire is desired, it should not be established by extending its sovereignty over other nations; rather what should be extended is not its own sovereignty but its ideas and ideals and the respect they deserve through respecting the sovereignty of others. What should be extended are the political rights and national advantages recognized for the empire's own citizens to those of other countries. Such an empire would enlarge its dominion by recognizing in other nations what it accepts for itself or desires that other nations recognize. In antiquity, Alexander tried to establish such an empire, governing not only the Greeks by favoring them, but also the Persians and all the countries that belonged to his empire. The Roman Empire tried to do something similar. It was something that only force of circumstances compelled the empire of the West to do.

But there was something more to the Liberator's dream, something that he had inherited from the dreams of the Iberian reformers. He dreamed of another kind of empire, one that would coordinate the efforts of all nations and all mankind and guide them toward a common goal. It would be a common objective for common efforts, a coordination of efforts directed toward the realization of a whole series of values. What values? Those pertaining to Western culture, but in their widest sense. Values of a culture that began in Greece, was enlarged in Rome, extended into Christianity, and reached its height during modern times when it spread all over the world. A culture in which the individual's rights are coordinated with the needs of the community, and the nation's freedom and sovereignty with the need for universal peace and for agreements guaranteeing that freedom and sovereignty. In that culture the freedom of the individual and of nations need not be incompatible with social justice and international coexistence. A culture therefore, in which the humanism of its creators prevails over the personal egotism which deprives it of substance.

DATE DUE